Dear Nathan,
I thought
you would enjoy
this book—
Love Always
forever
mom xx ooo
August 30, 2004
Happy 13th Birthday

W9-CJL-290

From Couch Potato
to Mouse Potato

by Jeff MacNelly

TRIUMPH BOOKS

CHICAGO

© 2000 by Tribune Media Services. All rights reserved.

No part of this publication may be reproduced, stored in a retrieval system, or transmitted, in any form by any means, electronic, mechanical, photocopying, or otherwise, without the prior written permission of the publisher, Triumph Books, 601 South LaSalle Street, Suite 500, Chicago, Illinois 60605.

This book is available in quantity at special discounts for your group or organization. For further information, contact:

Triumph Books
601 South LaSalle Street
Chicago, Illinois 60605
(312) 939-3330
Fax (312) 663-3557

Printed in Canada.

Book design by Patricia Frey.
Cover design by Salvatore Concialdi.

ISBN 1-57243-384-1

Table of Contents

Chapter One

An Open Mind and a Shut Mouth

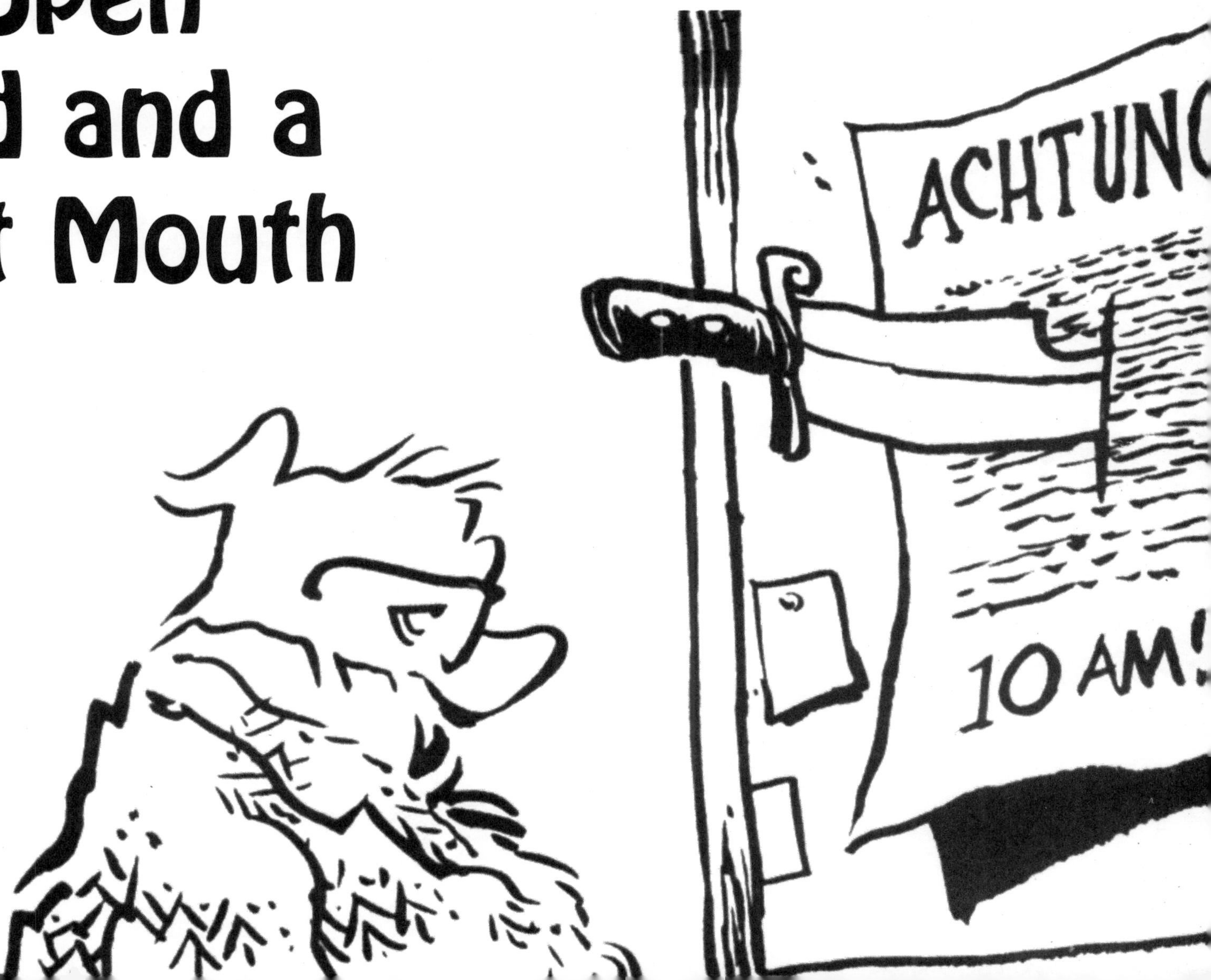
ACHTUNG
10 AM!

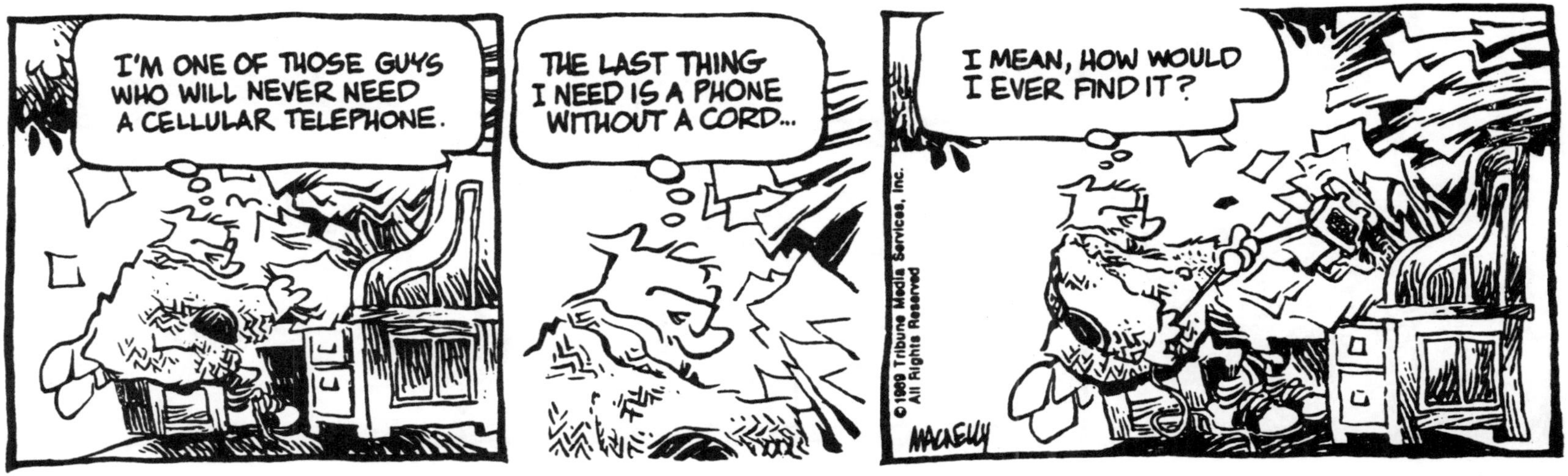
I'M ONE OF THOSE GUYS WHO WILL NEVER NEED A CELLULAR TELEPHONE.
THE LAST THING I NEED IS A PHONE WITHOUT A CORD...
I MEAN, HOW WOULD I EVER FIND IT?
© 1989 Tribune Media Services, Inc.
All Rights Reserved
MACNELLY

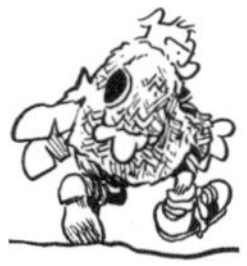

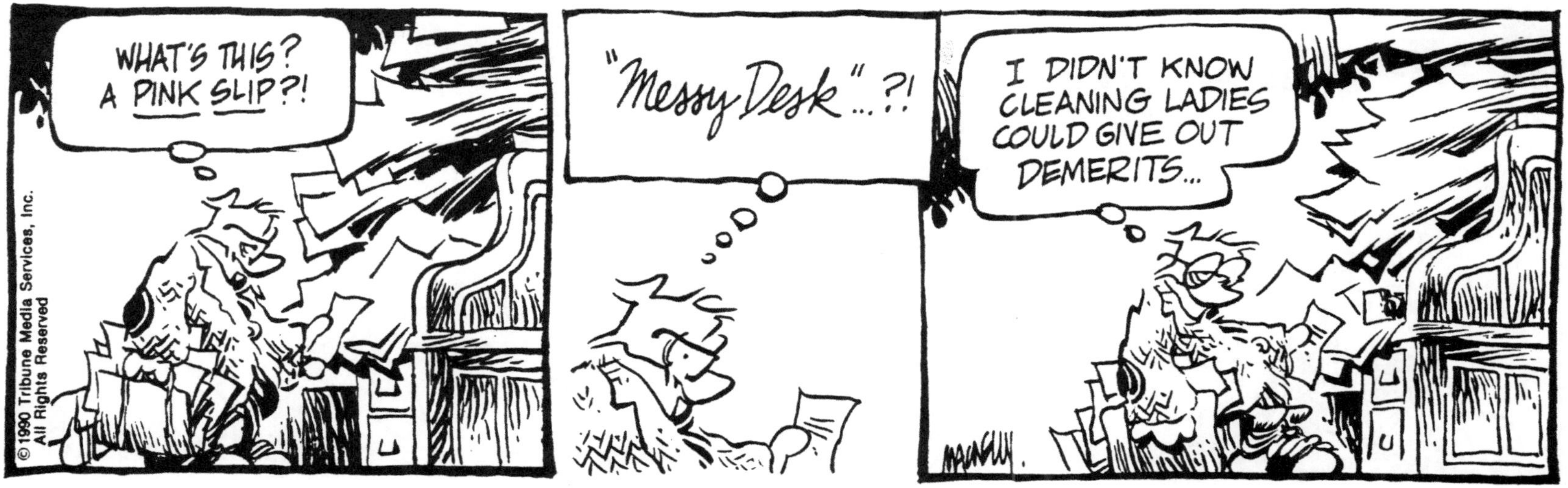
WHAT'S THIS? A PINK SLIP?!
© 1990 Tribune Media Services, Inc.
All Rights Reserved
"Messy Desk"...?!
I DIDN'T KNOW CLEANING LADIES COULD GIVE OUT DEMERITS...
MACNELLY

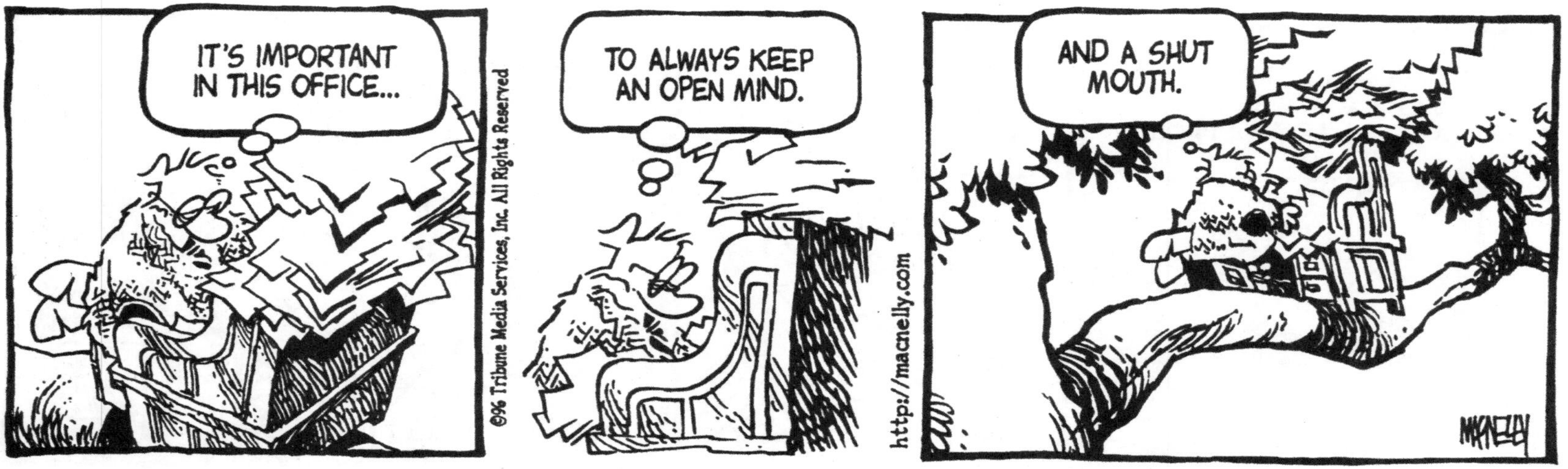
IT'S IMPORTANT IN THIS OFFICE...
TO ALWAYS KEEP AN OPEN MIND.
AND A SHUT MOUTH.
©96 Tribune Media Services, Inc. All Rights Reserved
http://macnelly.com
MACNELLY

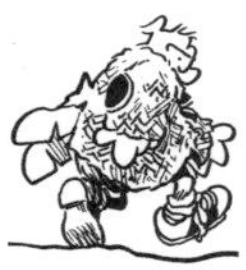

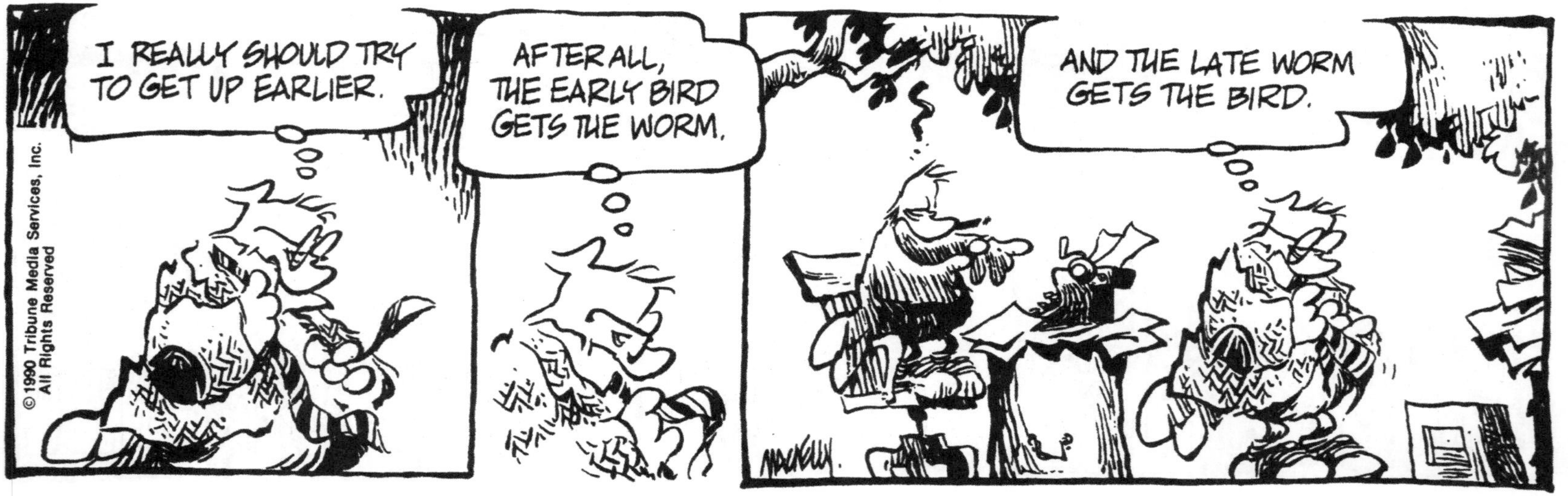
I REALLY SHOULD TRY TO GET UP EARLIER.
AFTER ALL, THE EARLY BIRD GETS THE WORM.
AND THE LATE WORM GETS THE BIRD.
© 1990 Tribune Media Services, Inc. All Rights Reserved
MACNELLY

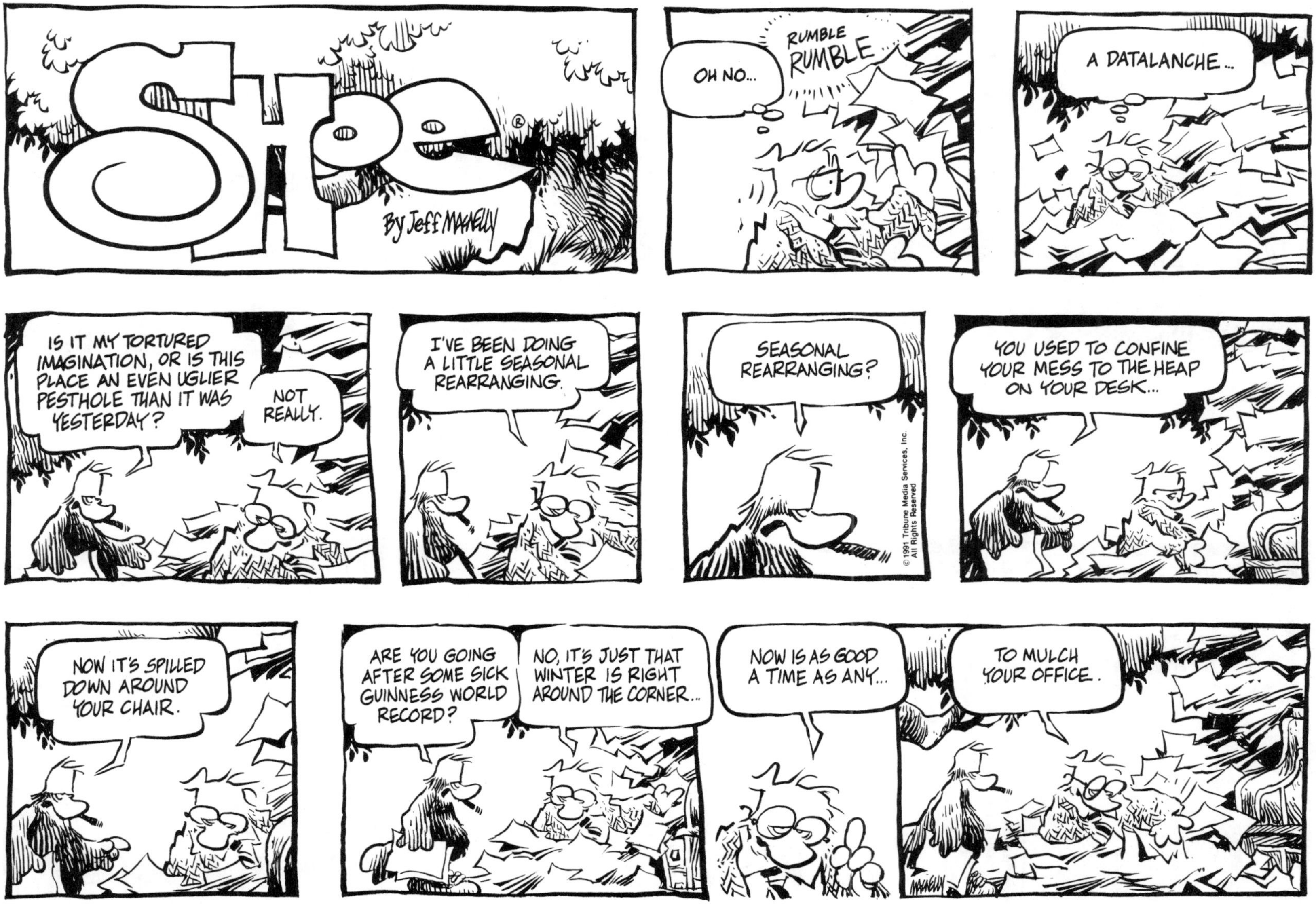
Shoe®
By Jeff MacNelly
OH NO...
RUMBLE RUMBLE...
A DATALANCHE...
IS IT MY TORTURED IMAGINATION, OR IS THIS PLACE AN EVEN UGLIER PESTHOLE THAN IT WAS YESTERDAY?
NOT REALLY.
I'VE BEEN DOING A LITTLE SEASONAL REARRANGING.
SEASONAL REARRANGING?
© 1991 Tribune Media Services, Inc. All Rights Reserved
YOU USED TO CONFINE YOUR MESS TO THE HEAP ON YOUR DESK...
NOW IT'S SPILLED DOWN AROUND YOUR CHAIR.
ARE YOU GOING AFTER SOME SICK GUINNESS WORLD RECORD?
NO, IT'S JUST THAT WINTER IS RIGHT AROUND THE CORNER...
NOW IS AS GOOD A TIME AS ANY...
TO MULCH YOUR OFFICE.

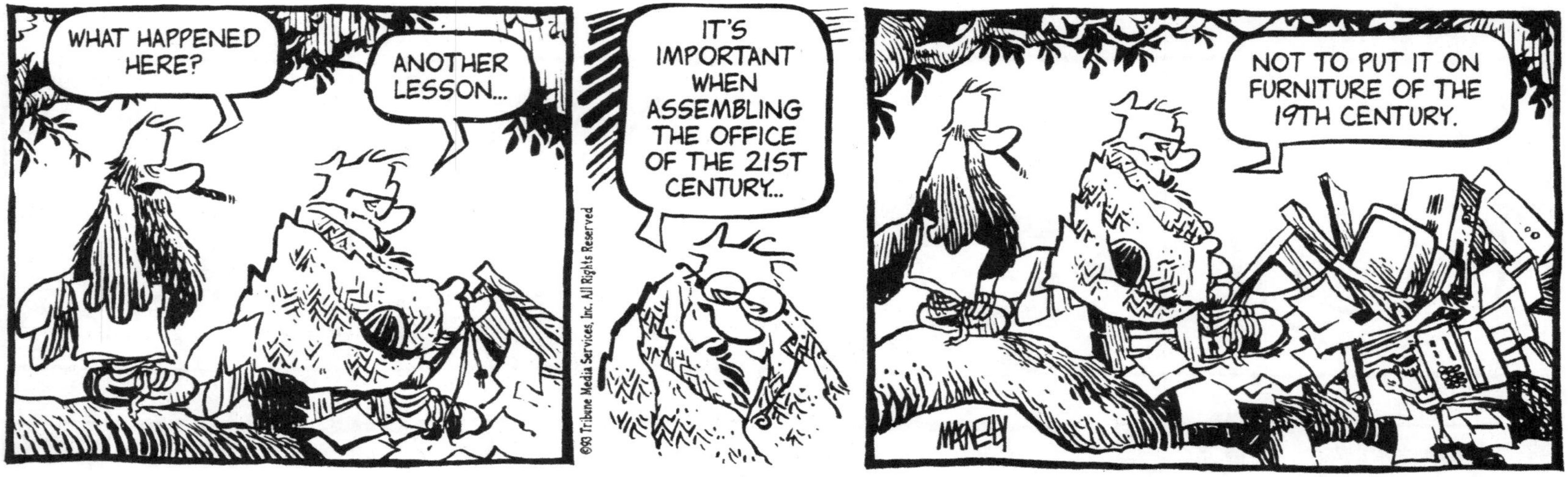
WHAT HAPPENED HERE?
ANOTHER LESSON...
IT'S IMPORTANT WHEN ASSEMBLING THE OFFICE OF THE 21ST CENTURY...
NOT TO PUT IT ON FURNITURE OF THE 19TH CENTURY.
©93 Tribune Media Services, Inc. All Rights Reserved
MACNELLY

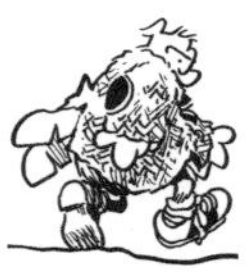

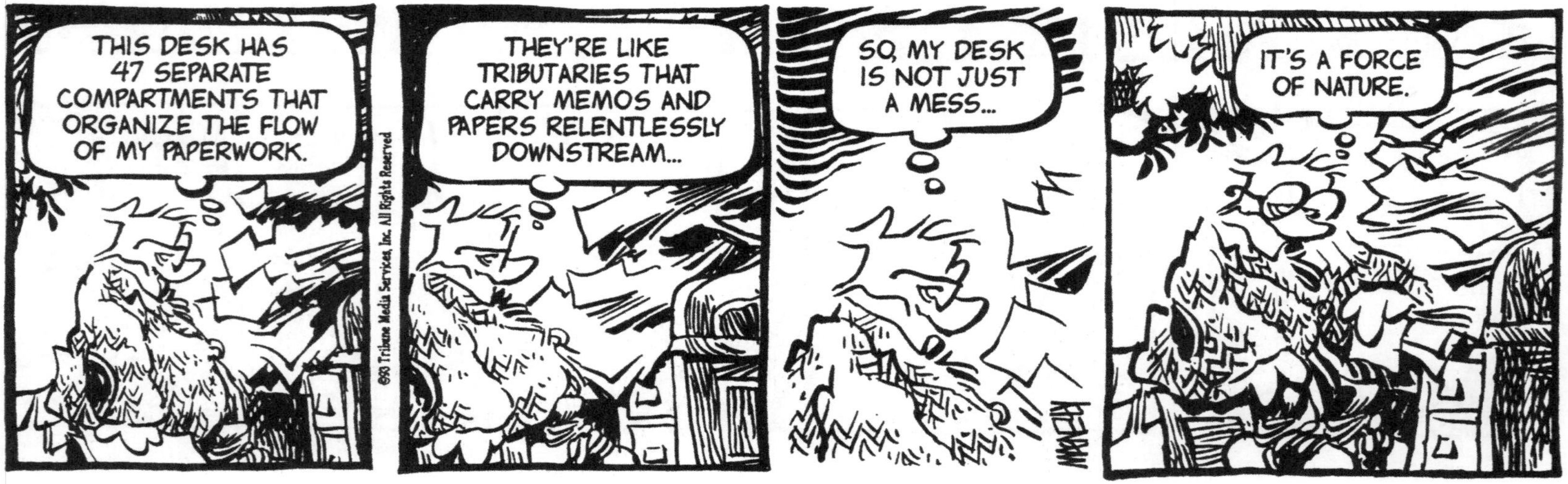
THIS DESK HAS 47 SEPARATE COMPARTMENTS THAT ORGANIZE THE FLOW OF MY PAPERWORK.
THEY'RE LIKE TRIBUTARIES THAT CARRY MEMOS AND PAPERS RELENTLESSLY DOWNSTREAM...
SO, MY DESK IS NOT JUST A MESS...
IT'S A FORCE OF NATURE.
©93 Tribune Media Services, Inc. All Rights Reserved

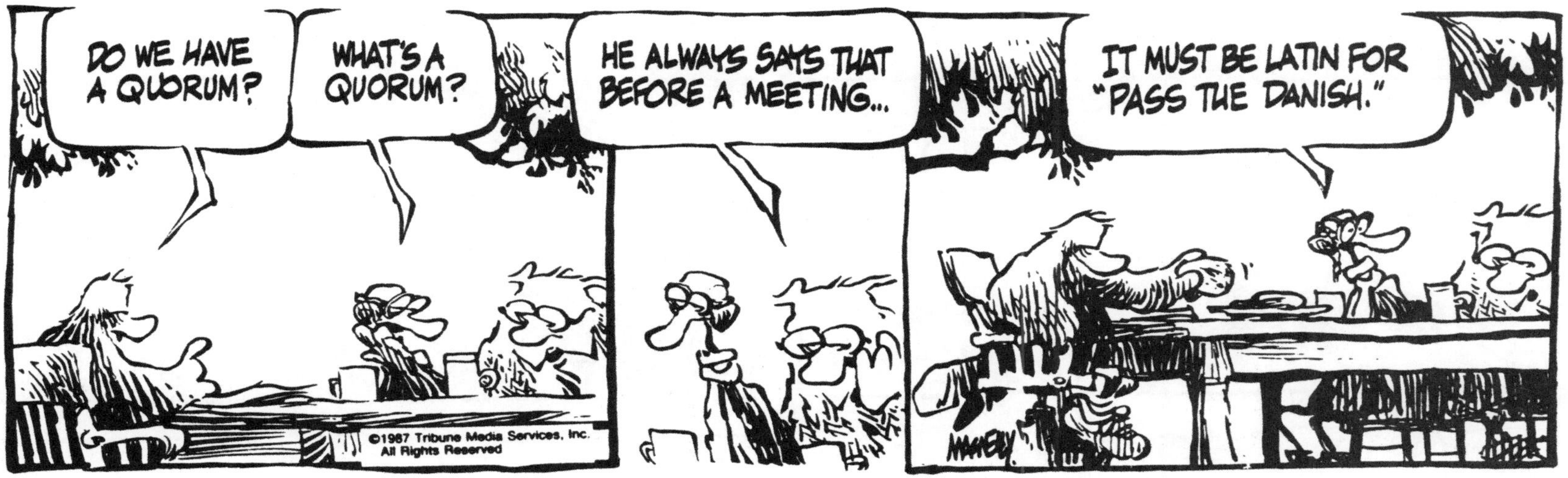
DO WE HAVE A QUORUM?
WHAT'S A QUORUM?
HE ALWAYS SAYS THAT BEFORE A MEETING...
IT MUST BE LATIN FOR "PASS THE DANISH."
©1987 Tribune Media Services, Inc. All Rights Reserved
MACNELLY

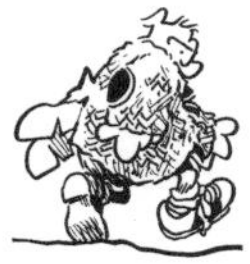

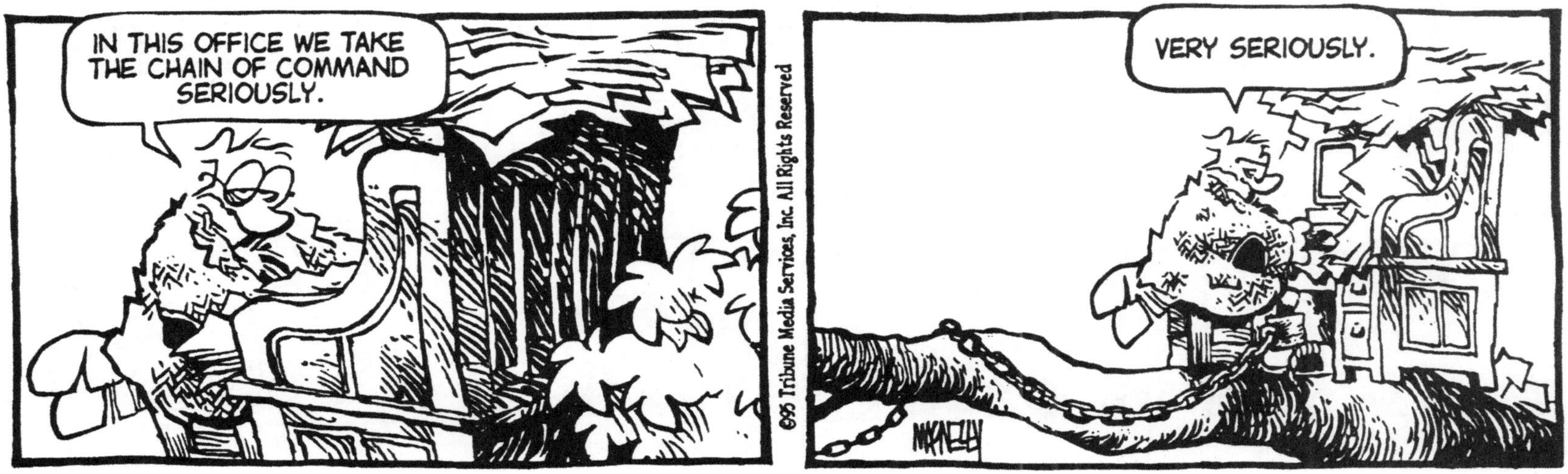
IN THIS OFFICE WE TAKE THE CHAIN OF COMMAND SERIOUSLY.
©95 Tribune Media Services, Inc. All Rights Reserved
VERY SERIOUSLY.
MACNELLY

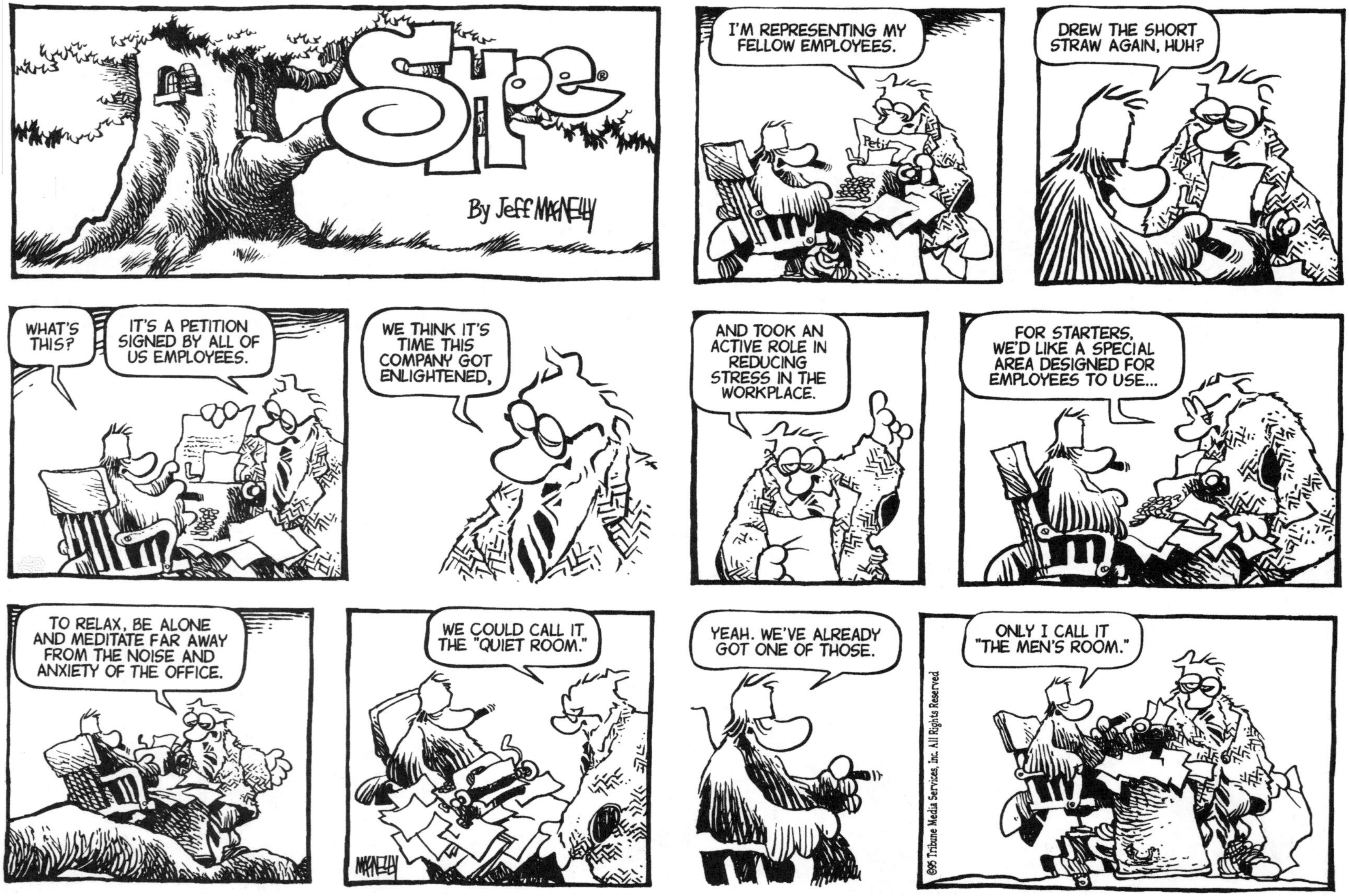
Shoe®
By Jeff MacNelly
I'M REPRESENTING MY FELLOW EMPLOYEES.
DREW THE SHORT STRAW AGAIN, HUH?
WHAT'S THIS?
IT'S A PETITION SIGNED BY ALL OF US EMPLOYEES.
WE THINK IT'S TIME THIS COMPANY GOT ENLIGHTENED,
AND TOOK AN ACTIVE ROLE IN REDUCING STRESS IN THE WORKPLACE.
FOR STARTERS, WE'D LIKE A SPECIAL AREA DESIGNED FOR EMPLOYEES TO USE...
TO RELAX, BE ALONE AND MEDITATE FAR AWAY FROM THE NOISE AND ANXIETY OF THE OFFICE.
WE COULD CALL IT THE "QUIET ROOM."
MACNELLY
YEAH. WE'VE ALREADY GOT ONE OF THOSE.
©95 Tribune Media Services, Inc. All Rights Reserved
ONLY I CALL IT "THE MEN'S ROOM."

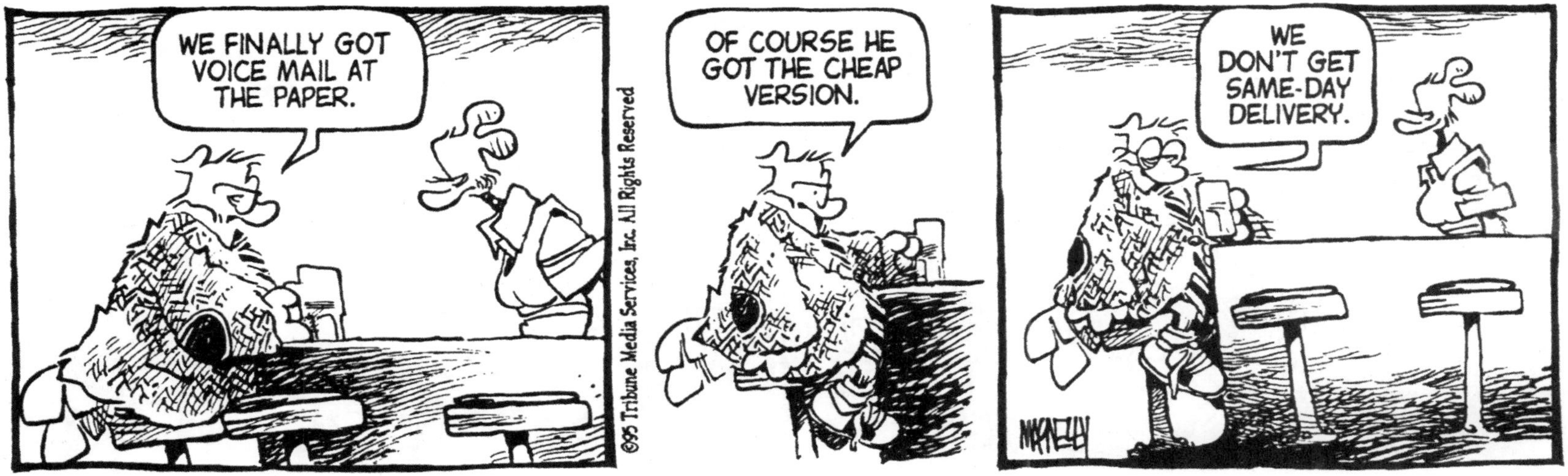
WE FINALLY GOT VOICE MAIL AT THE PAPER.
OF COURSE HE GOT THE CHEAP VERSION.
WE DON'T GET SAME-DAY DELIVERY.
©95 Tribune Media Services, Inc. All Rights Reserved
MACNELLY

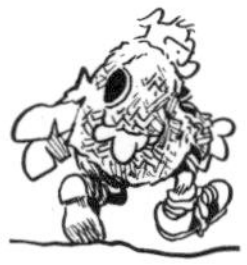

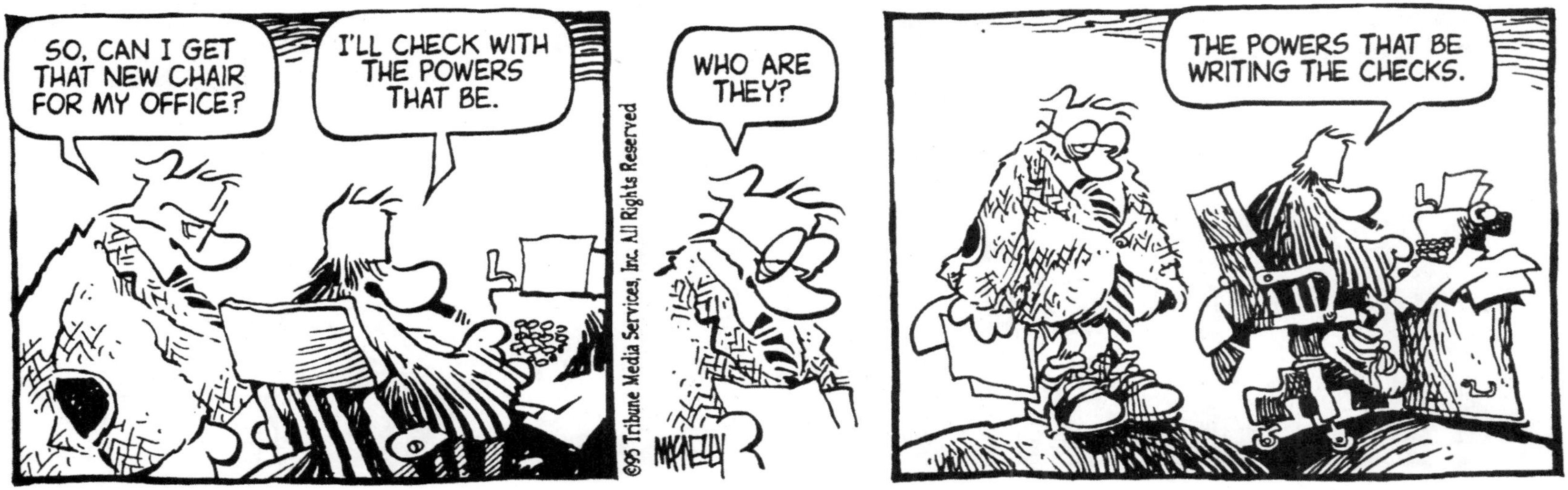
SO, CAN I GET THAT NEW CHAIR FOR MY OFFICE?
I'LL CHECK WITH THE POWERS THAT BE.
WHO ARE THEY?
THE POWERS THAT BE WRITING THE CHECKS.
©95 Tribune Media Services, Inc. All Rights Reserved
MACNELLY

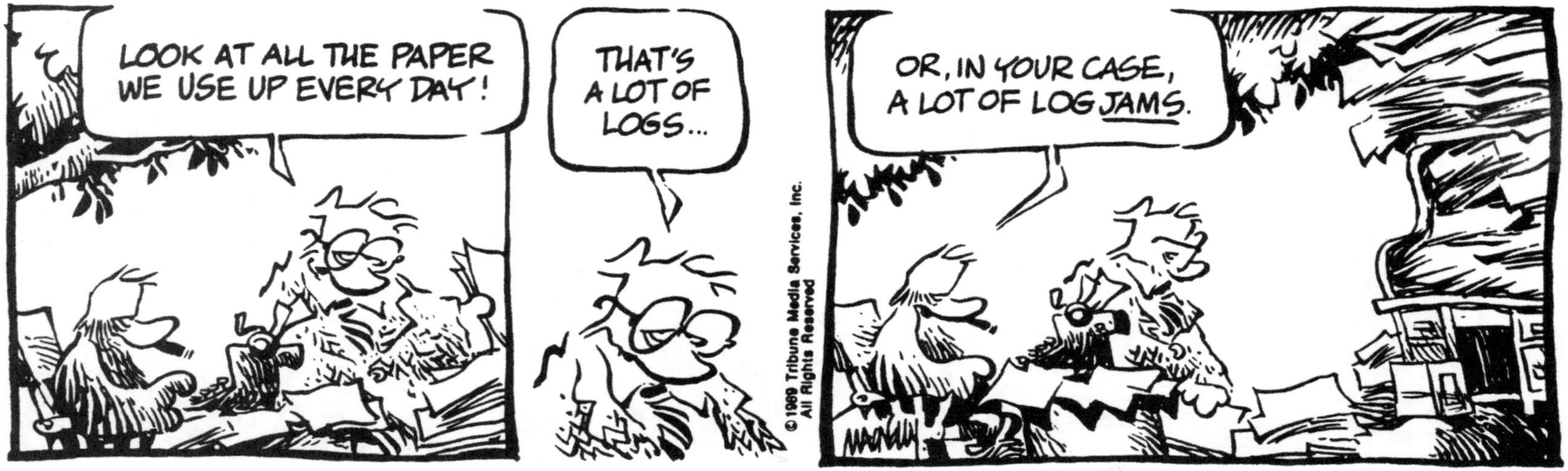
LOOK AT ALL THE PAPER WE USE UP EVERY DAY!
THAT'S A LOT OF LOGS...
©1989 Tribune Media Services, Inc. All Rights Reserved
OR, IN YOUR CASE, A LOT OF LOG JAMS.
MACNELLY

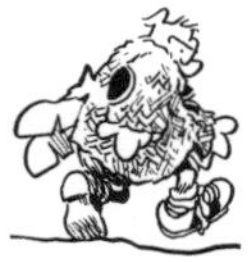

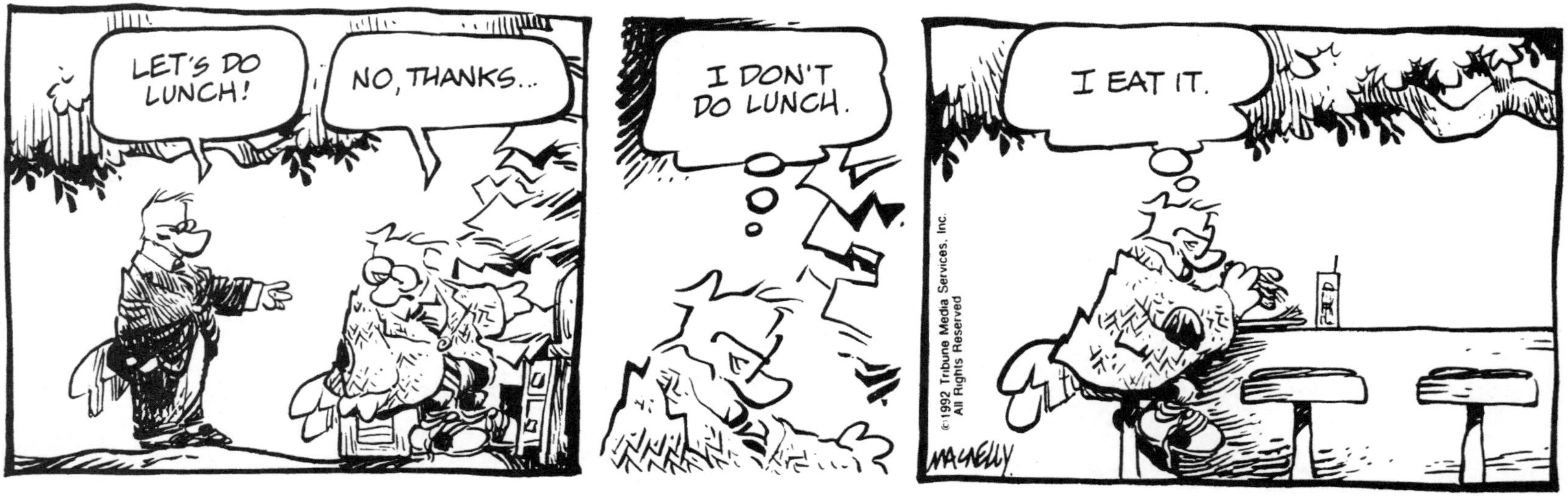
LET'S DO LUNCH!
NO, THANKS...
I DON'T DO LUNCH.
©1992 Tribune Media Services, Inc. All Rights Reserved
I EAT IT.
MACNELLY

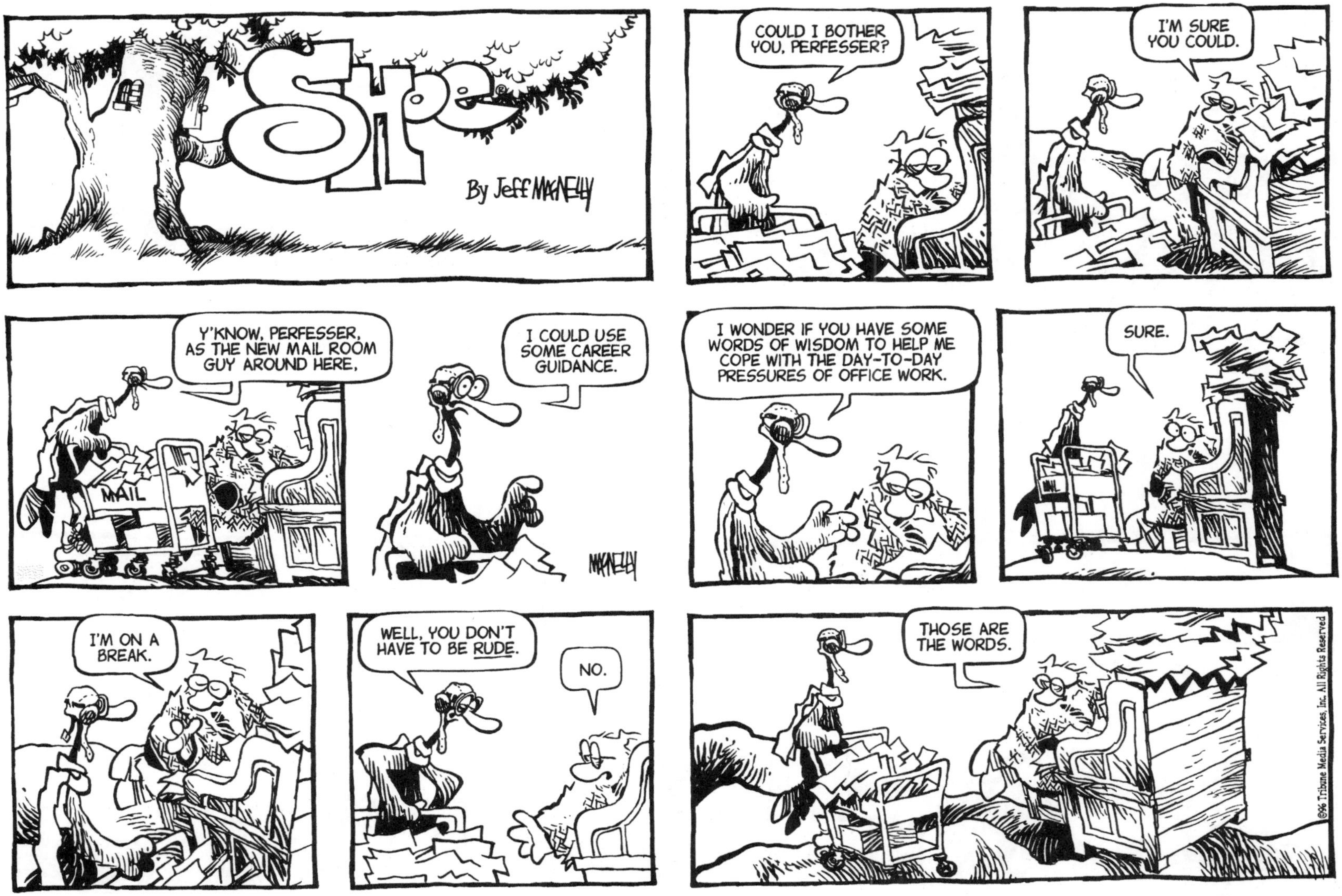
Shoe®
By Jeff MacNelly
COULD I BOTHER YOU, PERFESSER?
I'M SURE YOU COULD.
Y'KNOW, PERFESSER, AS THE NEW MAIL ROOM GUY AROUND HERE,
MAIL
I COULD USE SOME CAREER GUIDANCE.
MACNELLY
I WONDER IF YOU HAVE SOME WORDS OF WISDOM TO HELP ME COPE WITH THE DAY-TO-DAY PRESSURES OF OFFICE WORK.
SURE.
I'M ON A BREAK.
WELL, YOU DON'T HAVE TO BE RUDE.
NO.
THOSE ARE THE WORDS.
©96 Tribune Media Services, Inc. All Rights Reserved

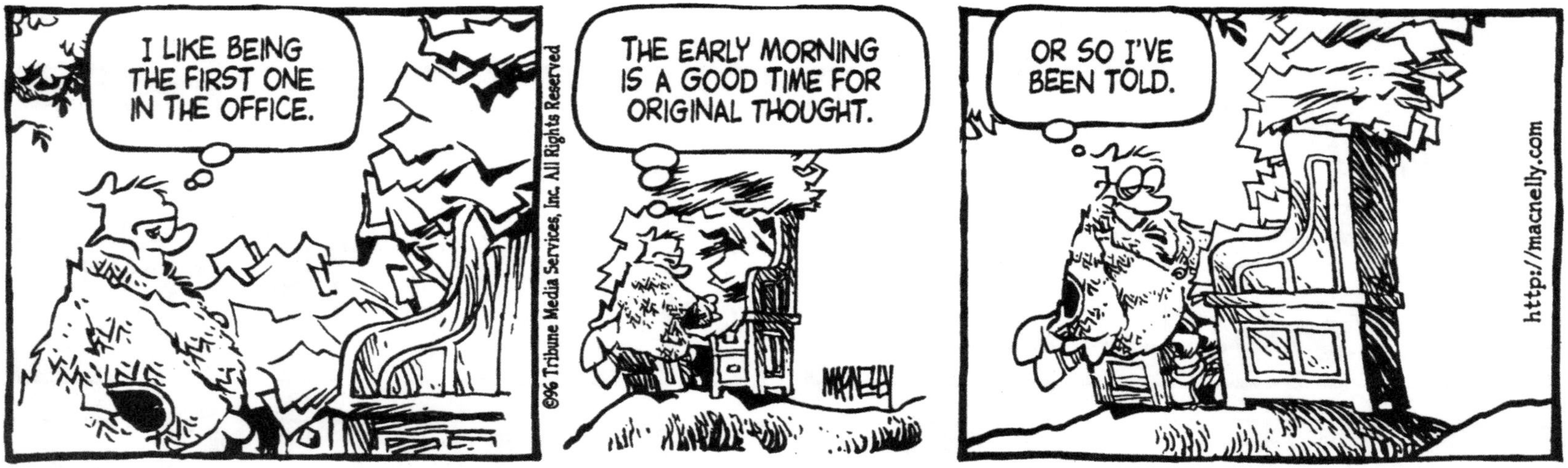

I LIKE BEING THE FIRST ONE IN THE OFFICE.
©96 Tribune Media Services, Inc. All Rights Reserved
THE EARLY MORNING IS A GOOD TIME FOR ORIGINAL THOUGHT.
MACNELLY
OR SO I'VE BEEN TOLD.
http://macnelly.com

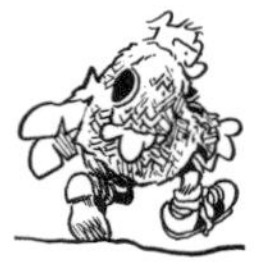

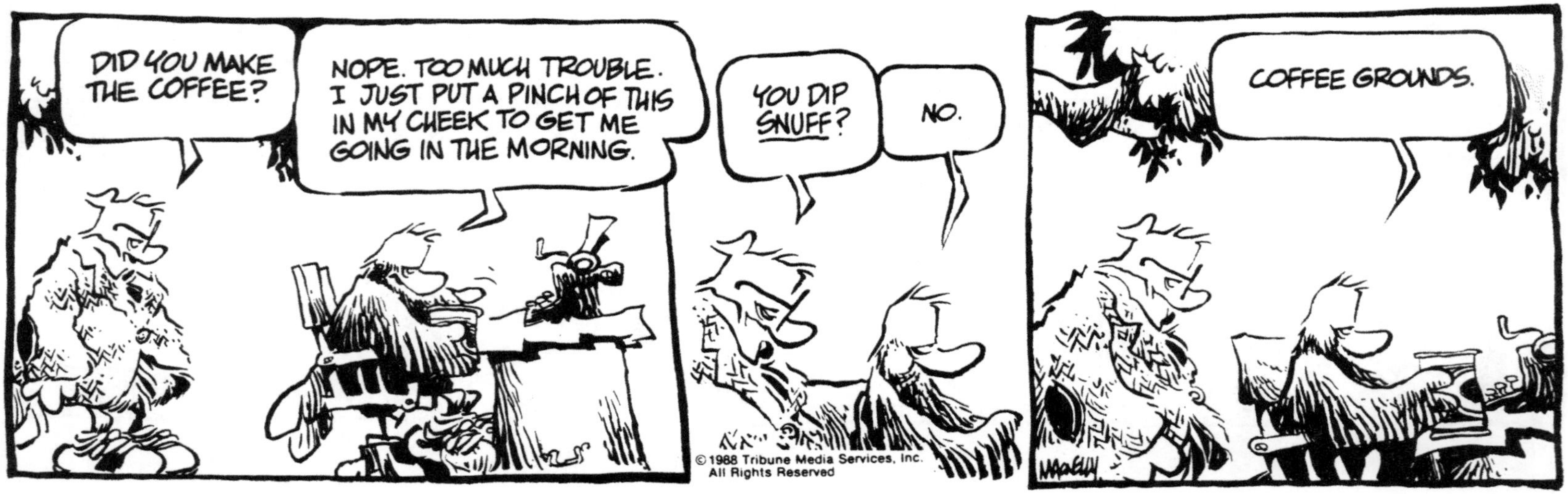

DID YOU MAKE THE COFFEE?
NOPE. TOO MUCH TROUBLE. I JUST PUT A PINCH OF THIS IN MY CHEEK TO GET ME GOING IN THE MORNING.
YOU DIP SNUFF?
NO.
© 1988 Tribune Media Services, Inc. All Rights Reserved
COFFEE GROUNDS.
MACNELLY

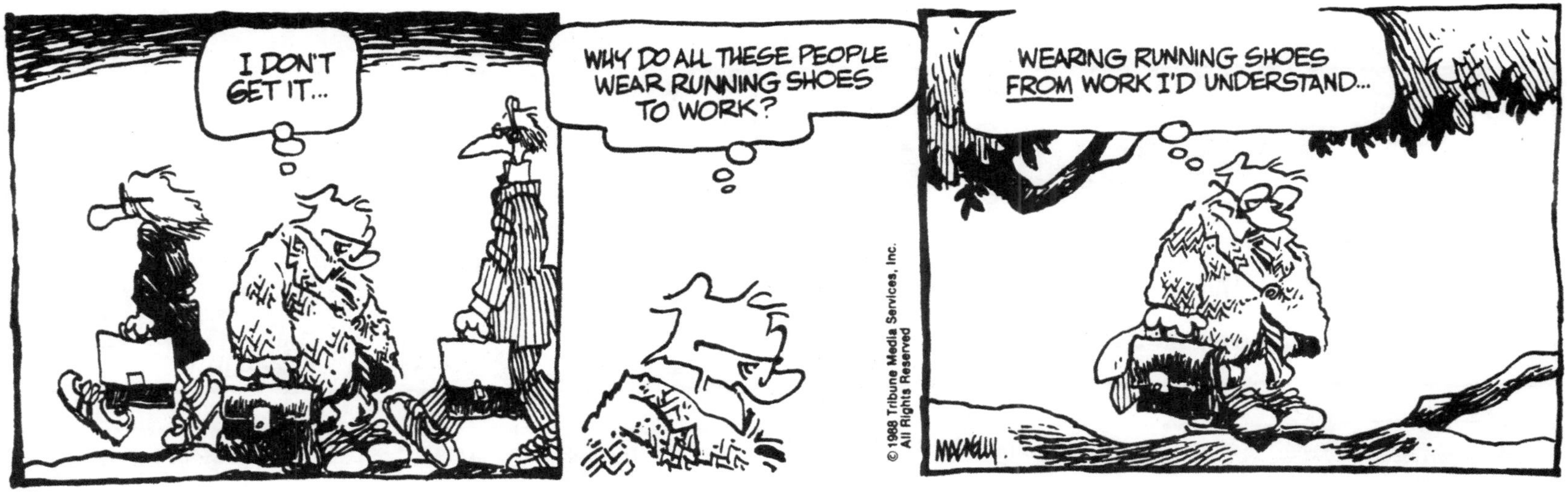
I DON'T GET IT...
WHY DO ALL THESE PEOPLE WEAR RUNNING SHOES TO WORK?
WEARING RUNNING SHOES FROM WORK I'D UNDERSTAND...
© 1988 Tribune Media Services, Inc. All Rights Reserved
MACNELLY

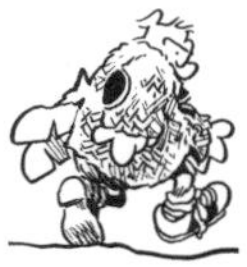

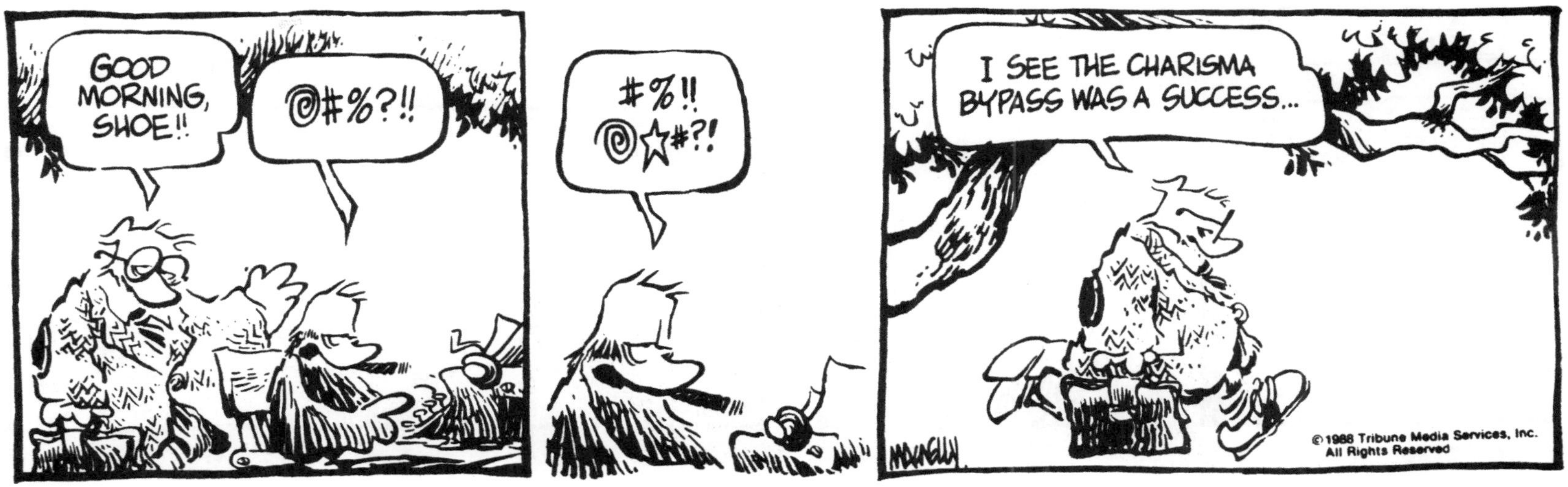
GOOD MORNING, SHOE!!
@#%?!!
#%!! @☆#?!
I SEE THE CHARISMA BYPASS WAS A SUCCESS...
MACNELLY
© 1988 Tribune Media Services, Inc. All Rights Reserved

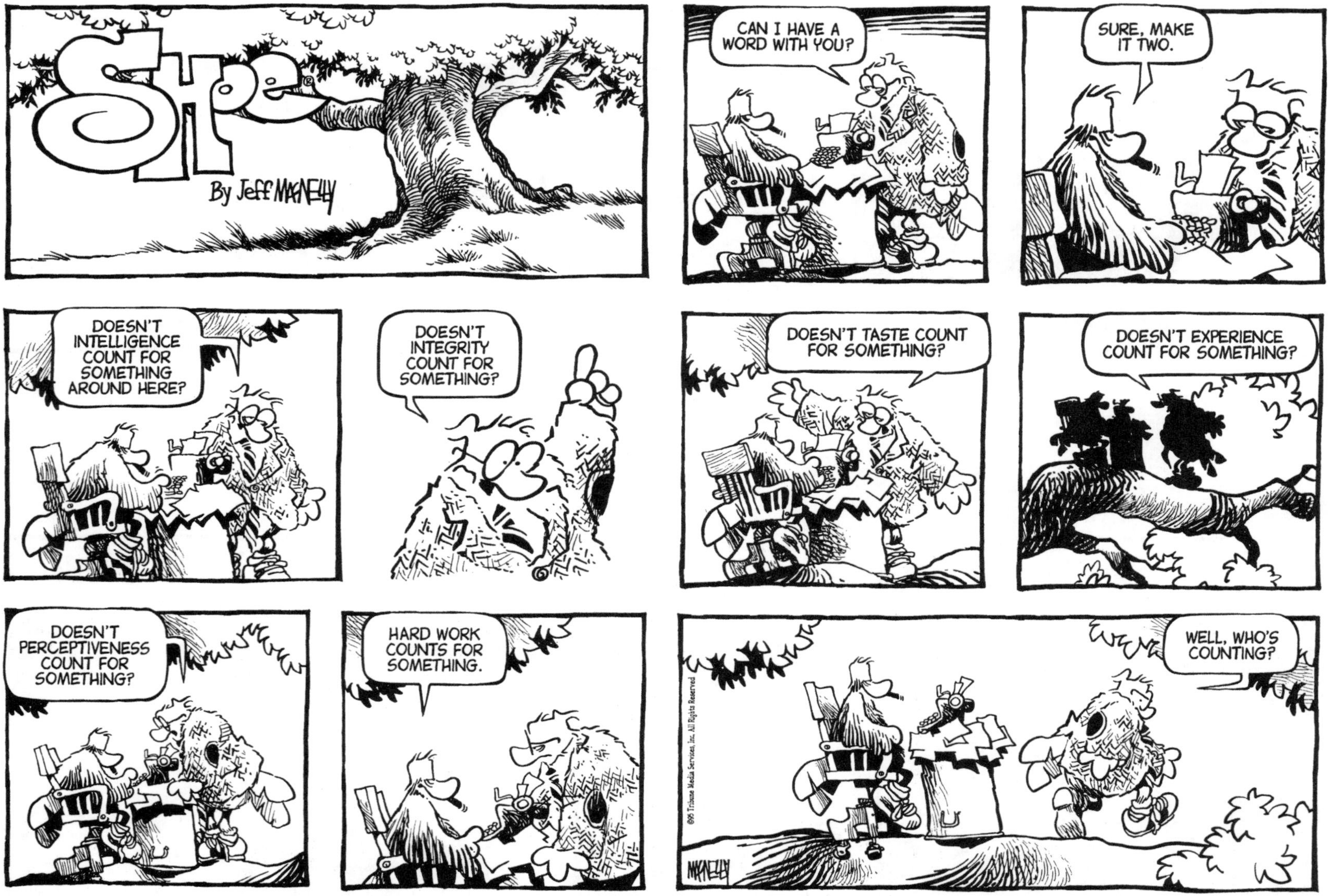
Shoe
By Jeff MacNelly
CAN I HAVE A WORD WITH YOU?
SURE, MAKE IT TWO.
DOESN'T INTELLIGENCE COUNT FOR SOMETHING AROUND HERE?
DOESN'T INTEGRITY COUNT FOR SOMETHING?
DOESN'T TASTE COUNT FOR SOMETHING?
DOESN'T EXPERIENCE COUNT FOR SOMETHING?
DOESN'T PERCEPTIVENESS COUNT FOR SOMETHING?
HARD WORK COUNTS FOR SOMETHING.
WELL, WHO'S COUNTING?
©95 Tribune Media Services, Inc. All Rights Reserved
MacNelly

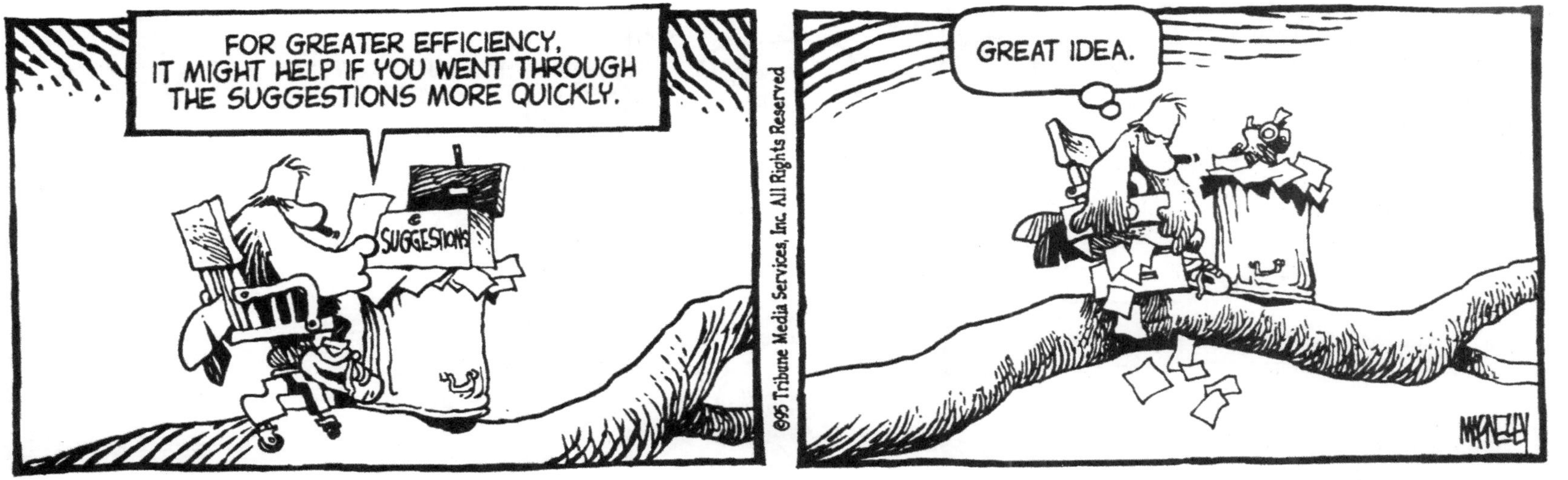
FOR GREATER EFFICIENCY, IT MIGHT HELP IF YOU WENT THROUGH THE SUGGESTIONS MORE QUICKLY.
SUGGESTIONS
©95 Tribune Media Services, Inc. All Rights Reserved
GREAT IDEA.
MACNELLY

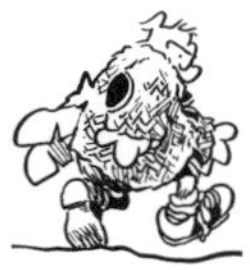

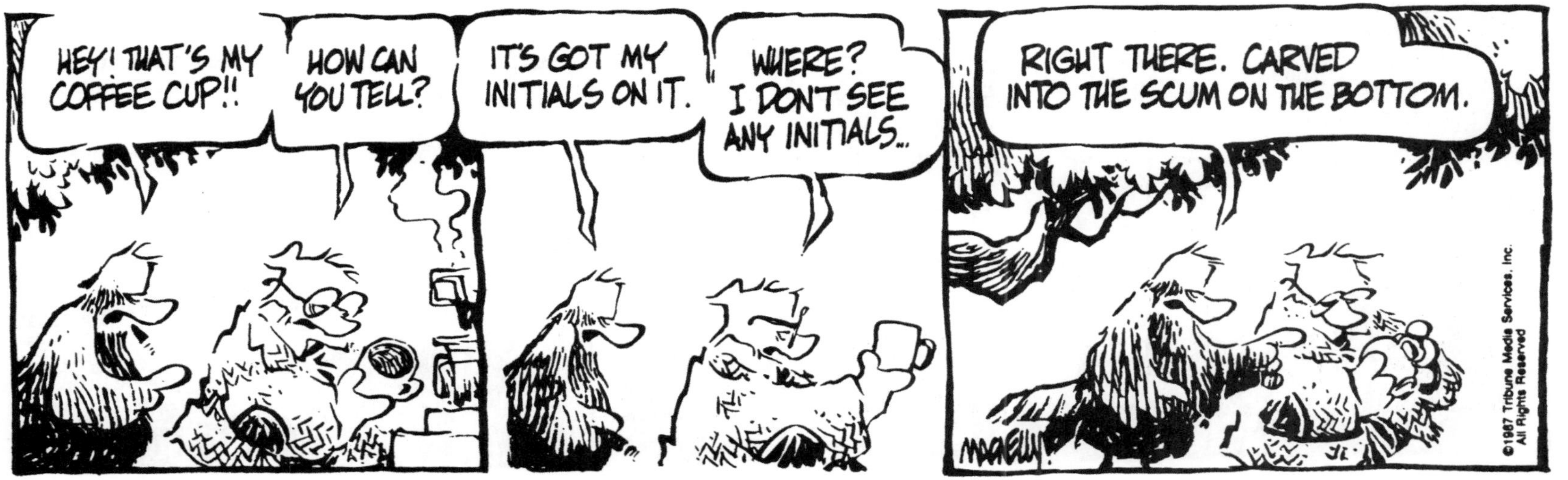
HEY! THAT'S MY COFFEE CUP!!
HOW CAN YOU TELL?
IT'S GOT MY INITIALS ON IT.
WHERE? I DON'T SEE ANY INITIALS...
RIGHT THERE. CARVED INTO THE SCUM ON THE BOTTOM.
MACNELLY
©1987 Tribune Media Services, Inc. All Rights Reserved

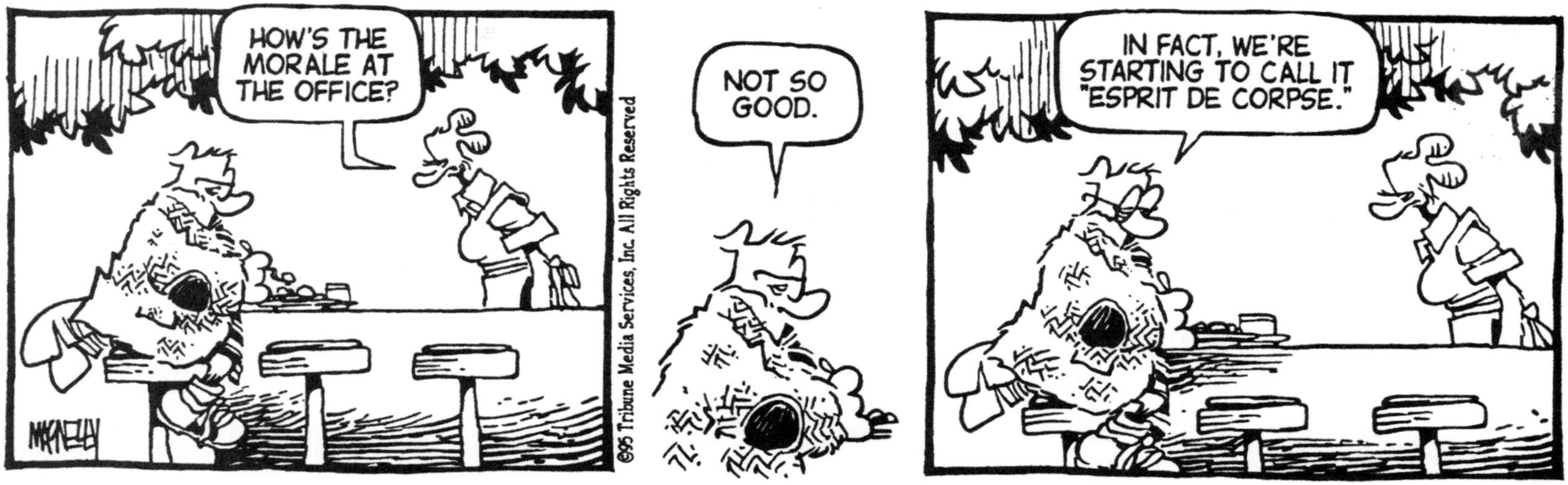
HOW'S THE MORALE AT THE OFFICE?
NOT SO GOOD.
IN FACT, WE'RE STARTING TO CALL IT "ESPRIT DE CORPSE."
©95 Tribune Media Services, Inc. All Rights Reserved

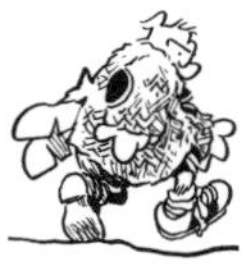

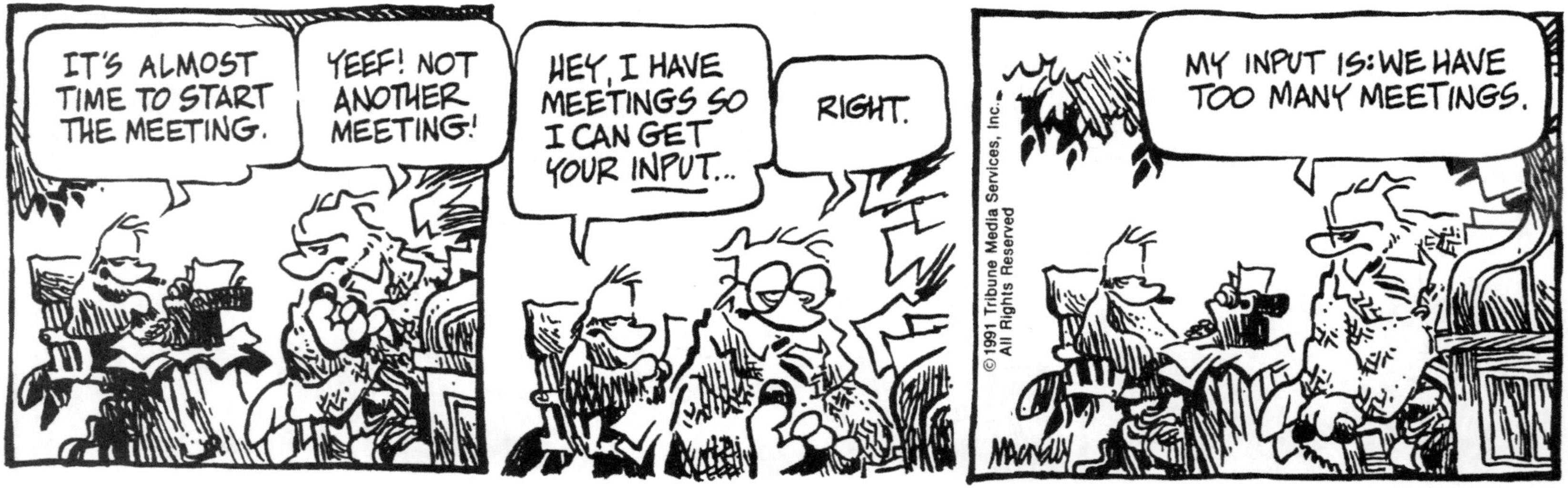
IT'S ALMOST TIME TO START THE MEETING.
YEEF! NOT ANOTHER MEETING!
HEY, I HAVE MEETINGS SO I CAN GET YOUR INPUT...
RIGHT.
MY INPUT IS: WE HAVE TOO MANY MEETINGS.
© 1991 Tribune Media Services, Inc. All Rights Reserved

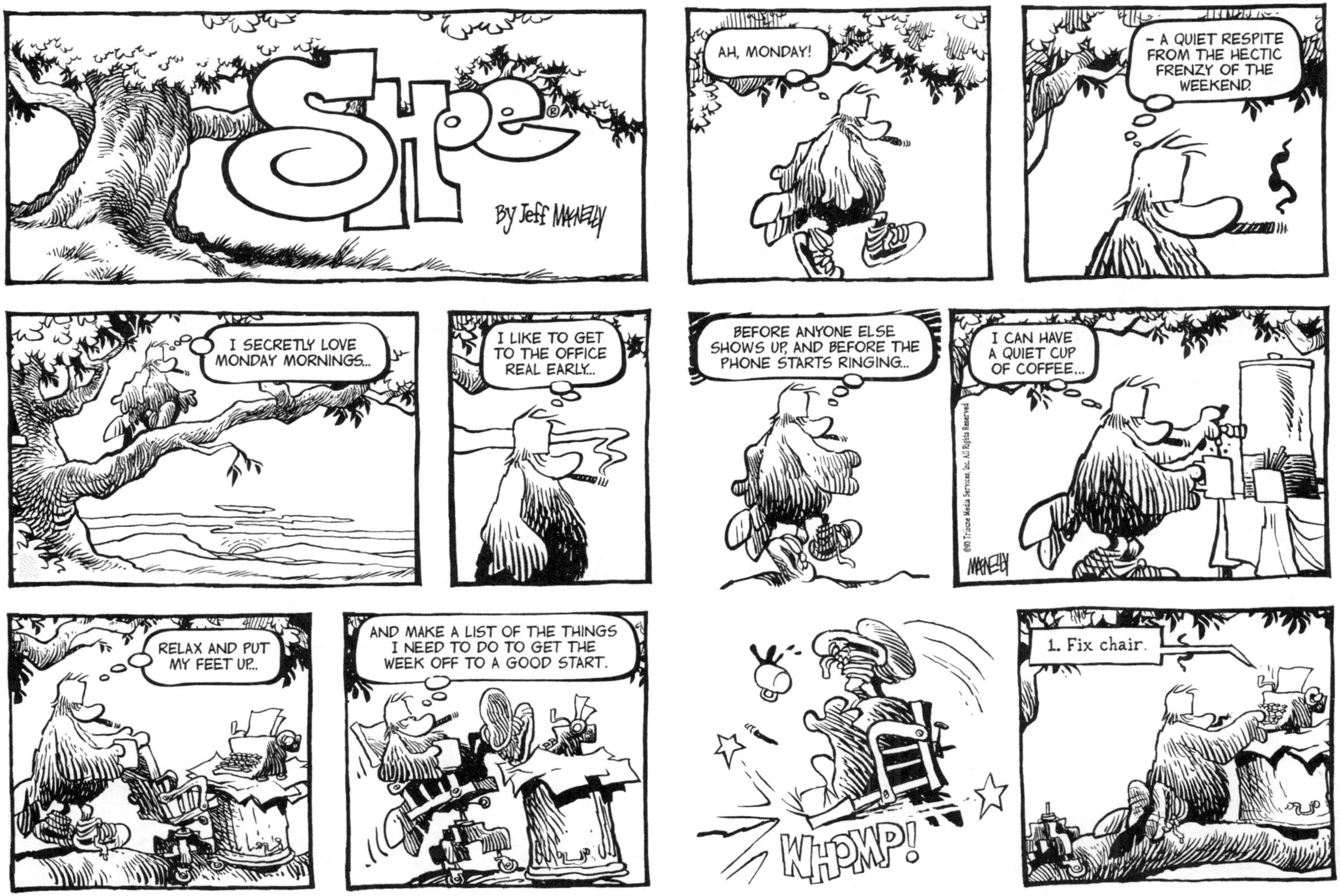
Shoe®
By Jeff MacNelly
AH, MONDAY!
– A QUIET RESPITE FROM THE HECTIC FRENZY OF THE WEEKEND.
I SECRETLY LOVE MONDAY MORNINGS...
I LIKE TO GET TO THE OFFICE REAL EARLY...
BEFORE ANYONE ELSE SHOWS UP, AND BEFORE THE PHONE STARTS RINGING...
I CAN HAVE A QUIET CUP OF COFFEE...
©93 Tribune Media Services, Inc. All Rights Reserved
MacNelly
RELAX AND PUT MY FEET UP...
AND MAKE A LIST OF THE THINGS I NEED TO DO TO GET THE WEEK OFF TO A GOOD START.
WHOMP!
1. Fix chair.

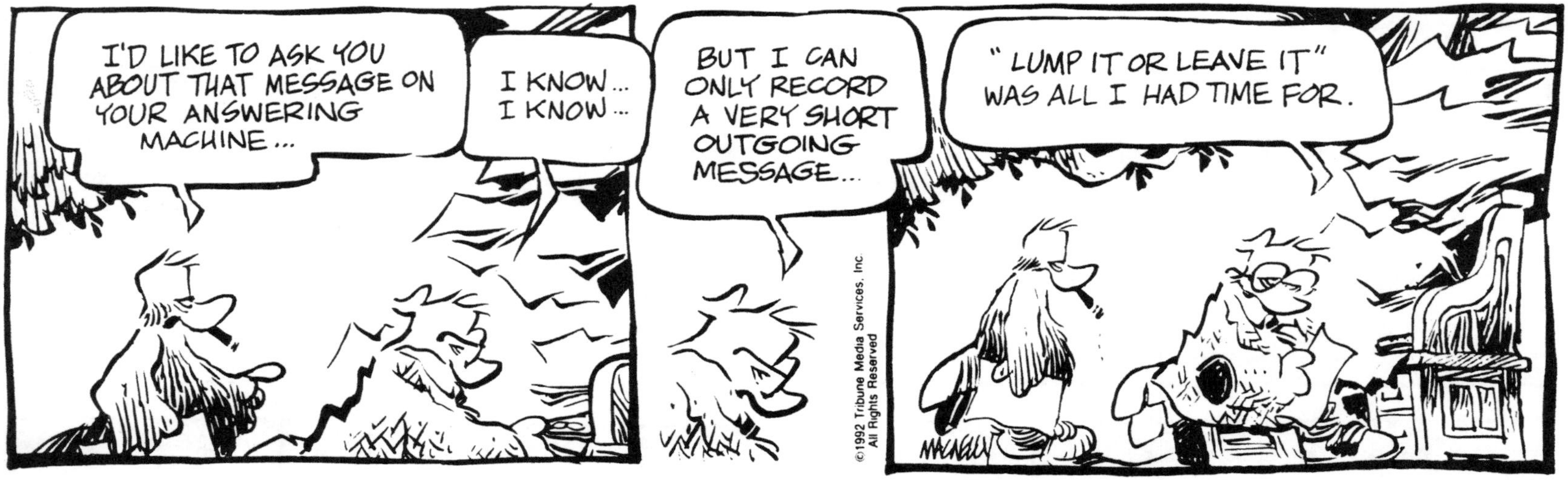
I'D LIKE TO ASK YOU ABOUT THAT MESSAGE ON YOUR ANSWERING MACHINE...
I KNOW... I KNOW...
BUT I CAN ONLY RECORD A VERY SHORT OUTGOING MESSAGE...
"LUMP IT OR LEAVE IT" WAS ALL I HAD TIME FOR.
©1992 Tribune Media Services, Inc. All Rights Reserved
MACNELLY

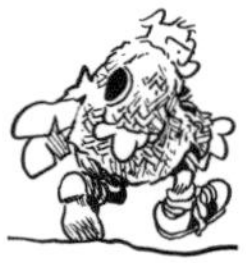

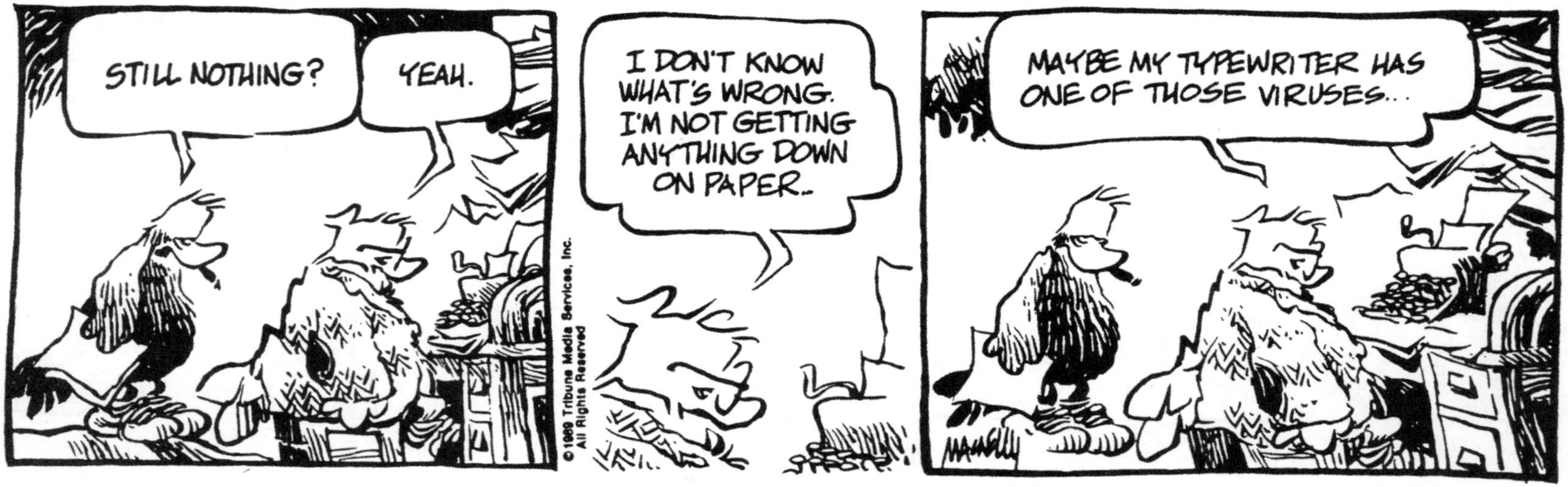
STILL NOTHING?
YEAH.
I DON'T KNOW WHAT'S WRONG. I'M NOT GETTING ANYTHING DOWN ON PAPER..
MAYBE MY TYPEWRITER HAS ONE OF THOSE VIRUSES...
©1989 Tribune Media Services, Inc. All Rights Reserved

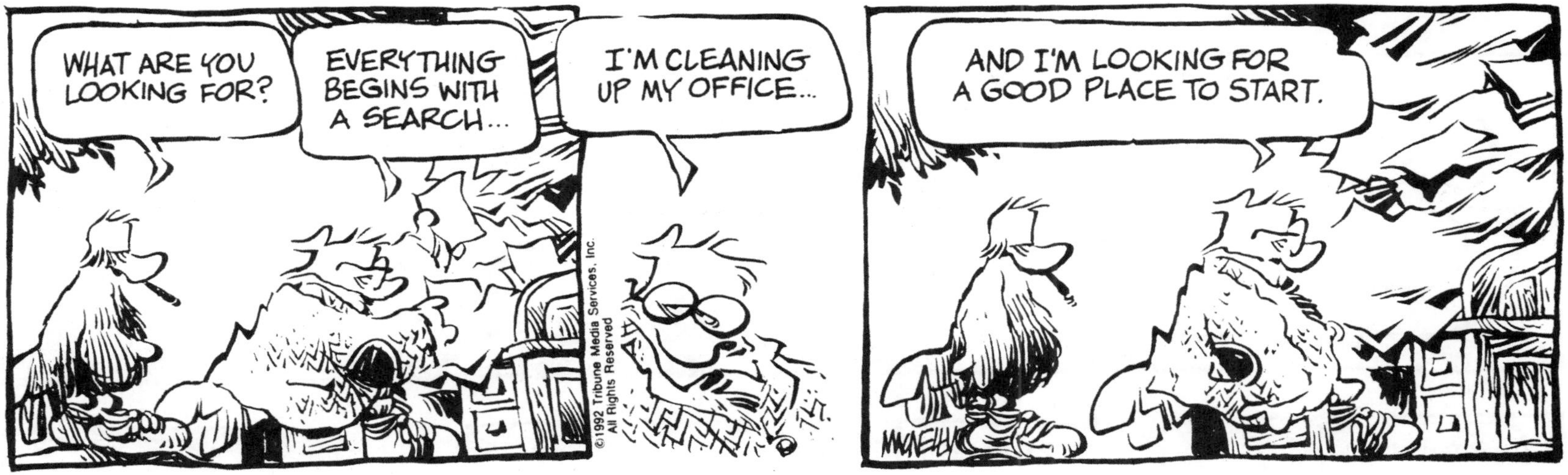
WHAT ARE YOU LOOKING FOR?
EVERYTHING BEGINS WITH A SEARCH...
I'M CLEANING UP MY OFFICE...
AND I'M LOOKING FOR A GOOD PLACE TO START.
©1992 Tribune Media Services, Inc. All Rights Reserved

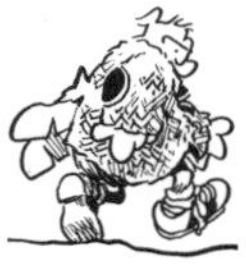

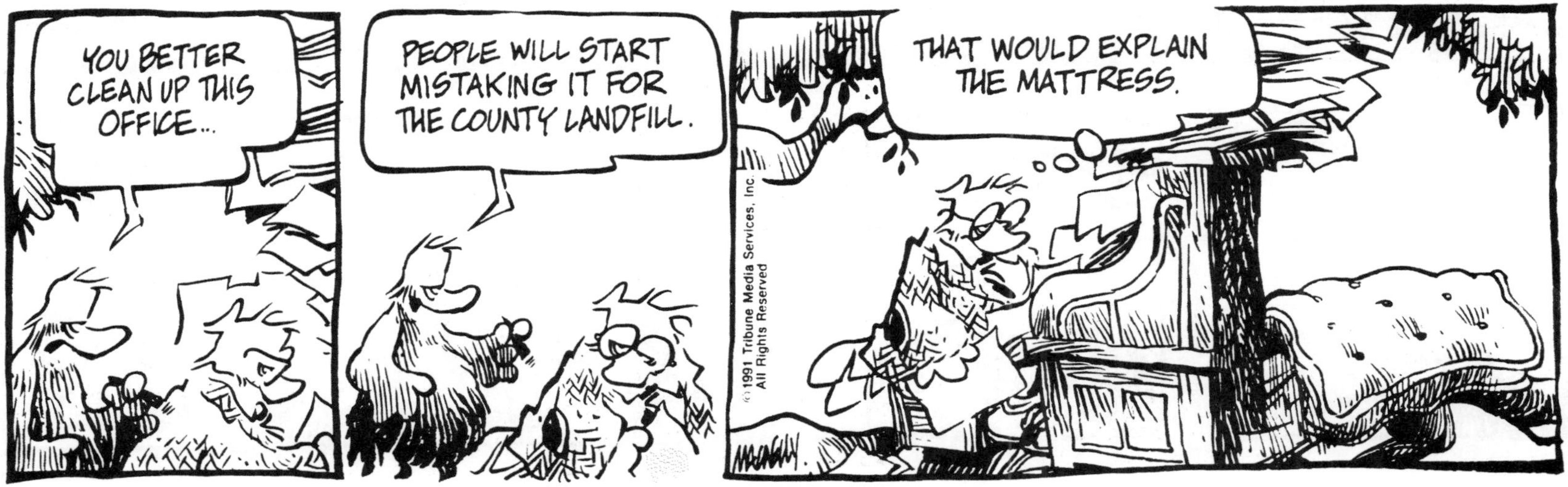
YOU BETTER CLEAN UP THIS OFFICE...
PEOPLE WILL START MISTAKING IT FOR THE COUNTY LANDFILL.
THAT WOULD EXPLAIN THE MATTRESS.
©1991 Tribune Media Services, Inc. All Rights Reserved

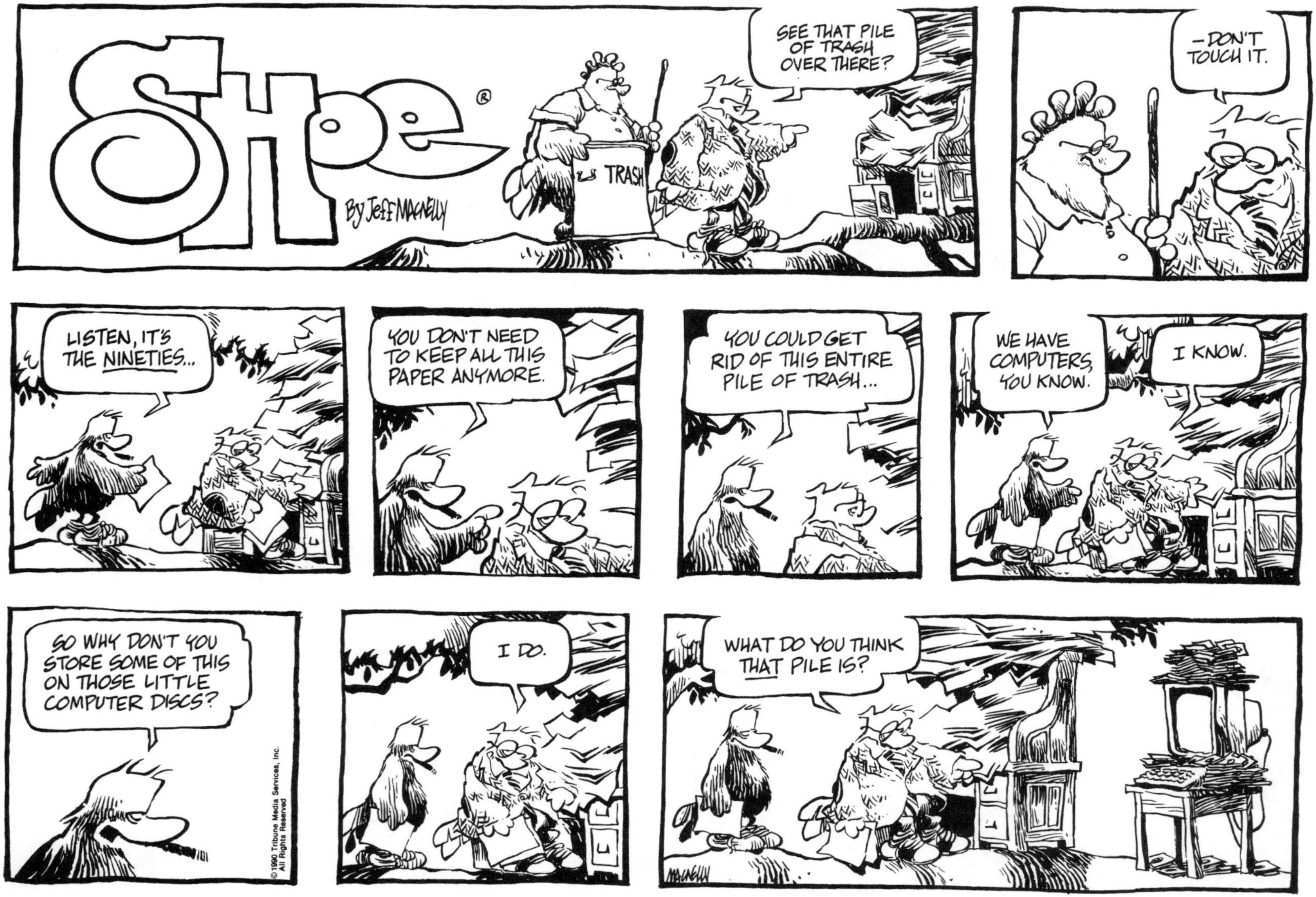
SHOE®
By Jeff MacNelly
TRASH
SEE THAT PILE OF TRASH OVER THERE?
—DON'T TOUCH IT.
LISTEN, IT'S THE NINETIES...
YOU DON'T NEED TO KEEP ALL THIS PAPER ANYMORE.
YOU COULD GET RID OF THIS ENTIRE PILE OF TRASH...
WE HAVE COMPUTERS, YOU KNOW.
I KNOW.
SO WHY DON'T YOU STORE SOME OF THIS ON THOSE LITTLE COMPUTER DISCS?
© 1990 Tribune Media Services, Inc. All Rights Reserved
I DO.
WHAT DO YOU THINK THAT PILE IS?
MACNELLY

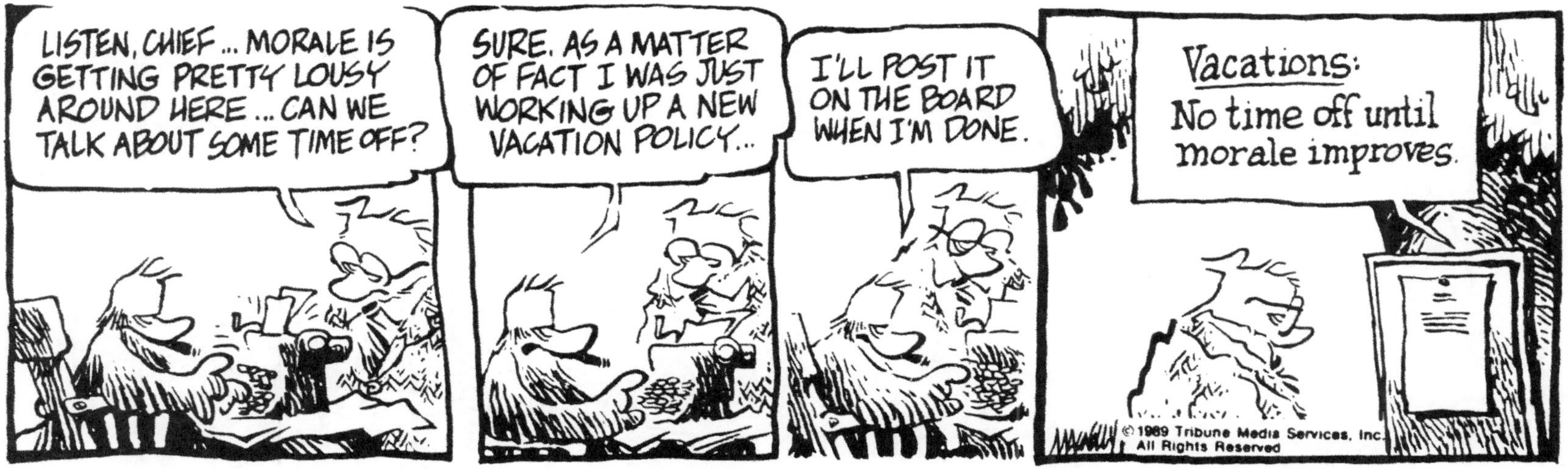
LISTEN, CHIEF ... MORALE IS GETTING PRETTY LOUSY AROUND HERE ... CAN WE TALK ABOUT SOME TIME OFF?
SURE. AS A MATTER OF FACT I WAS JUST WORKING UP A NEW VACATION POLICY...
I'LL POST IT ON THE BOARD WHEN I'M DONE.
Vacations:
No time off until morale improves.
© 1989 Tribune Media Services, Inc. All Rights Reserved

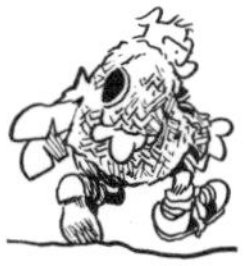

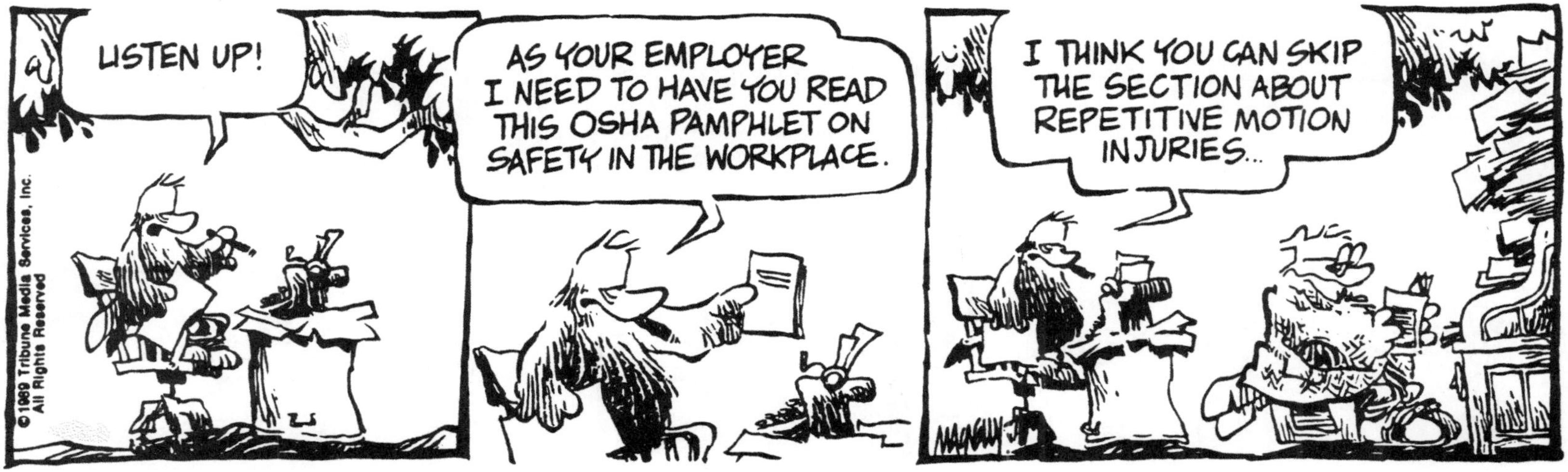
LISTEN UP!
AS YOUR EMPLOYER I NEED TO HAVE YOU READ THIS OSHA PAMPHLET ON SAFETY IN THE WORKPLACE.
I THINK YOU CAN SKIP THE SECTION ABOUT REPETITIVE MOTION INJURIES...
© 1989 Tribune Media Services, Inc. All Rights Reserved

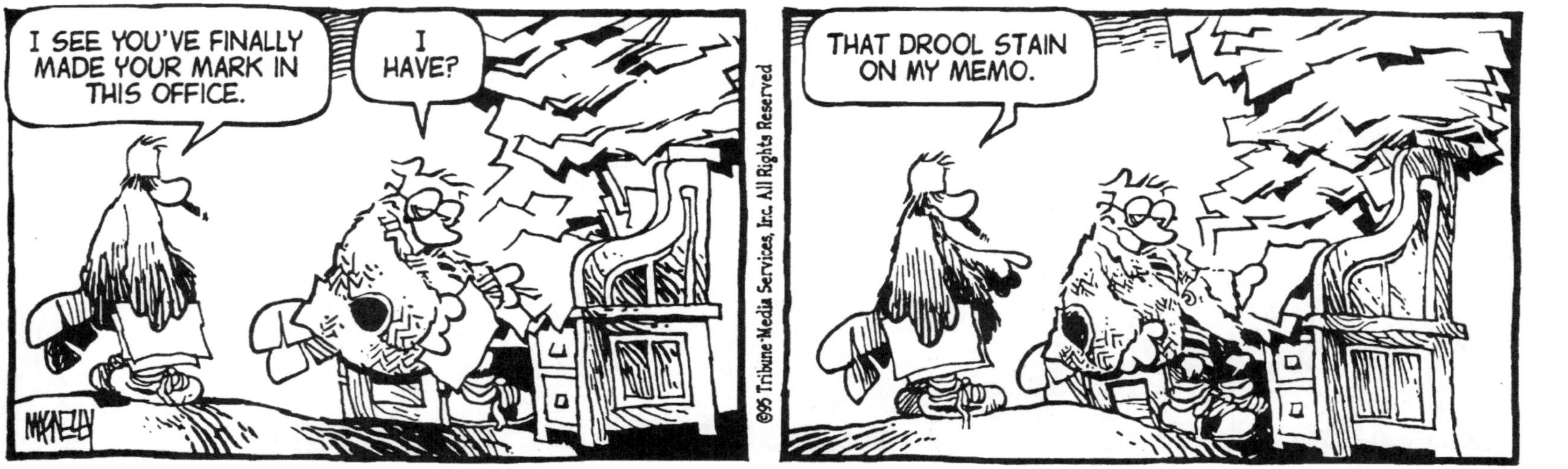
I SEE YOU'VE FINALLY MADE YOUR MARK IN THIS OFFICE.
I HAVE?
THAT DROOL STAIN ON MY MEMO.
©95 Tribune Media Services, Inc. All Rights Reserved

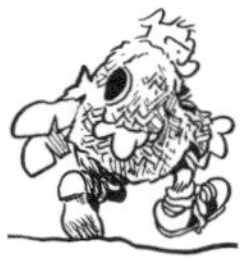

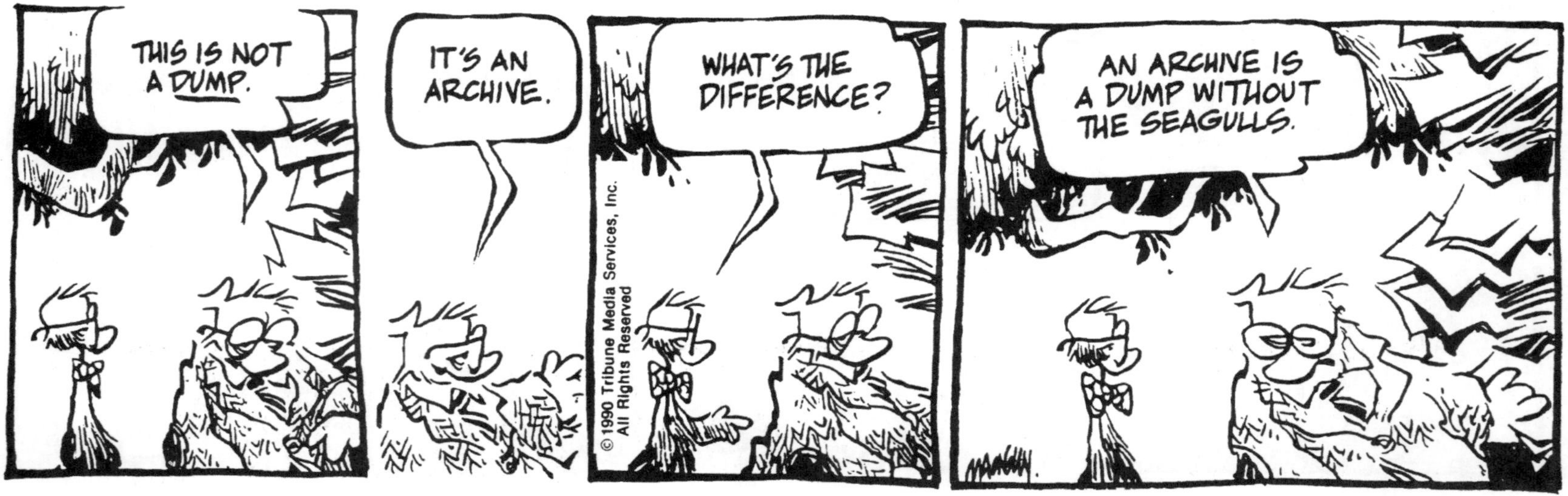
THIS IS NOT A DUMP.
IT'S AN ARCHIVE.
WHAT'S THE DIFFERENCE?
AN ARCHIVE IS A DUMP WITHOUT THE SEAGULLS.
© 1990 Tribune Media Services, Inc. All Rights Reserved

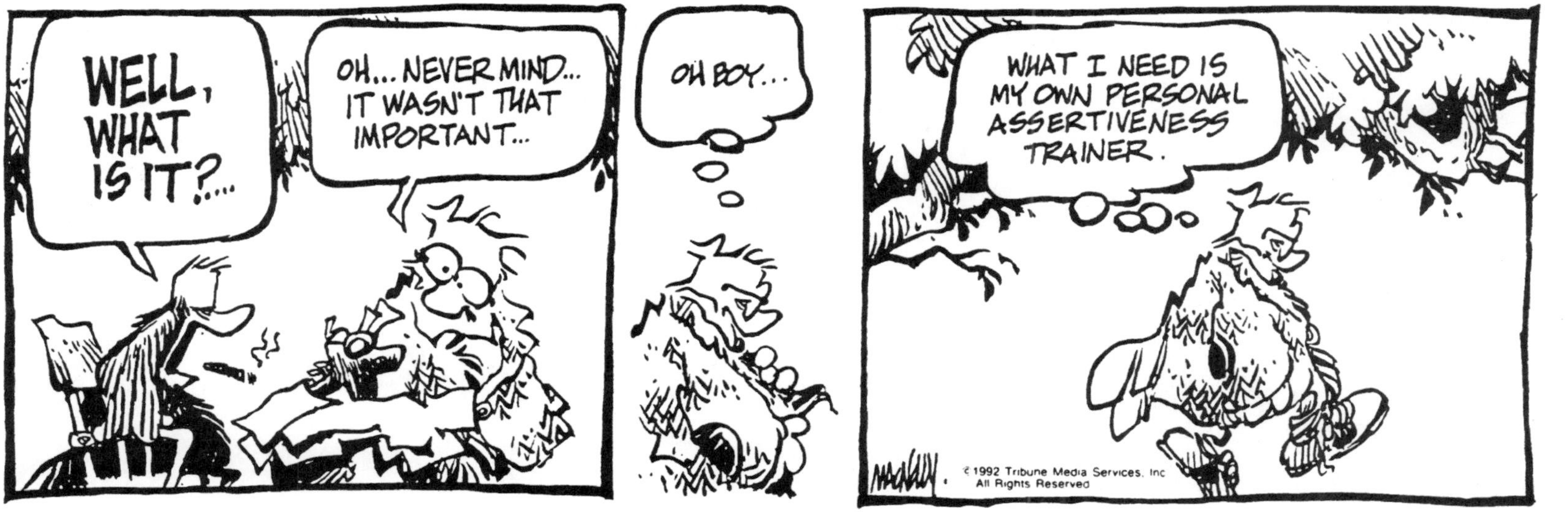
WELL, WHAT IS IT?....
OH... NEVER MIND... IT WASN'T THAT IMPORTANT...
OH BOY...
WHAT I NEED IS MY OWN PERSONAL ASSERTIVENESS TRAINER.
©1992 Tribune Media Services, Inc All Rights Reserved

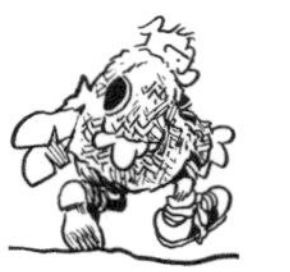

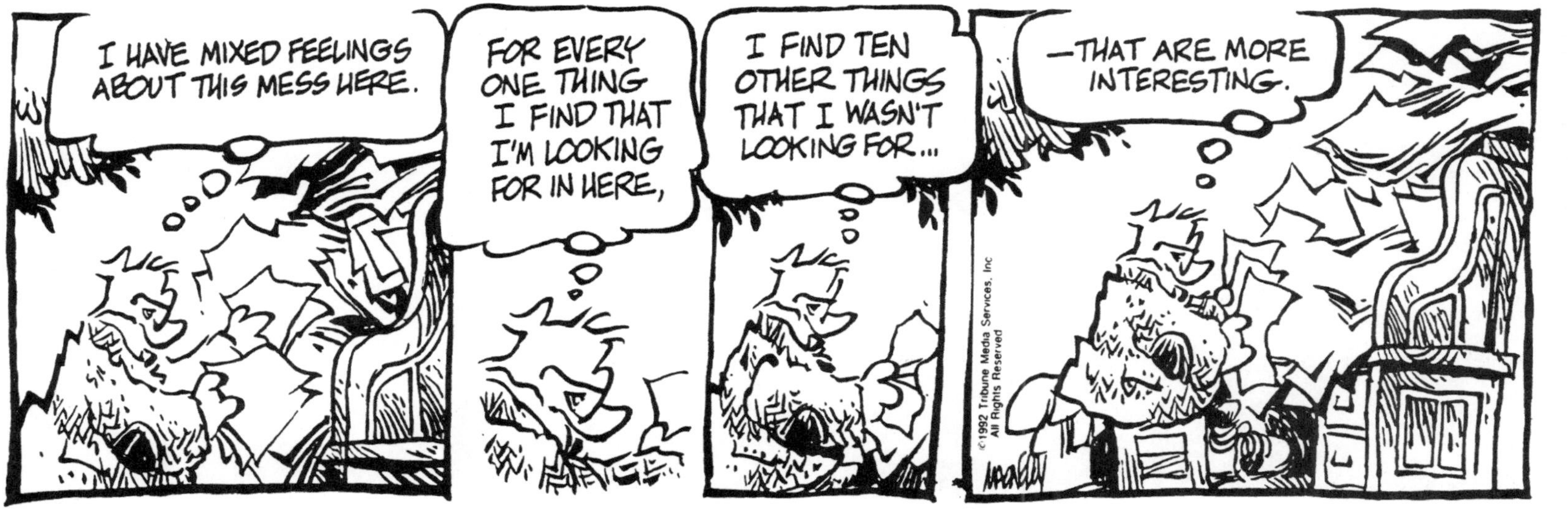
I HAVE MIXED FEELINGS ABOUT THIS MESS HERE.
FOR EVERY ONE THING I FIND THAT I'M LOOKING FOR IN HERE,
I FIND TEN OTHER THINGS THAT I WASN'T LOOKING FOR...
—THAT ARE MORE INTERESTING.
©1992 Tribune Media Services, Inc All Rights Reserved

Chapter Two

Datalanche!

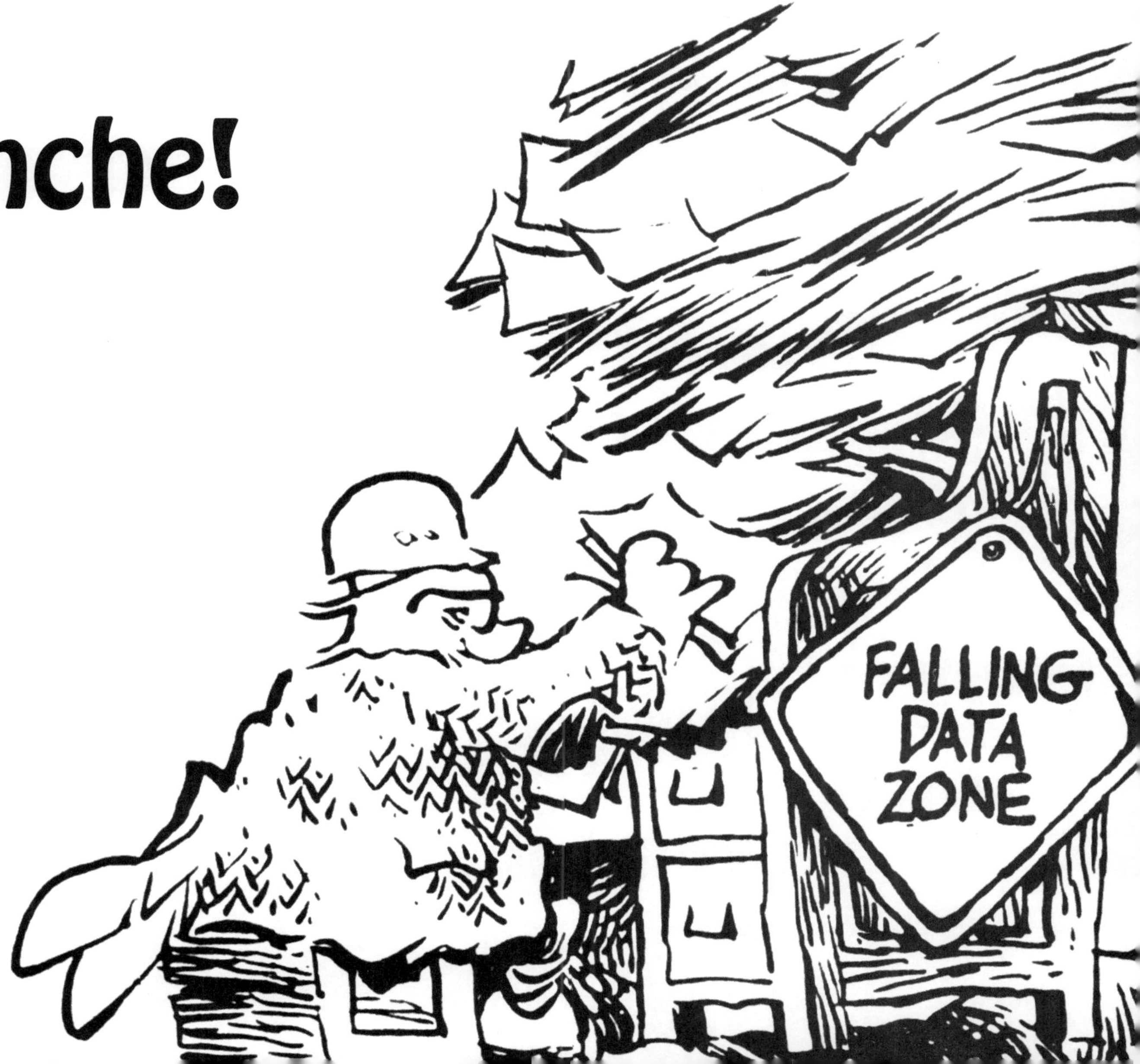
FALLING
DATA
ZONE

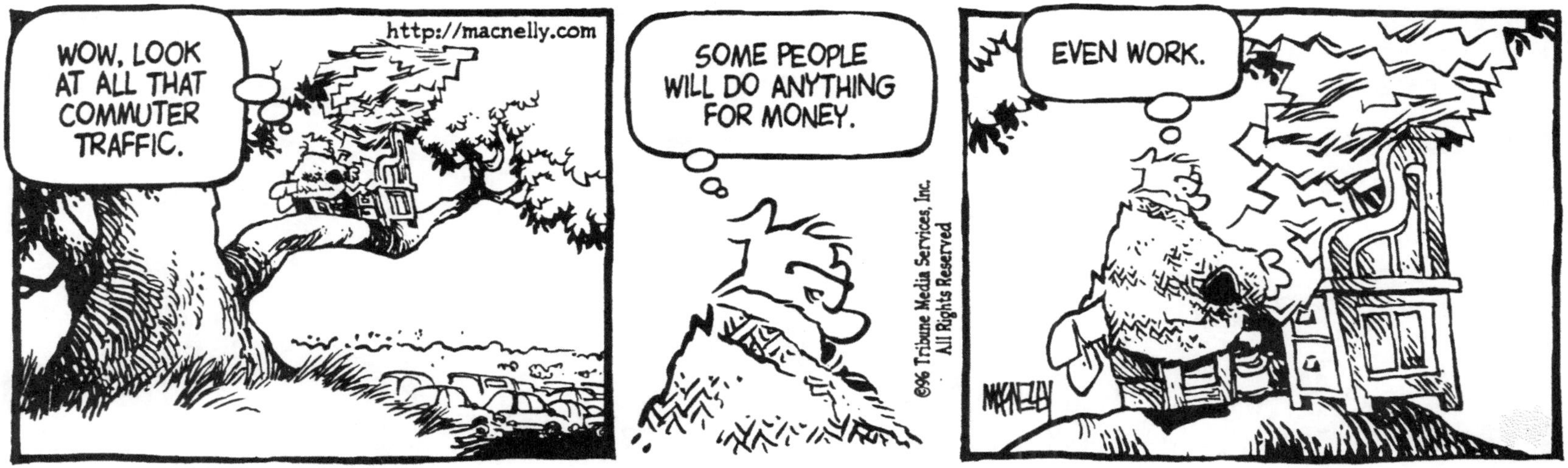
http://macnelly.com
WOW, LOOK AT ALL THAT COMMUTER TRAFFIC.
SOME PEOPLE WILL DO ANYTHING FOR MONEY.
©96 Tribune Media Services, Inc. All Rights Reserved
EVEN WORK.
MACNELLY

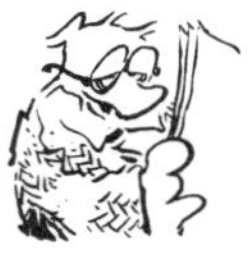

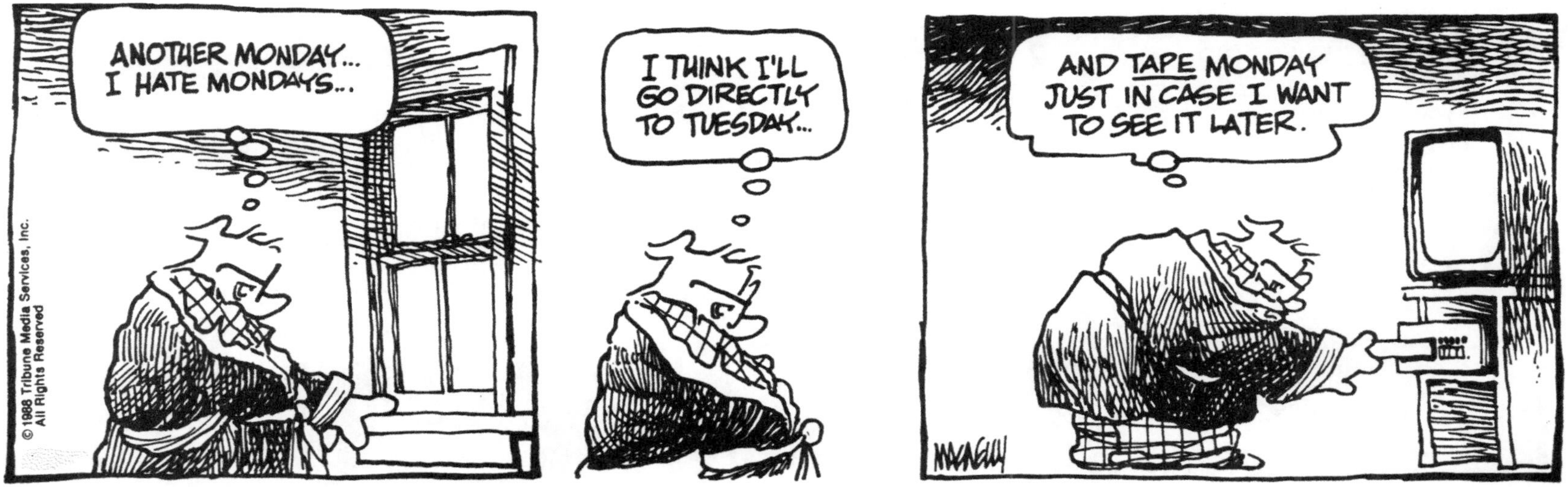
ANOTHER MONDAY... I HATE MONDAYS...
© 1988 Tribune Media Services, Inc. All Rights Reserved
I THINK I'LL GO DIRECTLY TO TUESDAY...
AND TAPE MONDAY JUST IN CASE I WANT TO SEE IT LATER.
MACNELLY

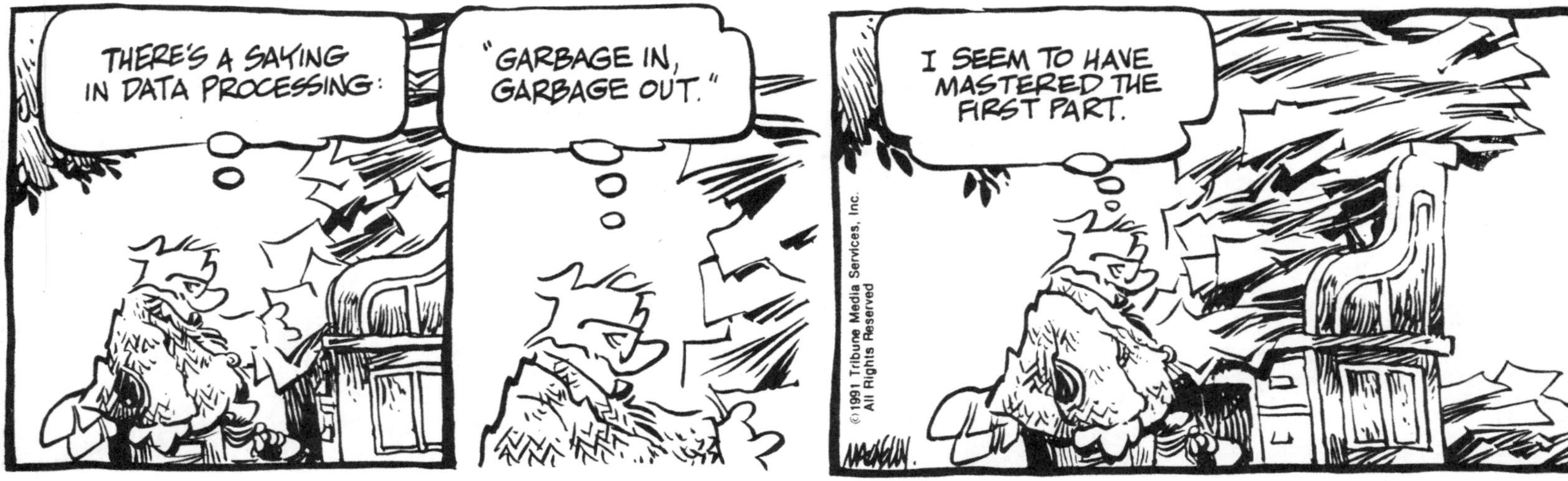
THERE'S A SAYING IN DATA PROCESSING:
"GARBAGE IN, GARBAGE OUT."
I SEEM TO HAVE MASTERED THE FIRST PART.
© 1991 Tribune Media Services, Inc. All Rights Reserved

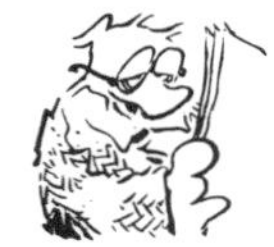

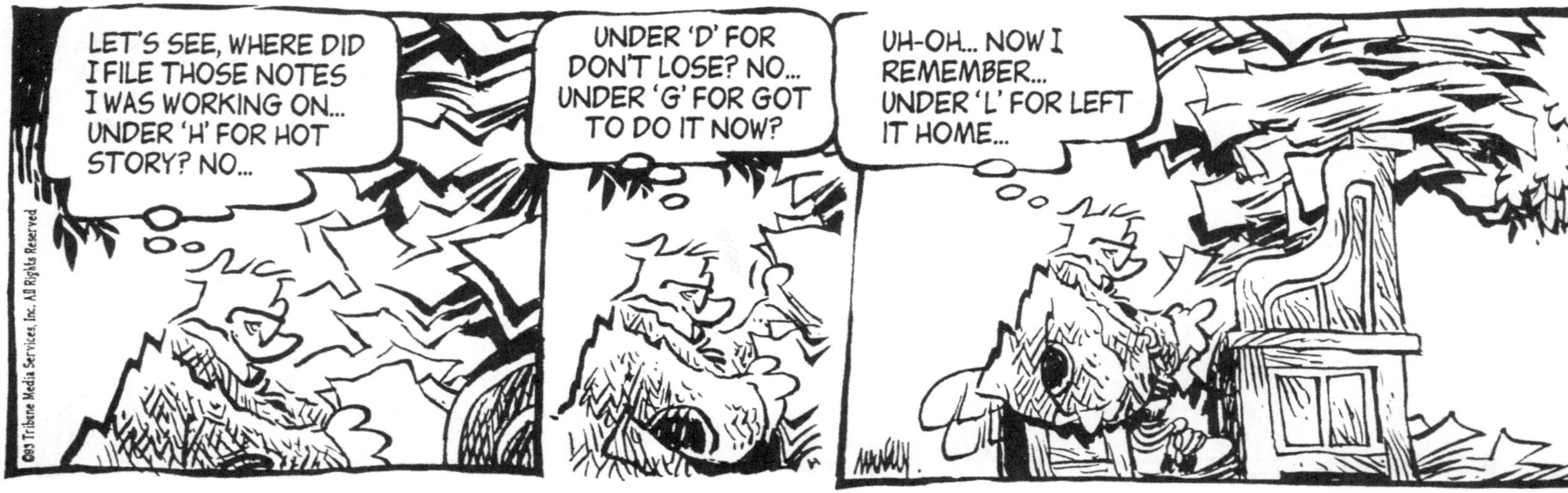
LET'S SEE, WHERE DID I FILE THOSE NOTES I WAS WORKING ON... UNDER 'H' FOR HOT STORY? NO...
UNDER 'D' FOR DON'T LOSE? NO... UNDER 'G' FOR GOT TO DO IT NOW?
UH-OH... NOW I REMEMBER... UNDER 'L' FOR LEFT IT HOME...
©93 Tribune Media Services, Inc. All Rights Reserved

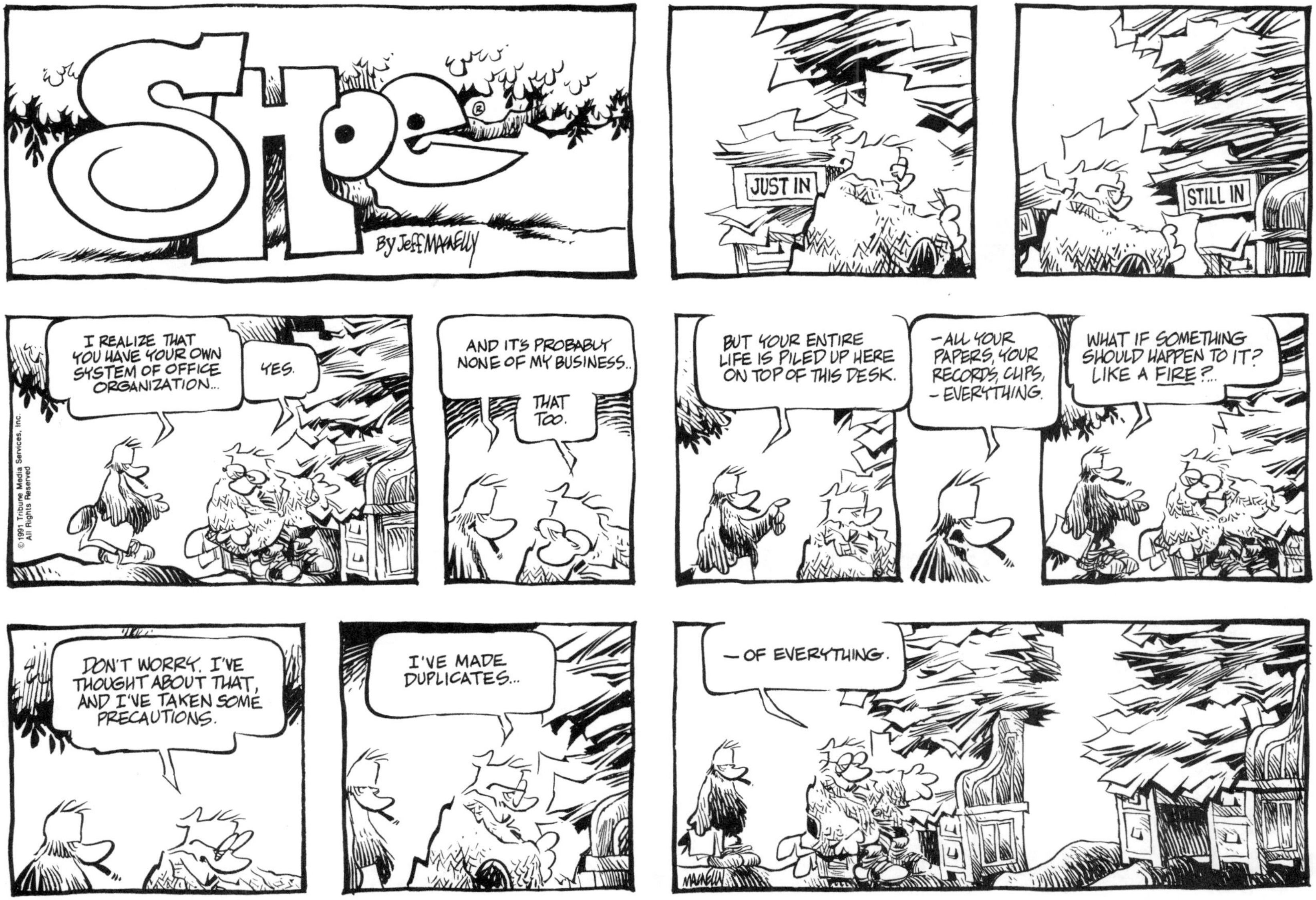
SHOE
By Jeff MacNelly
JUST IN
STILL IN
© 1991 Tribune Media Services, Inc. All Rights Reserved
I REALIZE THAT YOU HAVE YOUR OWN SYSTEM OF OFFICE ORGANIZATION...
YES.
AND IT'S PROBABLY NONE OF MY BUSINESS..
THAT TOO.
BUT YOUR ENTIRE LIFE IS PILED UP HERE ON TOP OF THIS DESK.
-ALL YOUR PAPERS, YOUR RECORDS, CLIPS, - EVERYTHING.
WHAT IF SOMETHING SHOULD HAPPEN TO IT? LIKE A FIRE?...
DON'T WORRY. I'VE THOUGHT ABOUT THAT, AND I'VE TAKEN SOME PRECAUTIONS.
I'VE MADE DUPLICATES...
— OF EVERYTHING.
MACNELLY

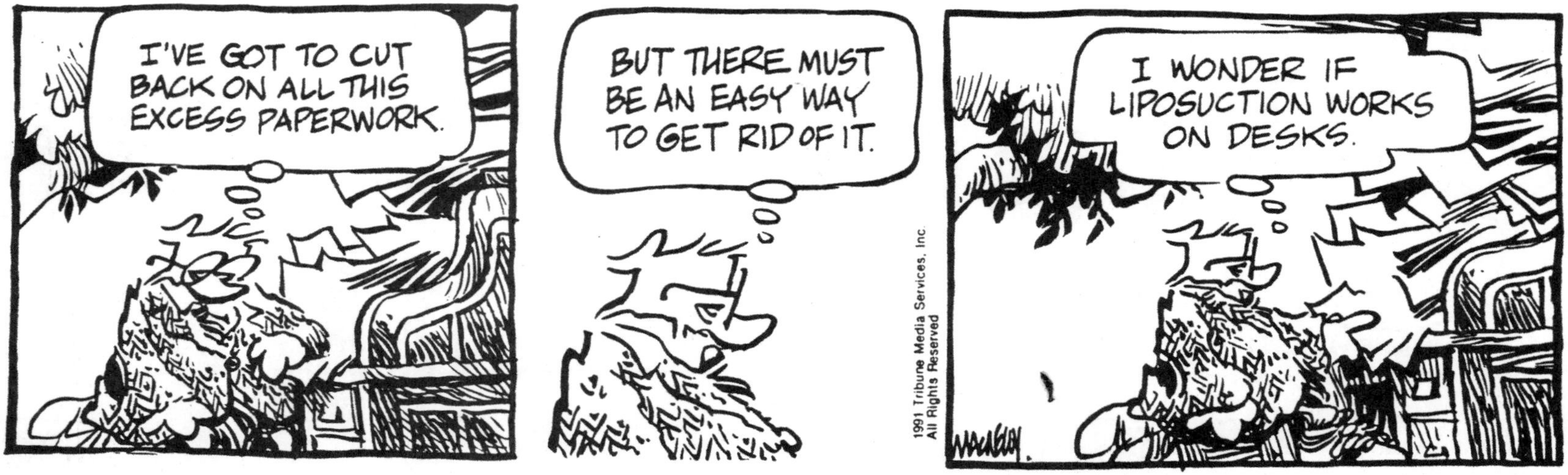
I'VE GOT TO CUT BACK ON ALL THIS EXCESS PAPERWORK.
BUT THERE MUST BE AN EASY WAY TO GET RID OF IT.
1991 Tribune Media Services, Inc
All Rights Reserved
I WONDER IF LIPOSUCTION WORKS ON DESKS.

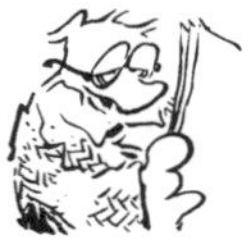

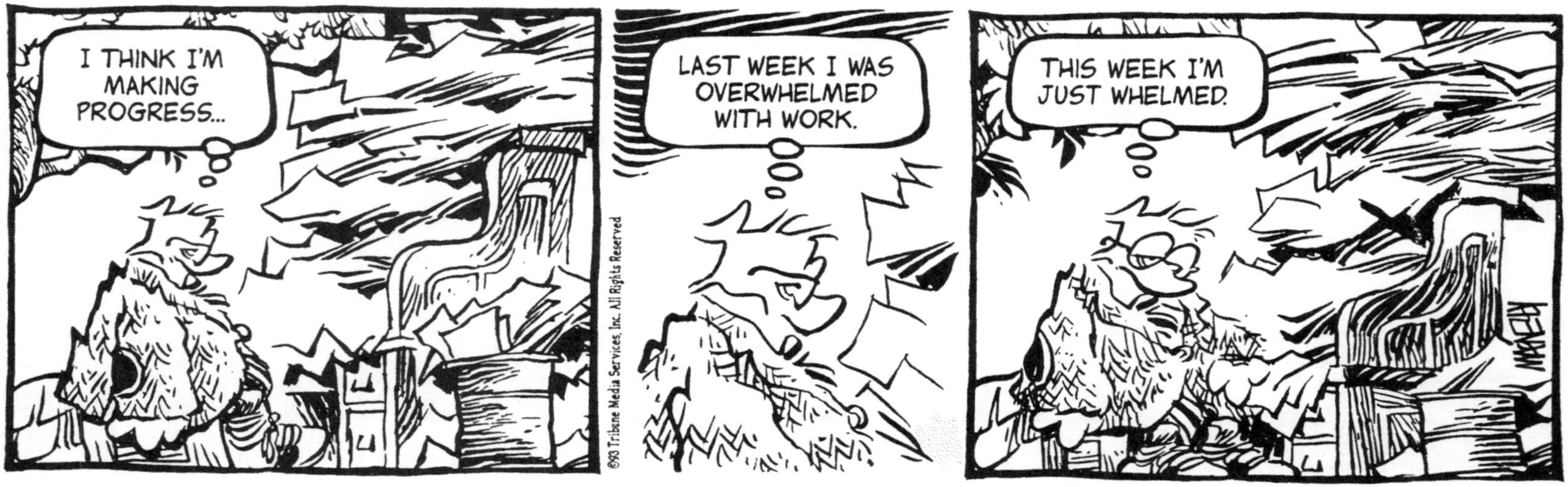
I THINK I'M MAKING PROGRESS...
©93 Tribune Media Services, Inc. All Rights Reserved
LAST WEEK I WAS OVERWHELMED WITH WORK.
THIS WEEK I'M JUST WHELMED.

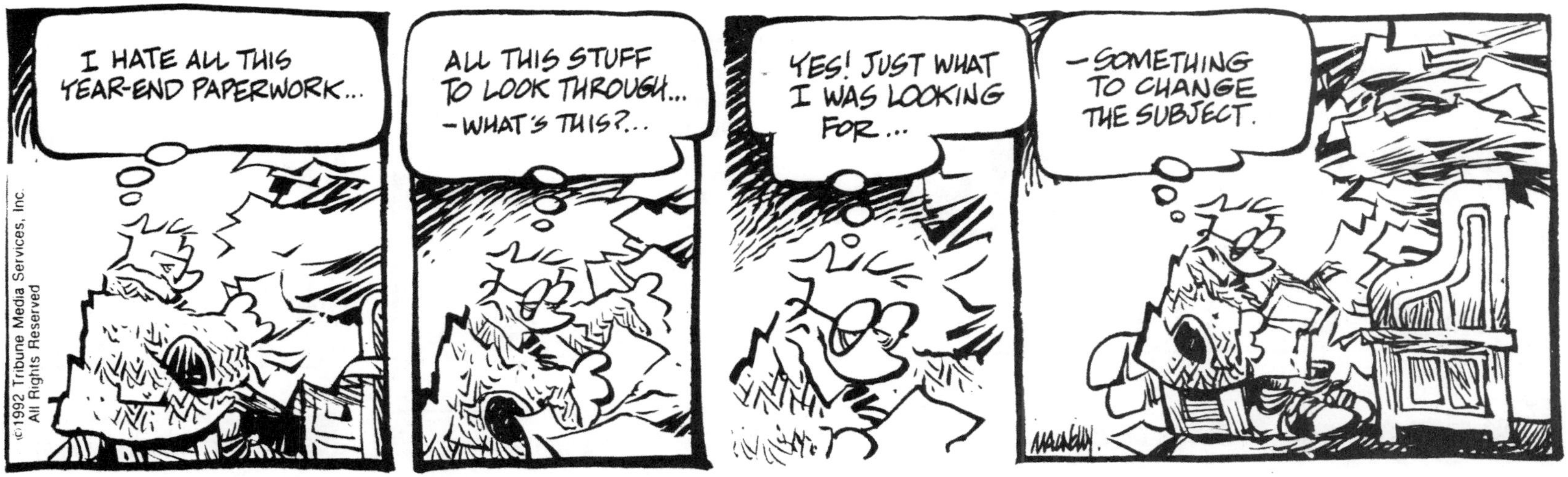

I HATE ALL THIS YEAR-END PAPERWORK...
ALL THIS STUFF TO LOOK THROUGH... -WHAT'S THIS?...
YES! JUST WHAT I WAS LOOKING FOR...
-SOMETHING TO CHANGE THE SUBJECT.
©1992 Tribune Media Services, Inc. All Rights Reserved

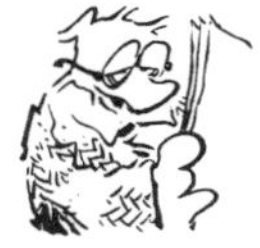

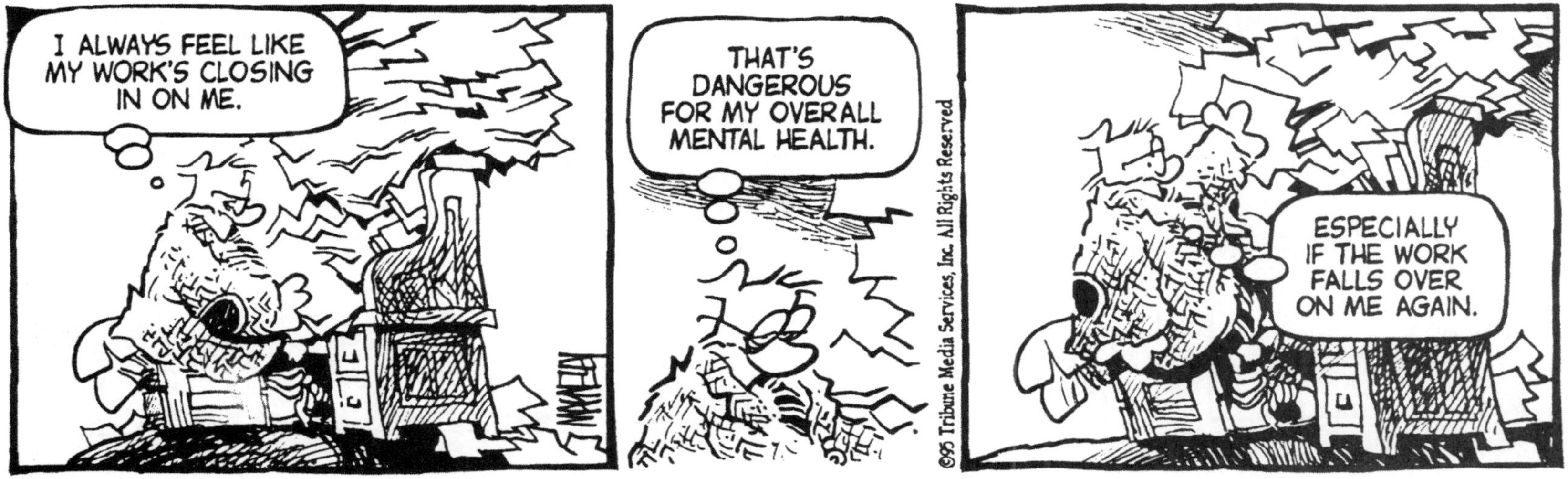

I ALWAYS FEEL LIKE MY WORK'S CLOSING IN ON ME.
THAT'S DANGEROUS FOR MY OVERALL MENTAL HEALTH.
ESPECIALLY IF THE WORK FALLS OVER ON ME AGAIN.
©95 Tribune Media Services, Inc. All Rights Reserved

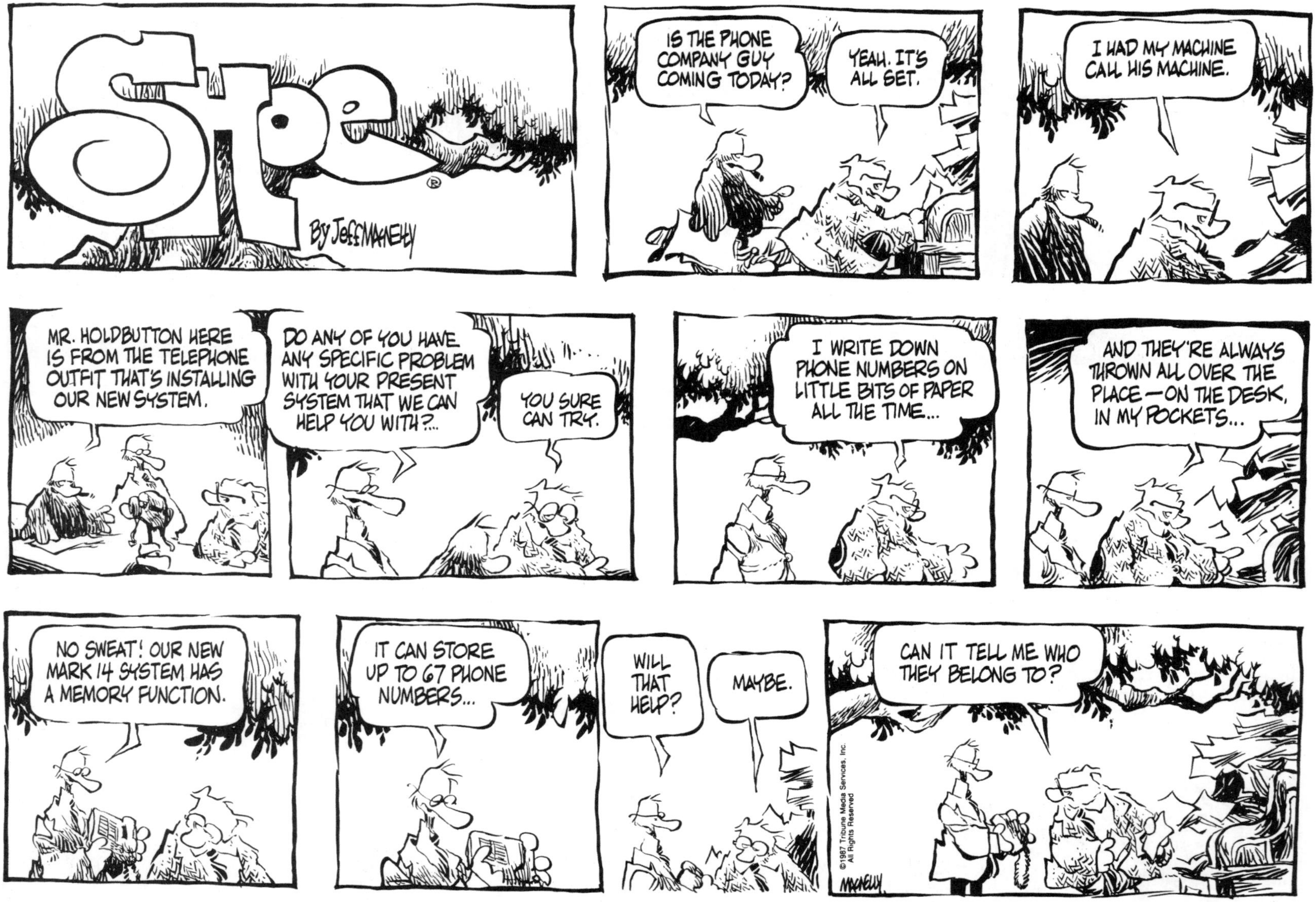
Shoe®
By Jeff MacNelly
IS THE PHONE COMPANY GUY COMING TODAY?
YEAH. IT'S ALL SET.
I HAD MY MACHINE CALL HIS MACHINE.
MR. HOLDBUTTON HERE IS FROM THE TELEPHONE OUTFIT THAT'S INSTALLING OUR NEW SYSTEM.
DO ANY OF YOU HAVE ANY SPECIFIC PROBLEM WITH YOUR PRESENT SYSTEM THAT WE CAN HELP YOU WITH?...
YOU SURE CAN TRY.
I WRITE DOWN PHONE NUMBERS ON LITTLE BITS OF PAPER ALL THE TIME...
AND THEY'RE ALWAYS THROWN ALL OVER THE PLACE—ON THE DESK, IN MY POCKETS...
NO SWEAT! OUR NEW MARK 14 SYSTEM HAS A MEMORY FUNCTION.
IT CAN STORE UP TO 67 PHONE NUMBERS...
WILL THAT HELP?
MAYBE.
CAN IT TELL ME WHO THEY BELONG TO?
©1987 Tribune Media Services, Inc. All Rights Reserved
MACNELLY

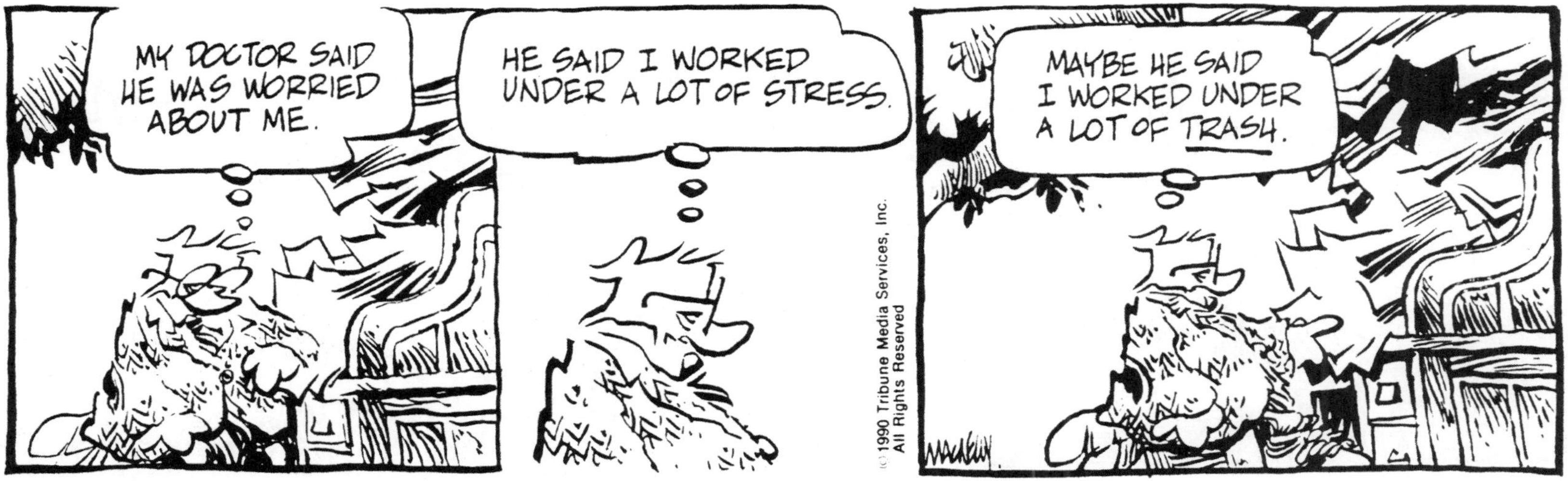
MY DOCTOR SAID HE WAS WORRIED ABOUT ME.
HE SAID I WORKED UNDER A LOT OF STRESS.
© 1990 Tribune Media Services, Inc. All Rights Reserved
MAYBE HE SAID I WORKED UNDER A LOT OF TRASH.

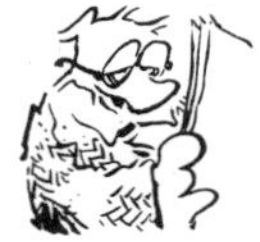

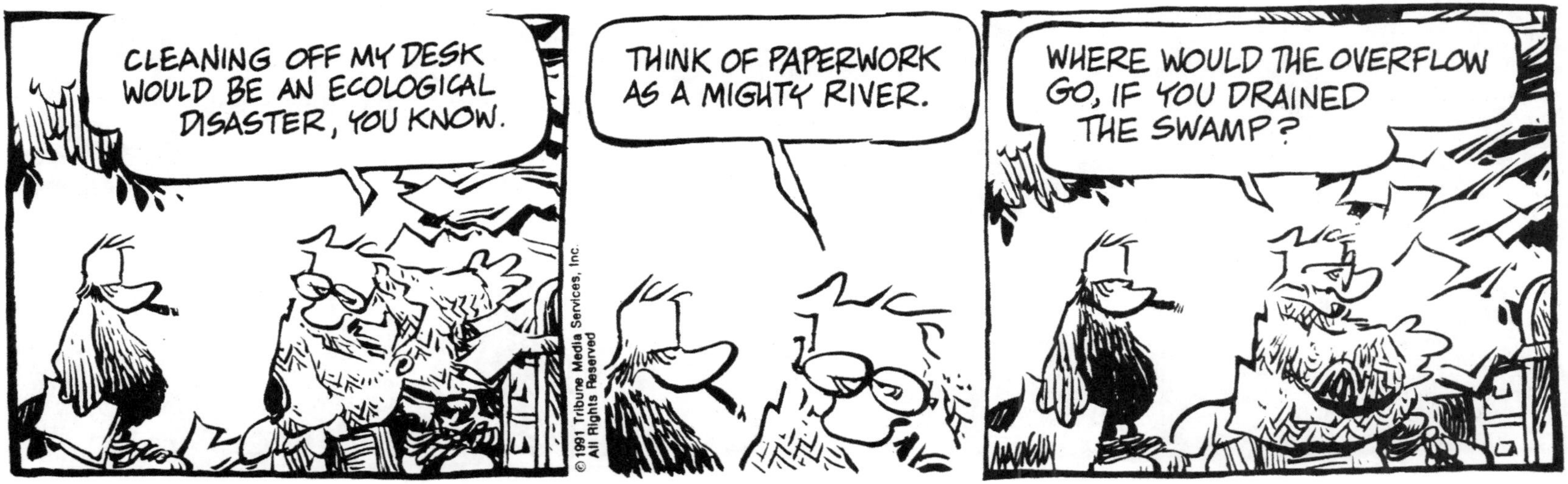
CLEANING OFF MY DESK WOULD BE AN ECOLOGICAL DISASTER, YOU KNOW.
© 1991 Tribune Media Services, Inc. All Rights Reserved
THINK OF PAPERWORK AS A MIGHTY RIVER.
WHERE WOULD THE OVERFLOW GO, IF YOU DRAINED THE SWAMP?

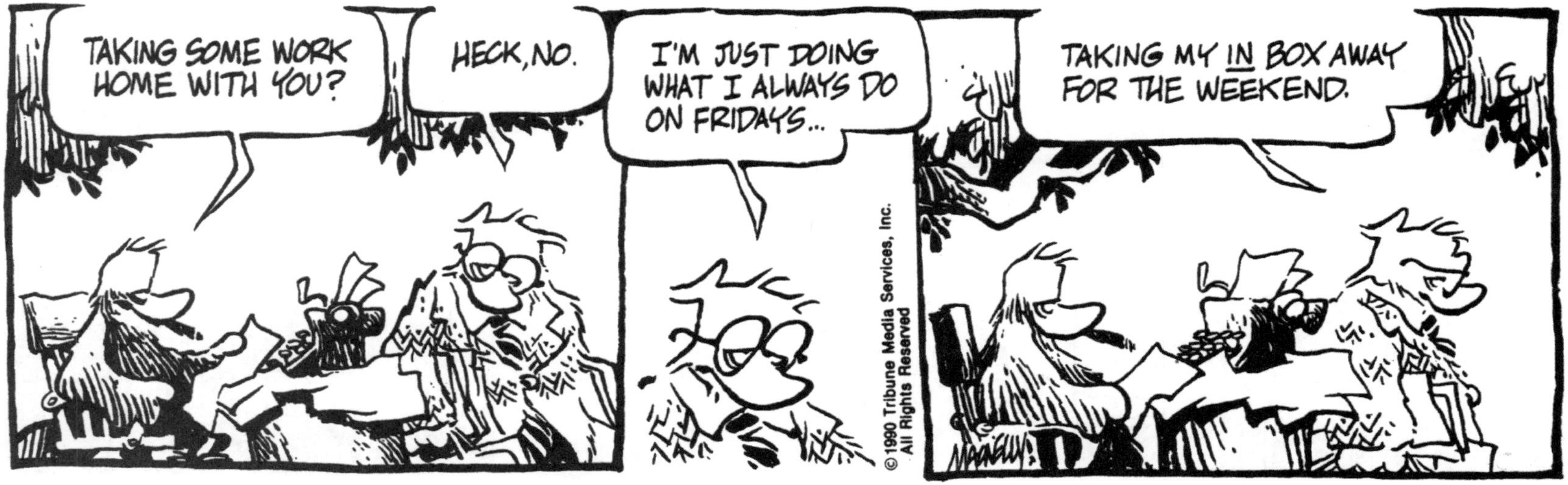
TAKING SOME WORK HOME WITH YOU?
HECK, NO.
I'M JUST DOING WHAT I ALWAYS DO ON FRIDAYS...
© 1990 Tribune Media Services, Inc. All Rights Reserved
TAKING MY IN BOX AWAY FOR THE WEEKEND.

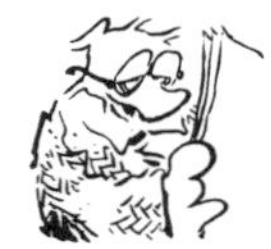

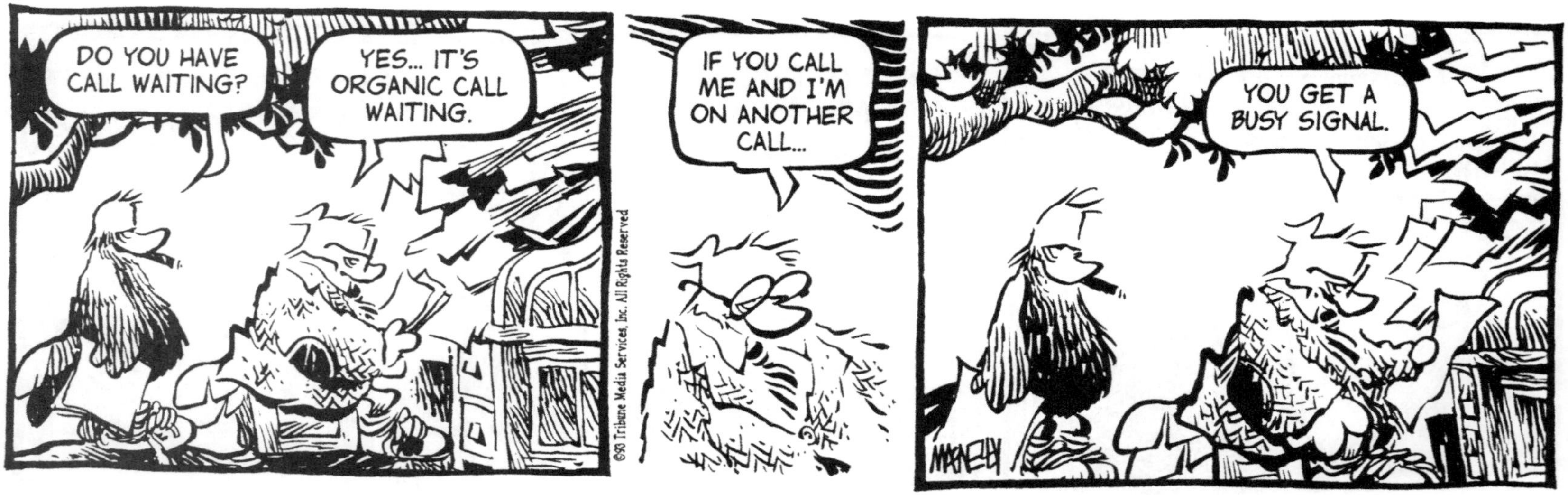
DO YOU HAVE CALL WAITING?
YES... IT'S ORGANIC CALL WAITING.
©93 Tribune Media Services, Inc. All Rights Reserved
IF YOU CALL ME AND I'M ON ANOTHER CALL...
YOU GET A BUSY SIGNAL.

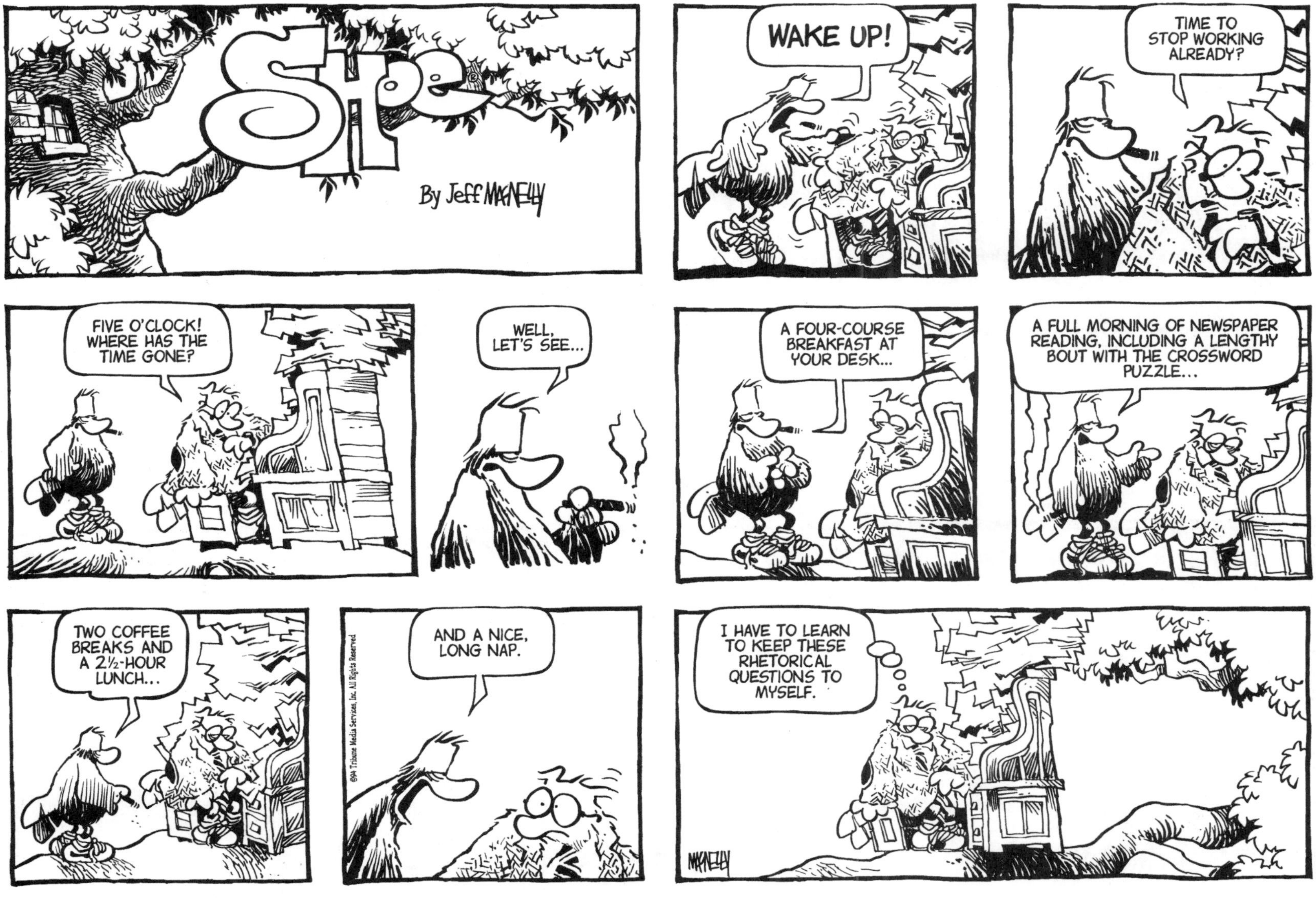
Shoe®
By Jeff MacNelly
WAKE UP!
TIME TO STOP WORKING ALREADY?
FIVE O'CLOCK! WHERE HAS THE TIME GONE?
WELL, LET'S SEE...
A FOUR-COURSE BREAKFAST AT YOUR DESK...
A FULL MORNING OF NEWSPAPER READING, INCLUDING A LENGTHY BOUT WITH THE CROSSWORD PUZZLE...
TWO COFFEE BREAKS AND A 2½-HOUR LUNCH...
©94 Tribune Media Services, Inc. All Rights Reserved
AND A NICE, LONG NAP.
I HAVE TO LEARN TO KEEP THESE RHETORICAL QUESTIONS TO MYSELF.
MacNelly

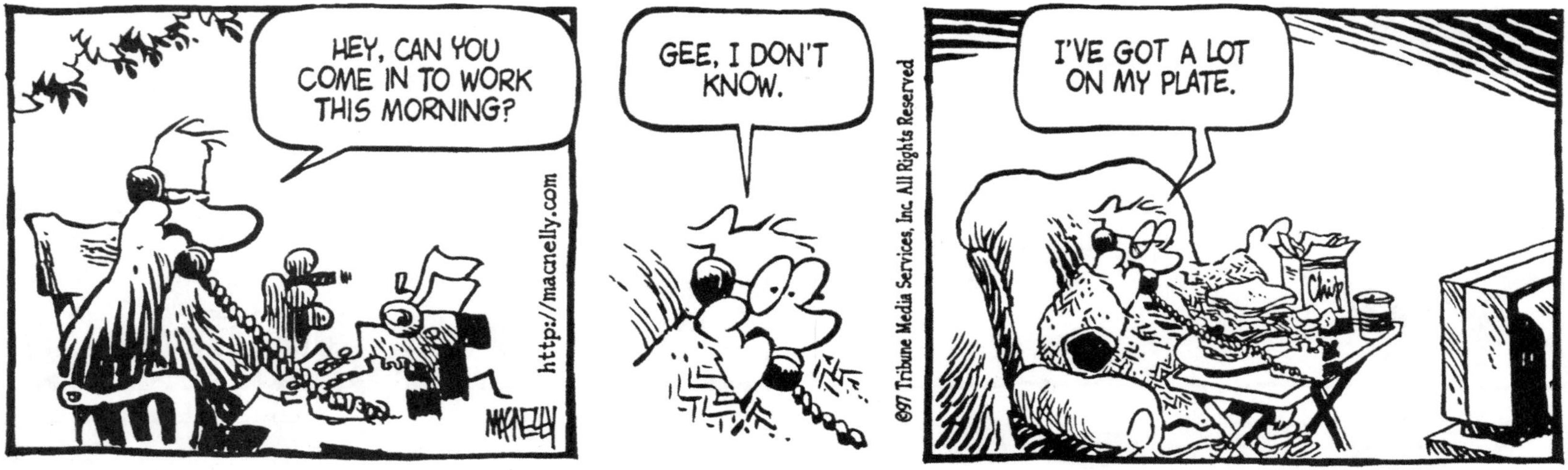
HEY, CAN YOU COME IN TO WORK THIS MORNING?
http://macnelly.com
MACNELLY
GEE, I DON'T KNOW.
©97 Tribune Media Services, Inc. All Rights Reserved
I'VE GOT A LOT ON MY PLATE.
Chip

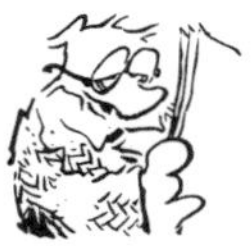

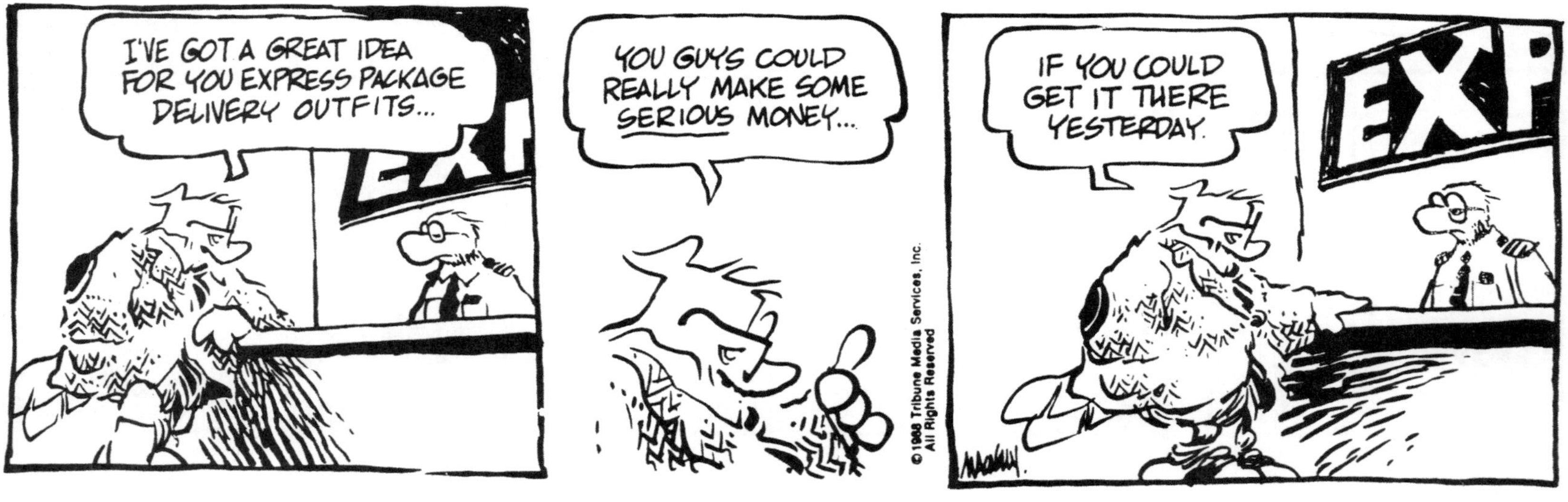
I'VE GOT A GREAT IDEA FOR YOU EXPRESS PACKAGE DELIVERY OUTFITS...
YOU GUYS COULD REALLY MAKE SOME SERIOUS MONEY...
© 1988 Tribune Media Services, Inc. All Rights Reserved
IF YOU COULD GET IT THERE YESTERDAY.
EXP
MACNELLY

ANYTHING HAPPEN WHILE I WAS GONE?

YES...

MOST OF THURSDAY.

©1987 Tribune Media Services, Inc. All Rights Reserved

WHAT DO YOU HAVE ON YOUR CALENDAR TODAY?

THE USUAL.

A BIG COFFEE STAIN...

©95 Tribune Media Services, Inc. All Rights Reserved

http://macnelly.com

AND SOME MUSTARD AND MAYO.

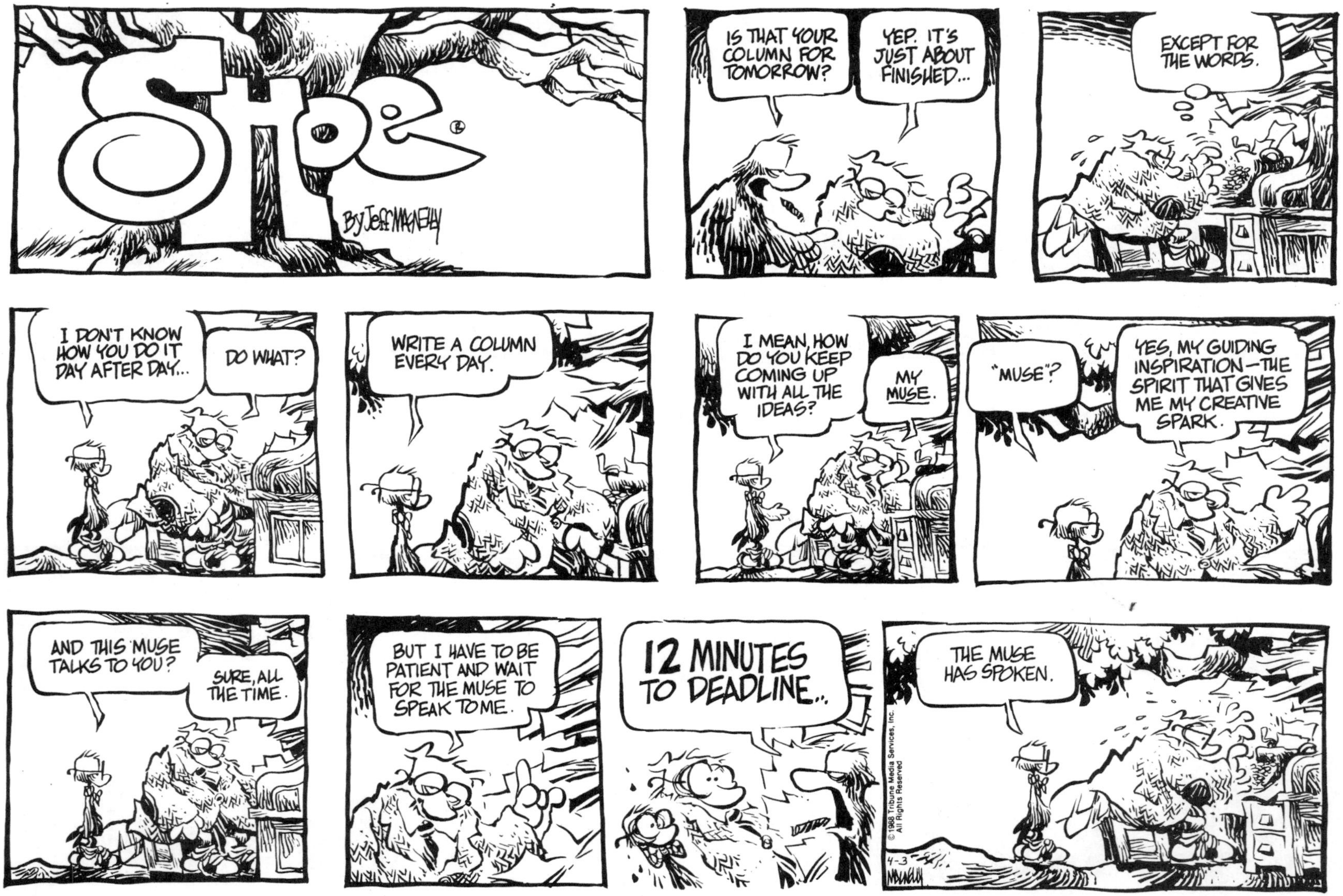
Shoe
By Jeff MacNelly
IS THAT YOUR COLUMN FOR TOMORROW?
YEP. IT'S JUST ABOUT FINISHED...
EXCEPT FOR THE WORDS.
I DON'T KNOW HOW YOU DO IT DAY AFTER DAY...
DO WHAT?
WRITE A COLUMN EVERY DAY.
I MEAN, HOW DO YOU KEEP COMING UP WITH ALL THE IDEAS?
MY MUSE.
"MUSE"?
YES, MY GUIDING INSPIRATION—THE SPIRIT THAT GIVES ME MY CREATIVE SPARK.
AND THIS MUSE TALKS TO YOU?
SURE, ALL THE TIME.
BUT I HAVE TO BE PATIENT AND WAIT FOR THE MUSE TO SPEAK TO ME.
12 MINUTES TO DEADLINE...
© 1988 Tribune Media Services, Inc. All Rights Reserved
4-3
THE MUSE HAS SPOKEN.

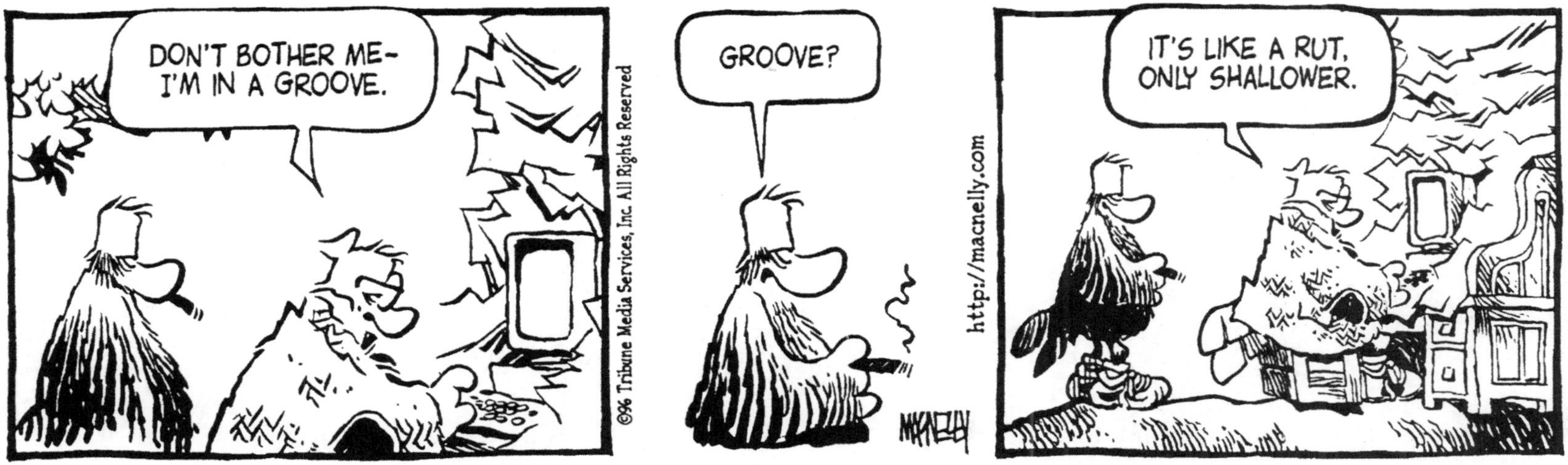
DON'T BOTHER ME-
I'M IN A GROOVE.
GROOVE?
IT'S LIKE A RUT, ONLY SHALLOWER.
©96 Tribune Media Services, Inc. All Rights Reserved
http://macnelly.com

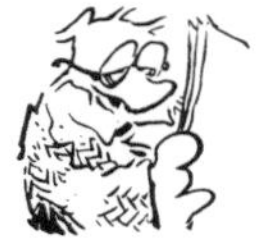

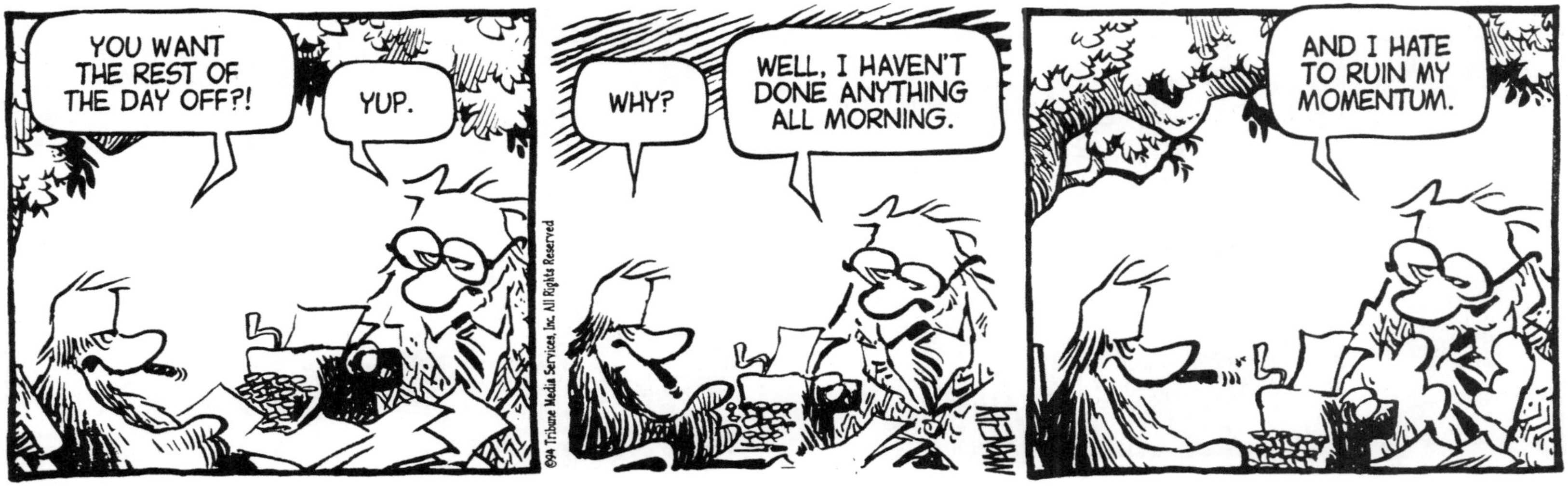
YOU WANT THE REST OF THE DAY OFF?!
YUP.
WHY?
WELL, I HAVEN'T DONE ANYTHING ALL MORNING.
AND I HATE TO RUIN MY MOMENTUM.
©94 Tribune Media Services, Inc. All Rights Reserved

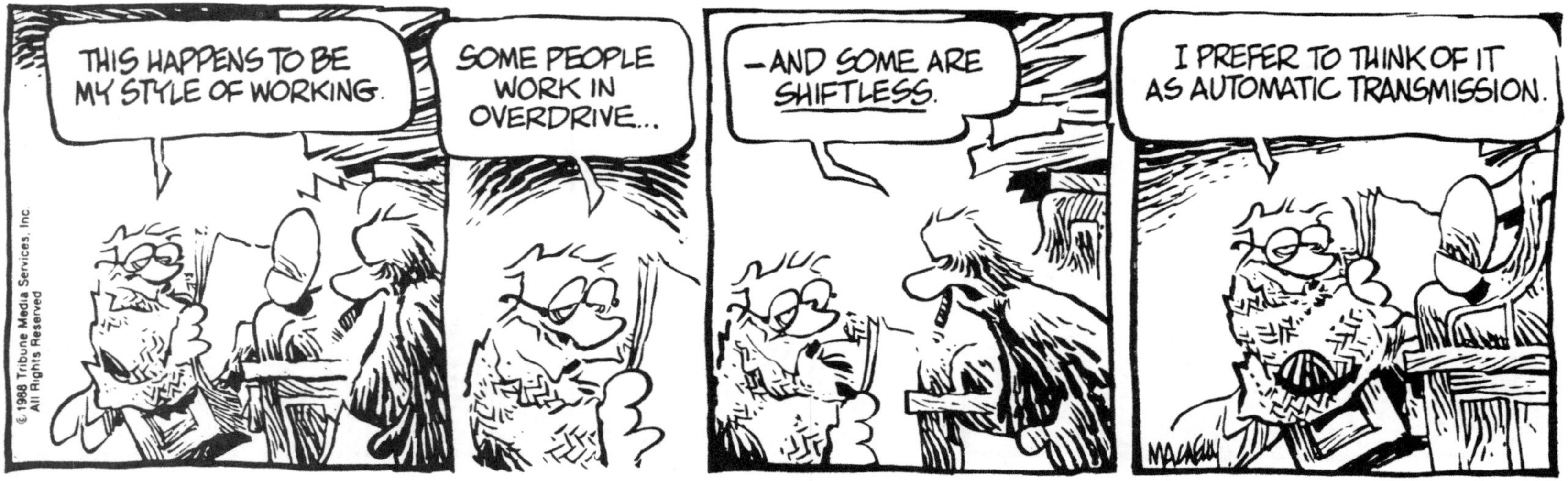
THIS HAPPENS TO BE MY STYLE OF WORKING.
SOME PEOPLE WORK IN OVERDRIVE...
—AND SOME ARE SHIFTLESS.
I PREFER TO THINK OF IT AS AUTOMATIC TRANSMISSION.
© 1988 Tribune Media Services, Inc. All Rights Reserved
MACNELLY

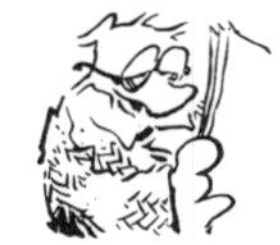

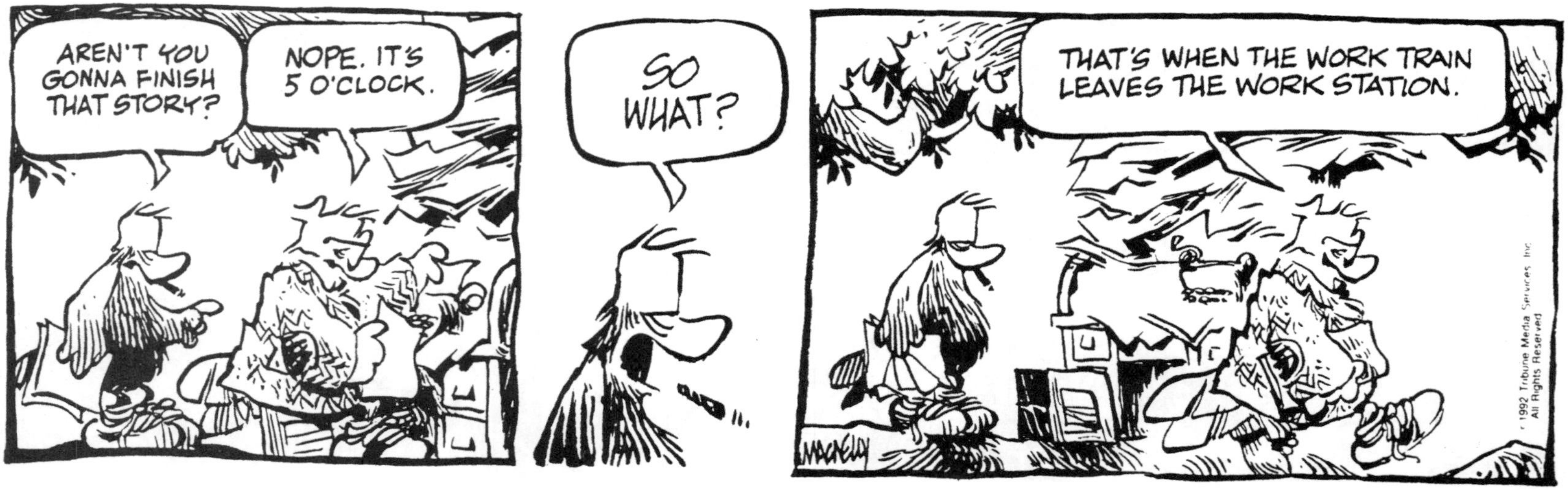
AREN'T YOU GONNA FINISH THAT STORY?
NOPE. IT'S 5 O'CLOCK.
SO WHAT?
THAT'S WHEN THE WORK TRAIN LEAVES THE WORK STATION.
MACNELLY
© 1992 Tribune Media Services, Inc. All Rights Reserved

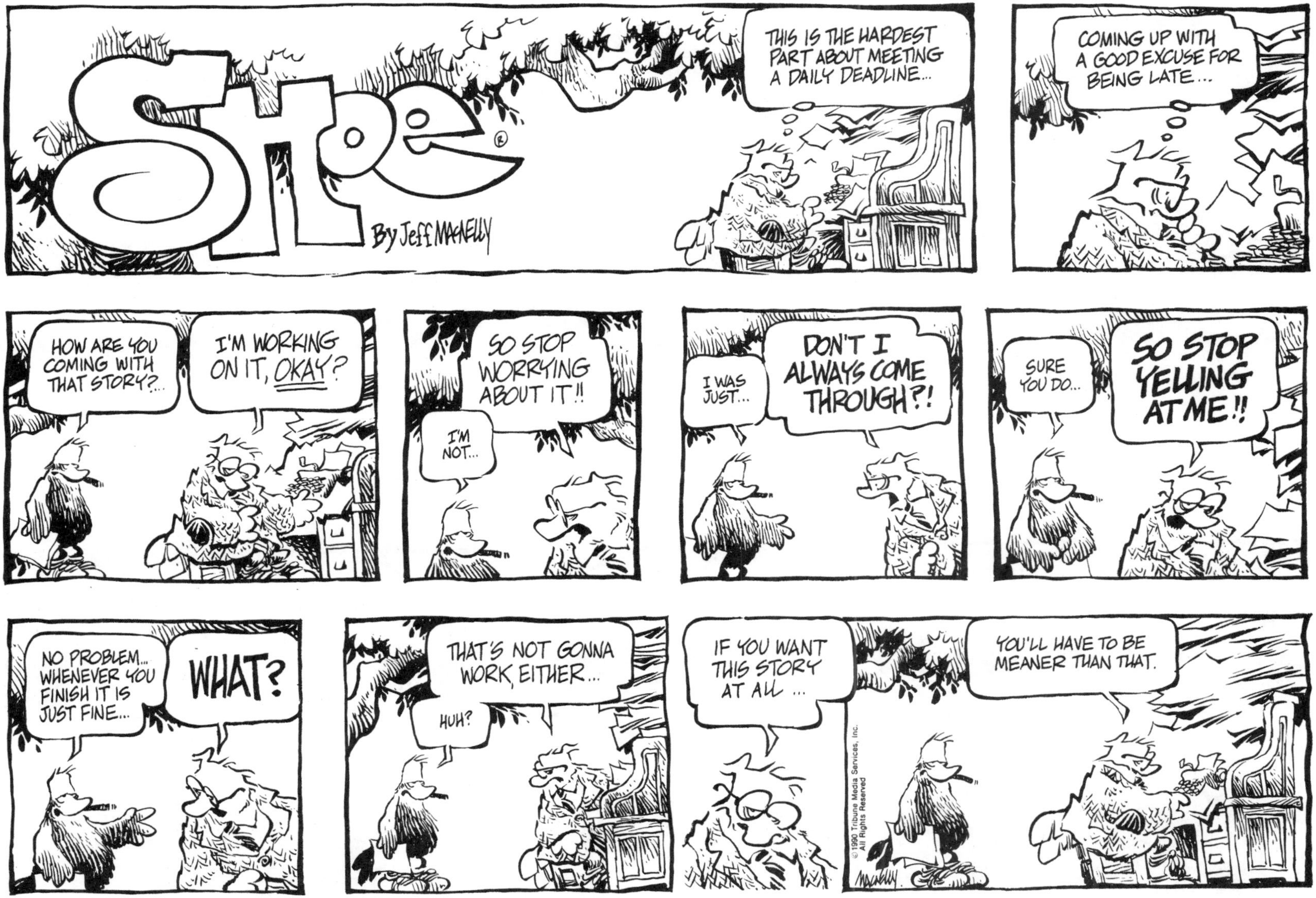
Shoe®
By Jeff MacNelly
THIS IS THE HARDEST PART ABOUT MEETING A DAILY DEADLINE...
COMING UP WITH A GOOD EXCUSE FOR BEING LATE...
HOW ARE YOU COMING WITH THAT STORY?...
I'M WORKING ON IT, OKAY?
SO STOP WORRYING ABOUT IT!!
I'M NOT...
I WAS JUST...
DON'T I ALWAYS COME THROUGH?!
SURE YOU DO...
SO STOP YELLING AT ME!!
NO PROBLEM... WHENEVER YOU FINISH IT IS JUST FINE...
WHAT?
THAT'S NOT GONNA WORK, EITHER...
HUH?
IF YOU WANT THIS STORY AT ALL ...
YOU'LL HAVE TO BE MEANER THAN THAT.
© 1990 Tribune Media Services, Inc. All Rights Reserved
MACNELLY

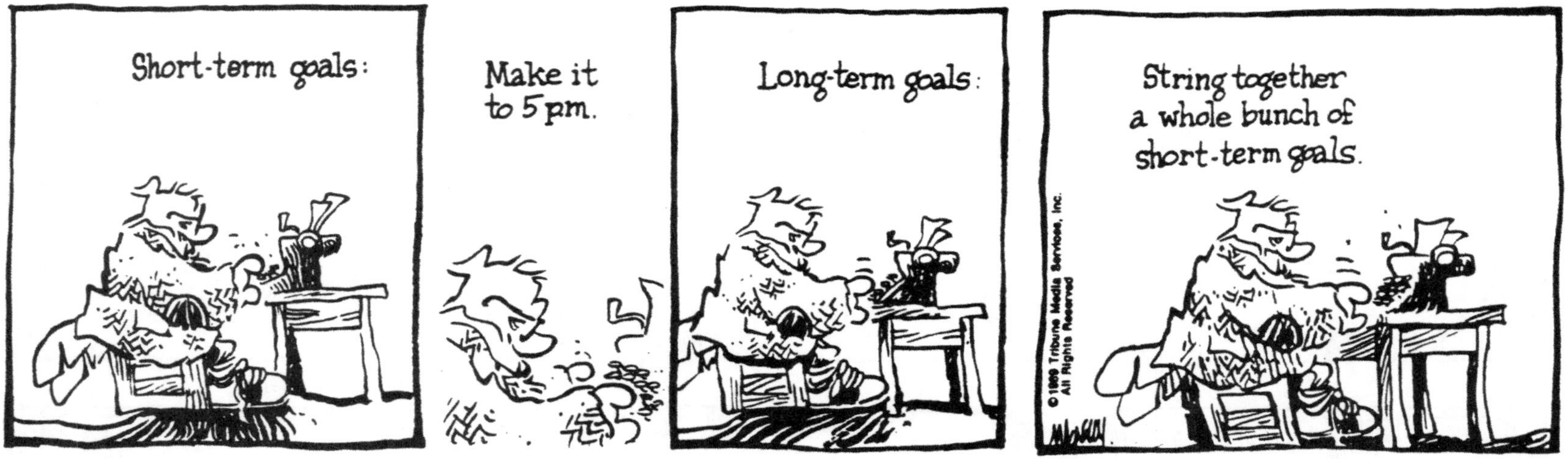
Short-term goals:
Make it to 5 p.m.
Long-term goals:
String together a whole bunch of short-term goals.
© 1989 Tribune Media Services, Inc. All Rights Reserved

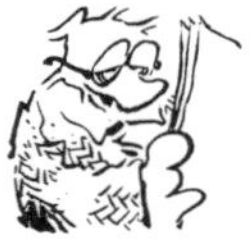

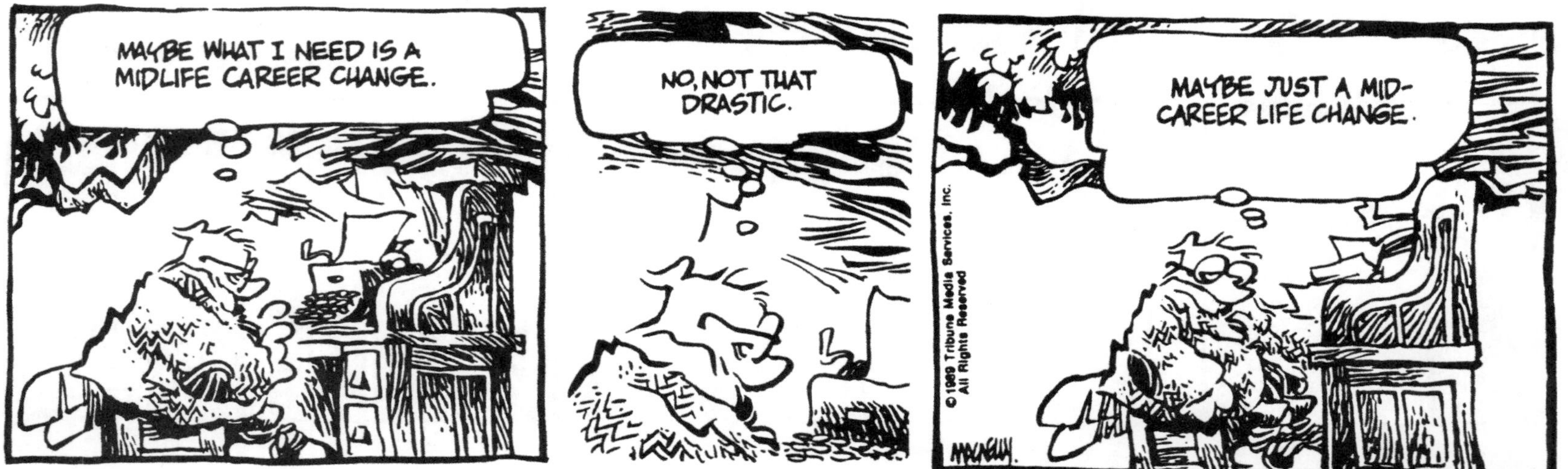
MAYBE WHAT I NEED IS A MIDLIFE CAREER CHANGE.
NO, NOT THAT DRASTIC.
MAYBE JUST A MID-CAREER LIFE CHANGE.
© 1989 Tribune Media Services, Inc. All Rights Reserved

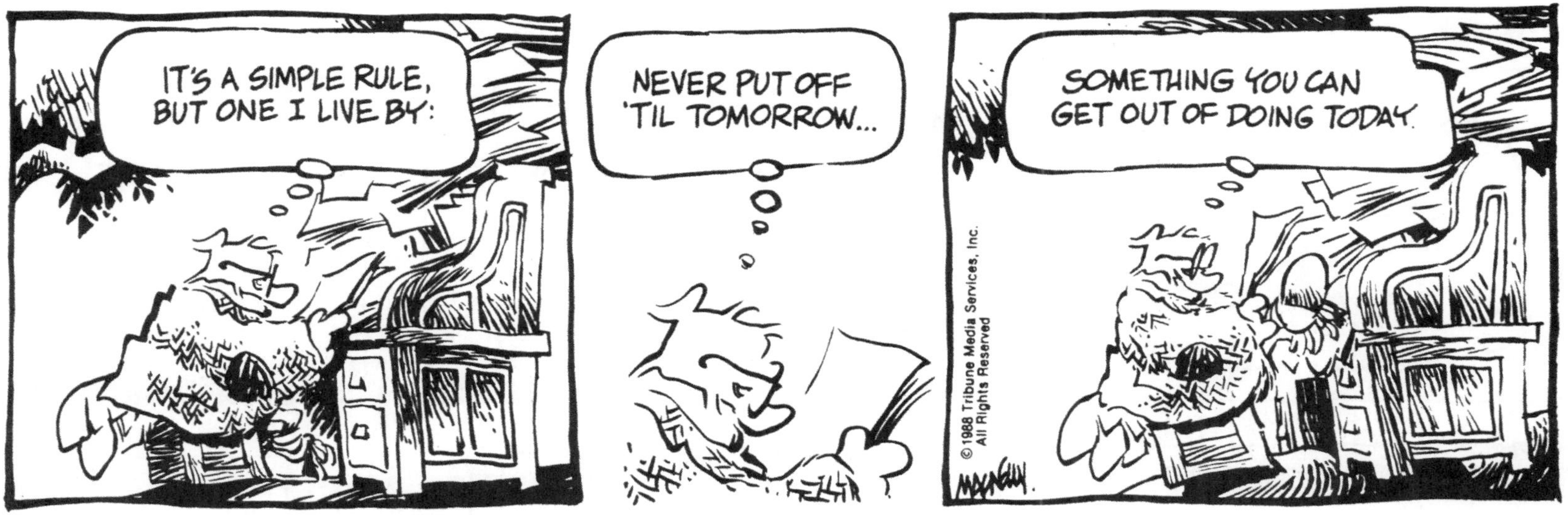
IT'S A SIMPLE RULE, BUT ONE I LIVE BY:
NEVER PUT OFF 'TIL TOMORROW...
SOMETHING YOU CAN GET OUT OF DOING TODAY.
© 1988 Tribune Media Services, Inc. All Rights Reserved

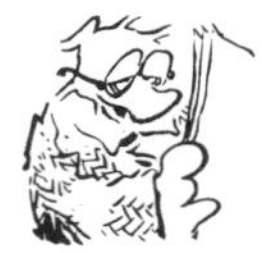

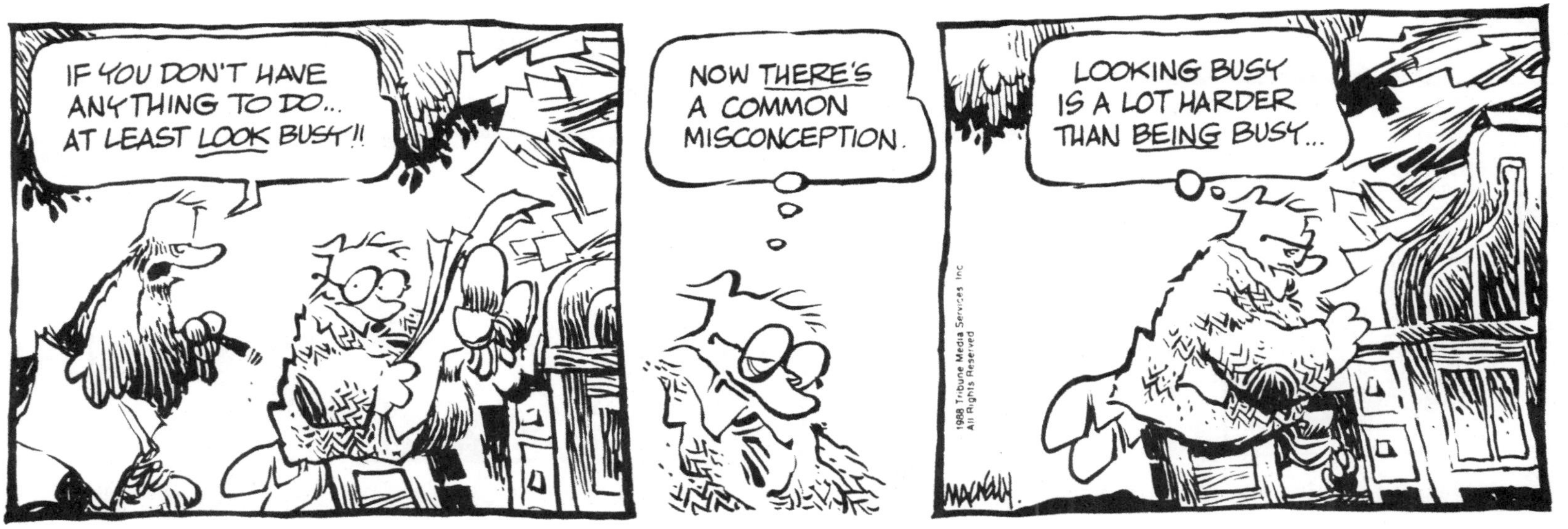
IF YOU DON'T HAVE ANYTHING TO DO... AT LEAST LOOK BUSY!!
NOW THERE'S A COMMON MISCONCEPTION.
LOOKING BUSY IS A LOT HARDER THAN BEING BUSY...
1988 Tribune Media Services Inc All Rights Reserved

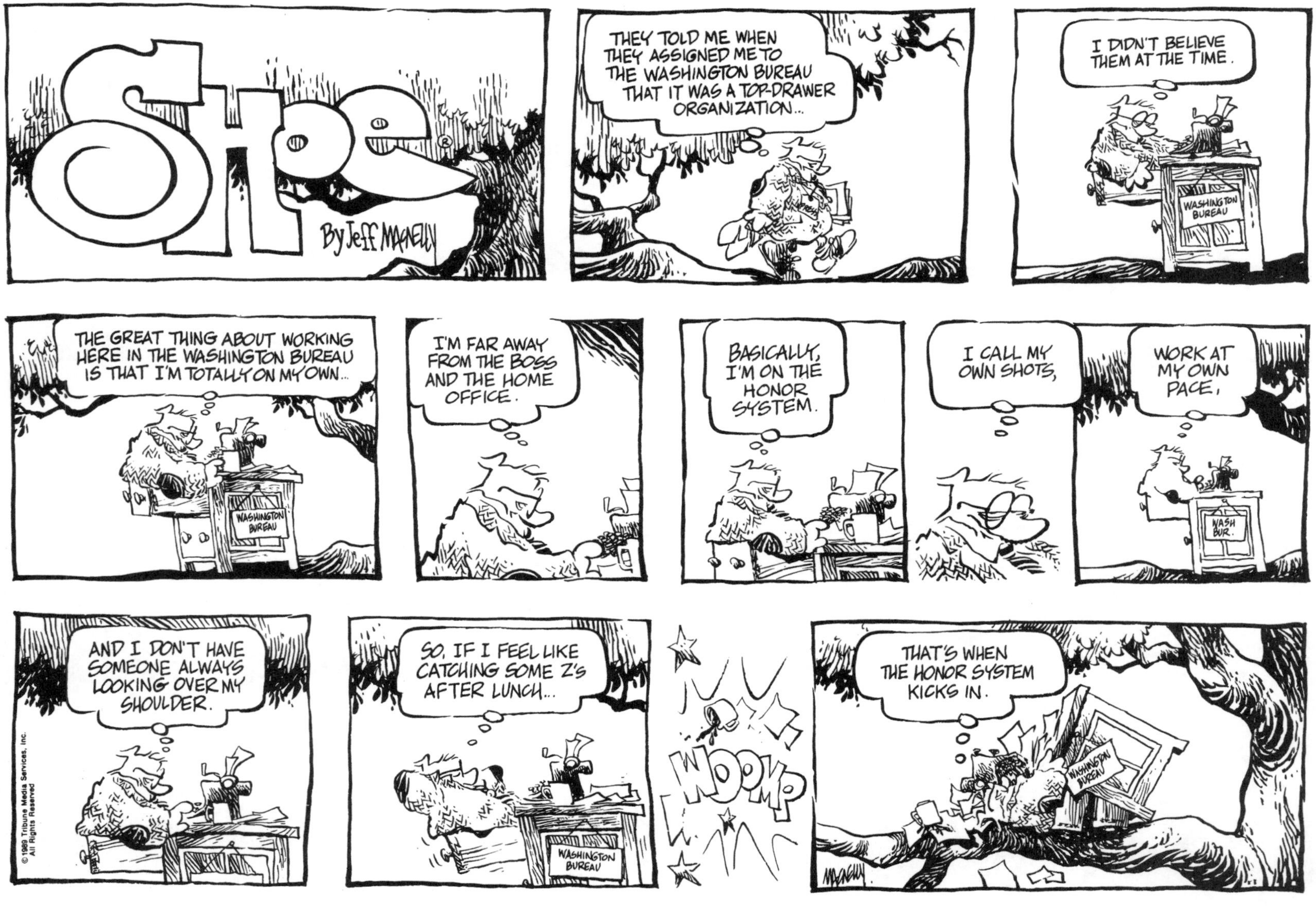
Shoe®
By Jeff MacNelly
THEY TOLD ME WHEN THEY ASSIGNED ME TO THE WASHINGTON BUREAU THAT IT WAS A TOP-DRAWER ORGANIZATION...
I DIDN'T BELIEVE THEM AT THE TIME.
WASHINGTON BUREAU
THE GREAT THING ABOUT WORKING HERE IN THE WASHINGTON BUREAU IS THAT I'M TOTALLY ON MY OWN...
WASHINGTON BUREAU
I'M FAR AWAY FROM THE BOSS AND THE HOME OFFICE.
BASICALLY, I'M ON THE HONOR SYSTEM.
I CALL MY OWN SHOTS,
WORK AT MY OWN PACE,
WASH BUR.
AND I DON'T HAVE SOMEONE ALWAYS LOOKING OVER MY SHOULDER.
SO, IF I FEEL LIKE CATCHING SOME Z's AFTER LUNCH...
WASHINGTON BUREAU
WOOMP
THAT'S WHEN THE HONOR SYSTEM KICKS IN.
WASHINGTON BUREAU
MACNELLY

GOSH, I'VE FALLEN SO FAR BEHIND IN MY PAPERWORK...
OH, WELL...
AS LONG AS I DON'T FALL UNDER MY PAPERWORK...
MACNELLY
© 1988 Tribune Media Services, Inc. All Rights Reserved

I'D NEVER GET ANYTHING DONE IF IT WEREN'T FOR THAT ONE KEY DAY.
– IT'S ALWAYS THE BUSIEST DAY OF ANY WORK WEEK:
TOMORROW.
MACNELLY
©94 Tribune Media Services, Inc. All Rights Reserved

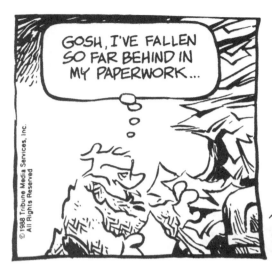

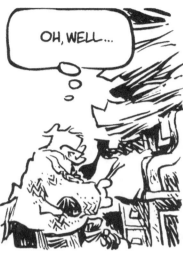

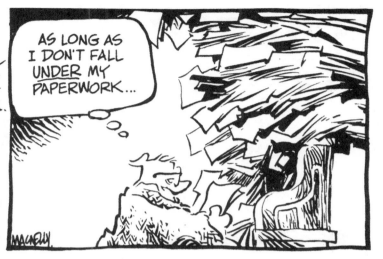

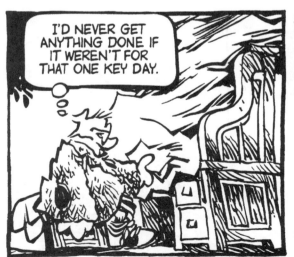

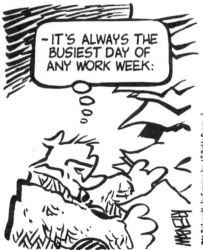

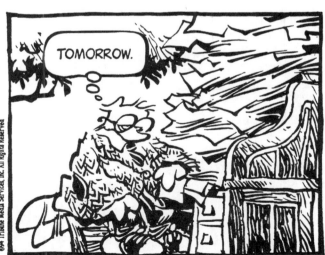

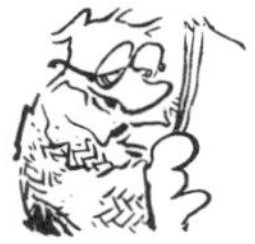

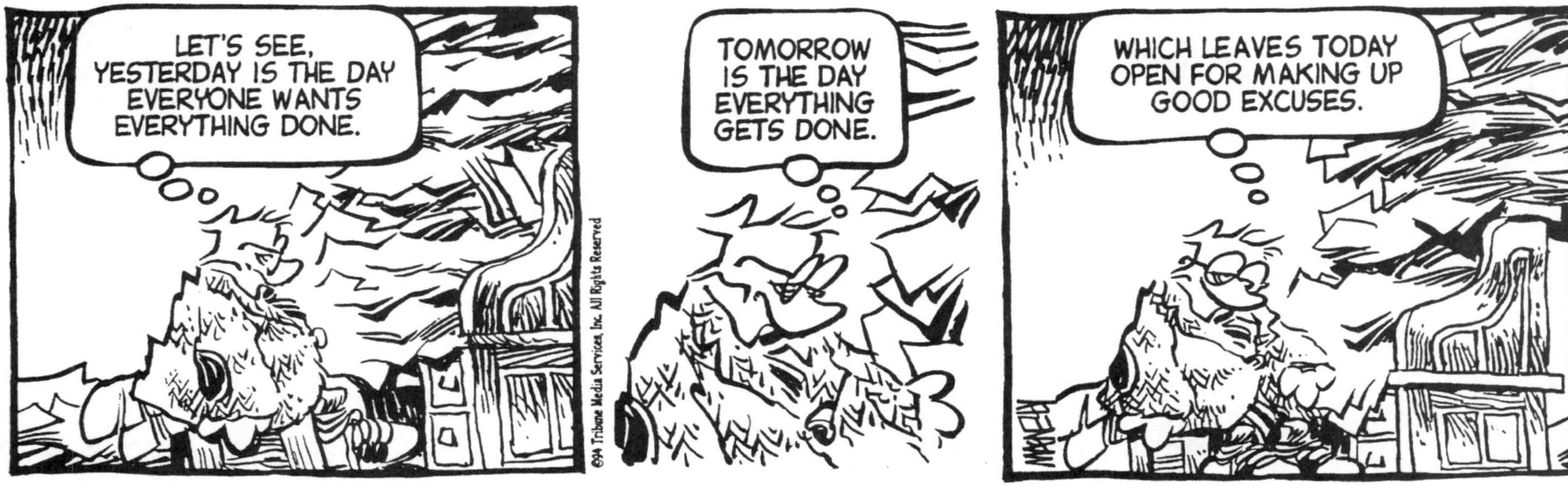
LET'S SEE, YESTERDAY IS THE DAY EVERYONE WANTS EVERYTHING DONE.
TOMORROW IS THE DAY EVERYTHING GETS DONE.
WHICH LEAVES TODAY OPEN FOR MAKING UP GOOD EXCUSES.
©94 Tribune Media Services, Inc. All Rights Reserved

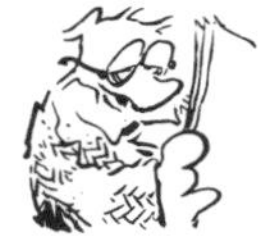

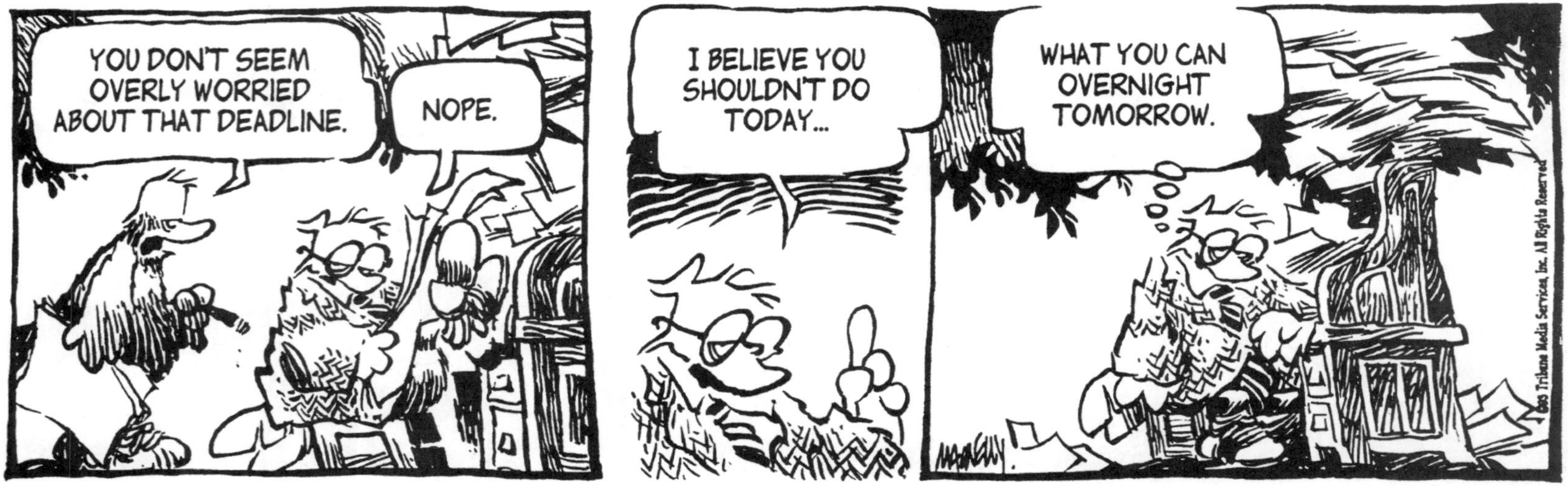
YOU DON'T SEEM OVERLY WORRIED ABOUT THAT DEADLINE.
NOPE.
I BELIEVE YOU SHOULDN'T DO TODAY...
WHAT YOU CAN OVERNIGHT TOMORROW.
©95 Tribune Media Services, Inc. All Rights Reserved

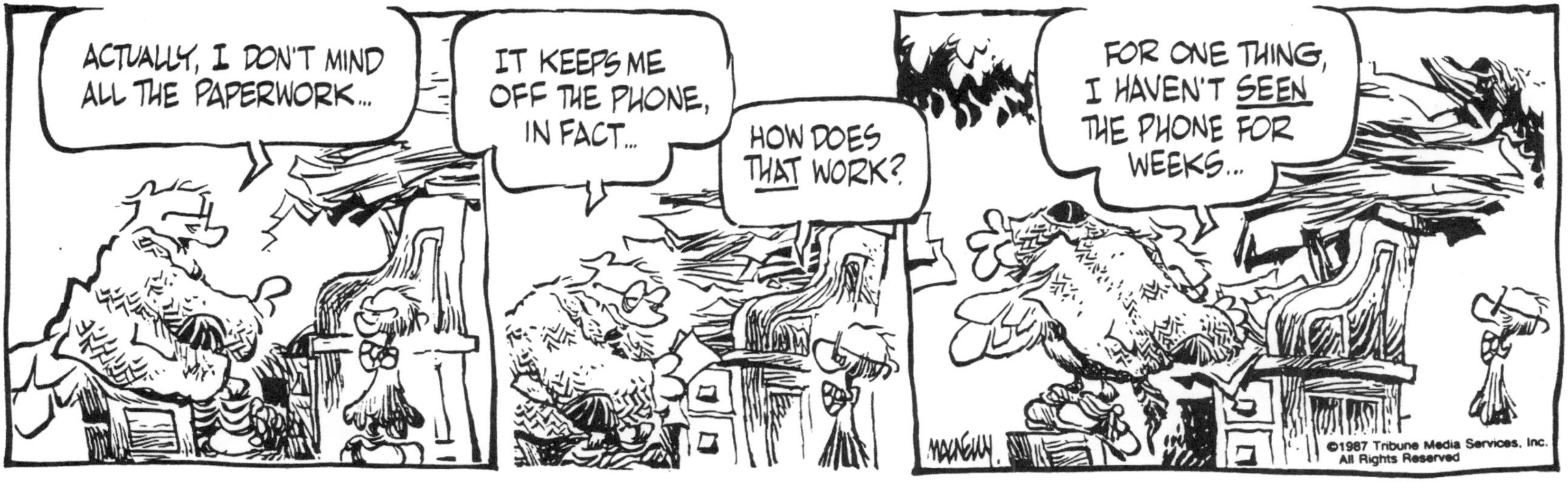
ACTUALLY, I DON'T MIND ALL THE PAPERWORK...
IT KEEPS ME OFF THE PHONE, IN FACT...
HOW DOES THAT WORK?
FOR ONE THING, I HAVEN'T SEEN THE PHONE FOR WEEKS...
©1987 Tribune Media Services, Inc. All Rights Reserved

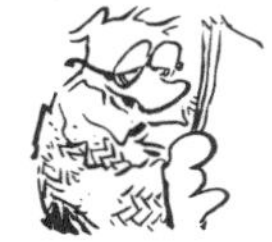

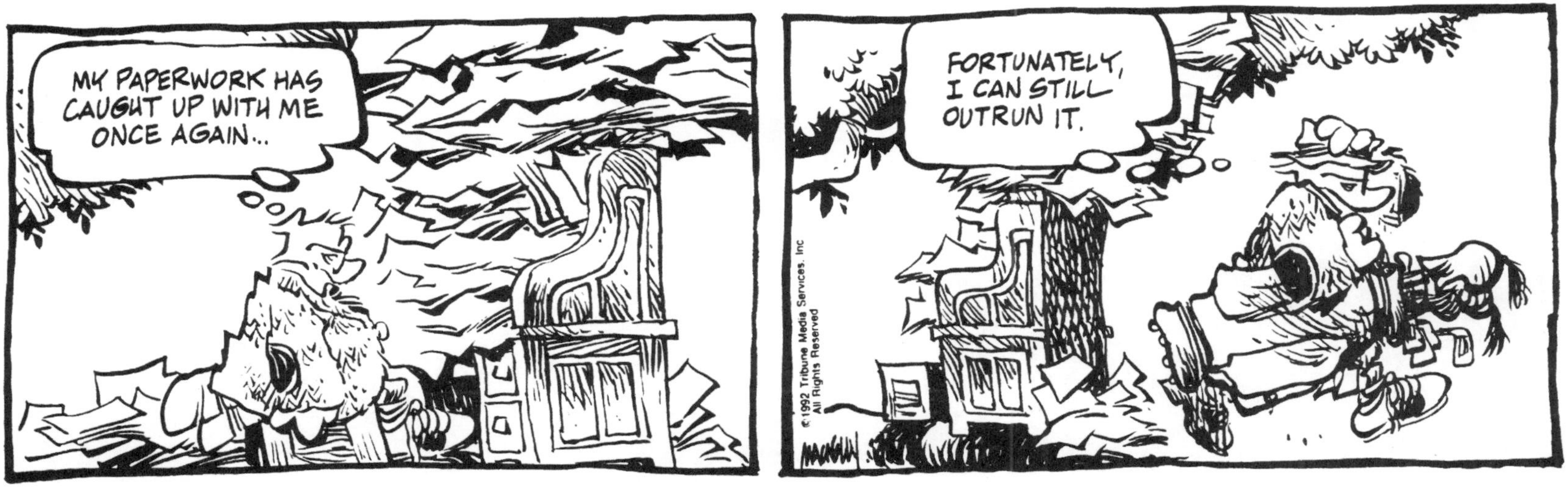
MY PAPERWORK HAS CAUGHT UP WITH ME ONCE AGAIN...
FORTUNATELY, I CAN STILL OUTRUN IT.
©1992 Tribune Media Services, Inc All Rights Reserved

Chapter Three

Stalled on the Information Superhighway

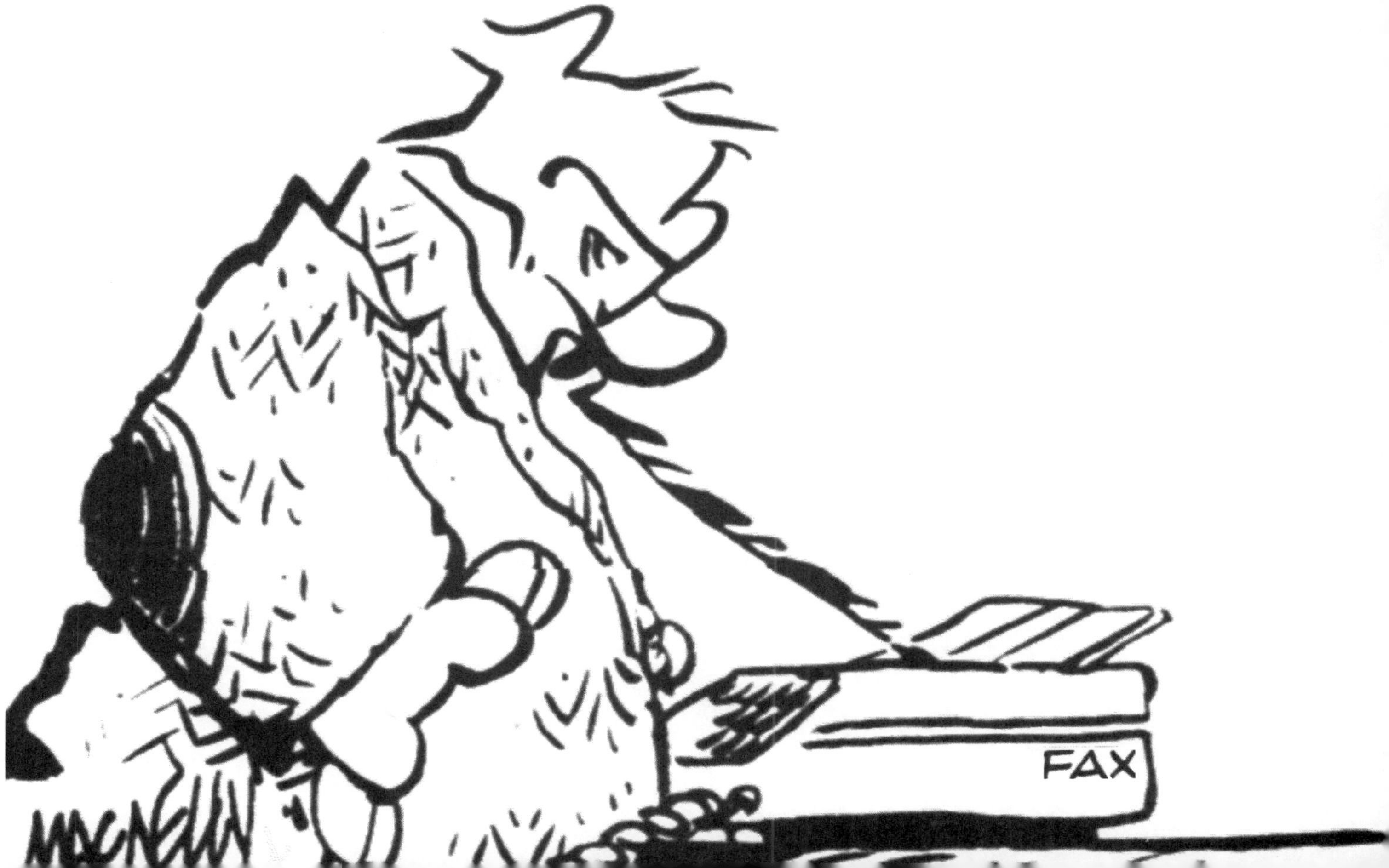
FAX
MACNELLY

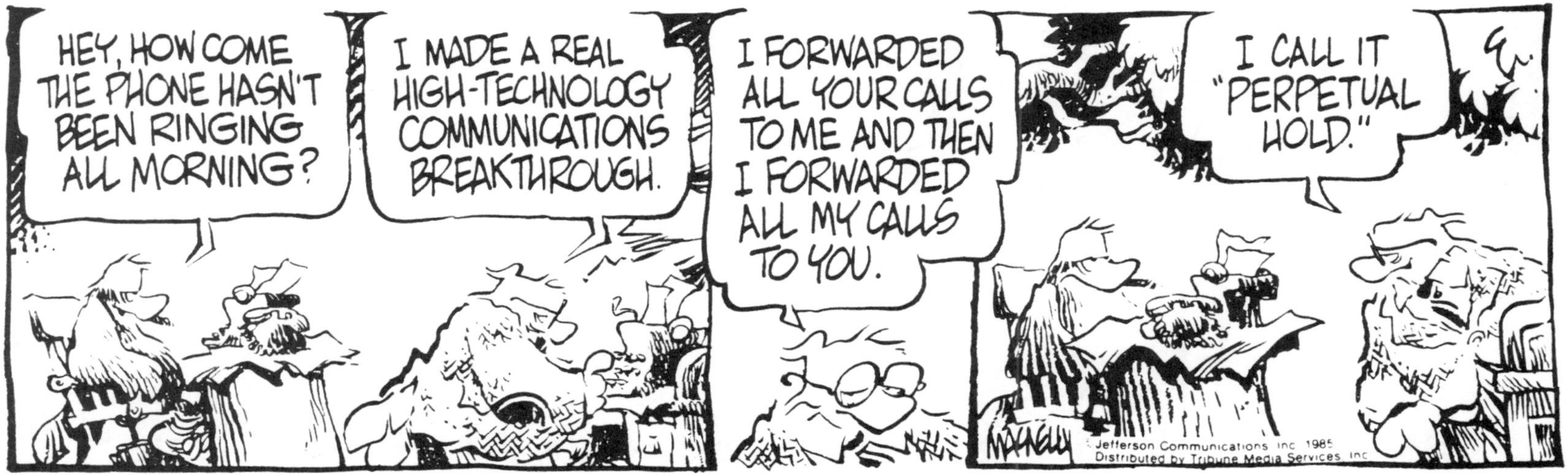
HEY, HOW COME THE PHONE HASN'T BEEN RINGING ALL MORNING?
I MADE A REAL HIGH-TECHNOLOGY COMMUNICATIONS BREAKTHROUGH.
I FORWARDED ALL YOUR CALLS TO ME AND THEN I FORWARDED ALL MY CALLS TO YOU.
I CALL IT "PERPETUAL HOLD."
© Jefferson Communications Inc 1985
Distributed by Tribune Media Services Inc

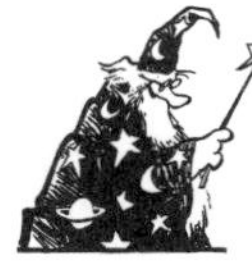

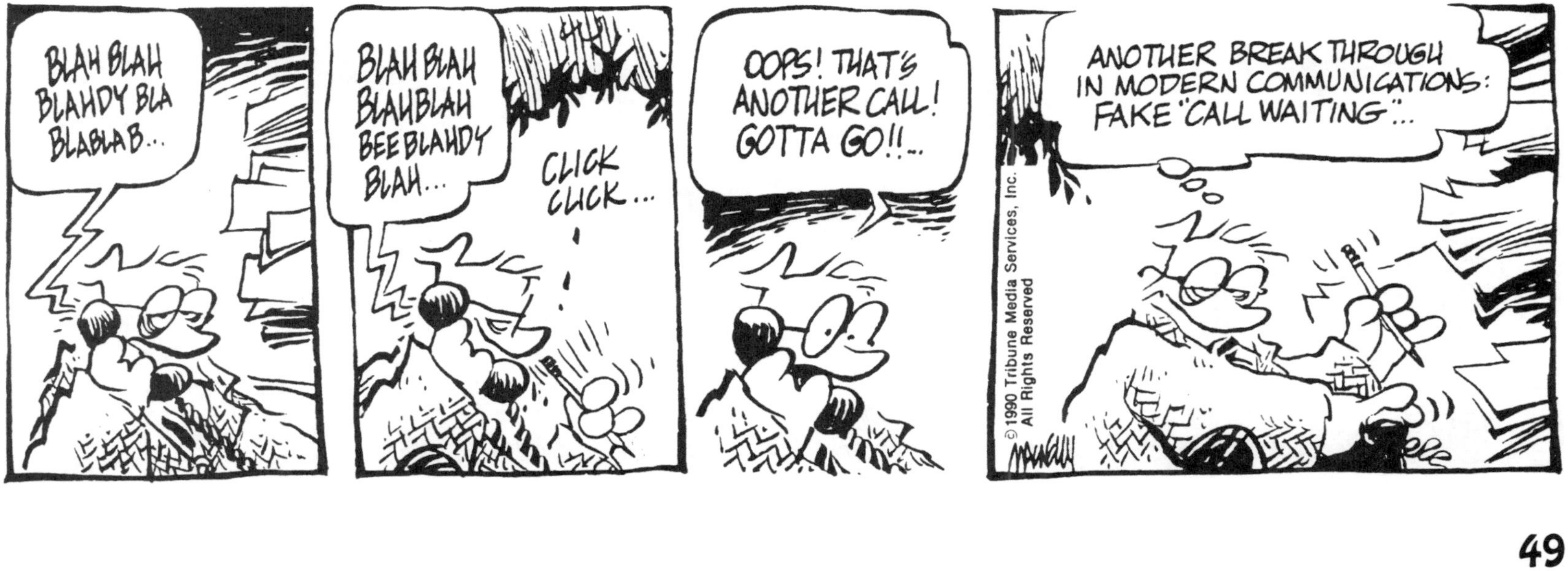
BLAH BLAH BLAHDY BLA BLABLAB...
BLAH BLAH BLAHBLAH BEE BLAHDY BLAH...
CLICK CLICK...
OOPS! THAT'S ANOTHER CALL! GOTTA GO!!..
© 1990 Tribune Media Services, Inc.
All Rights Reserved
ANOTHER BREAK THROUGH IN MODERN COMMUNICATIONS: FAKE "CALL WAITING"...

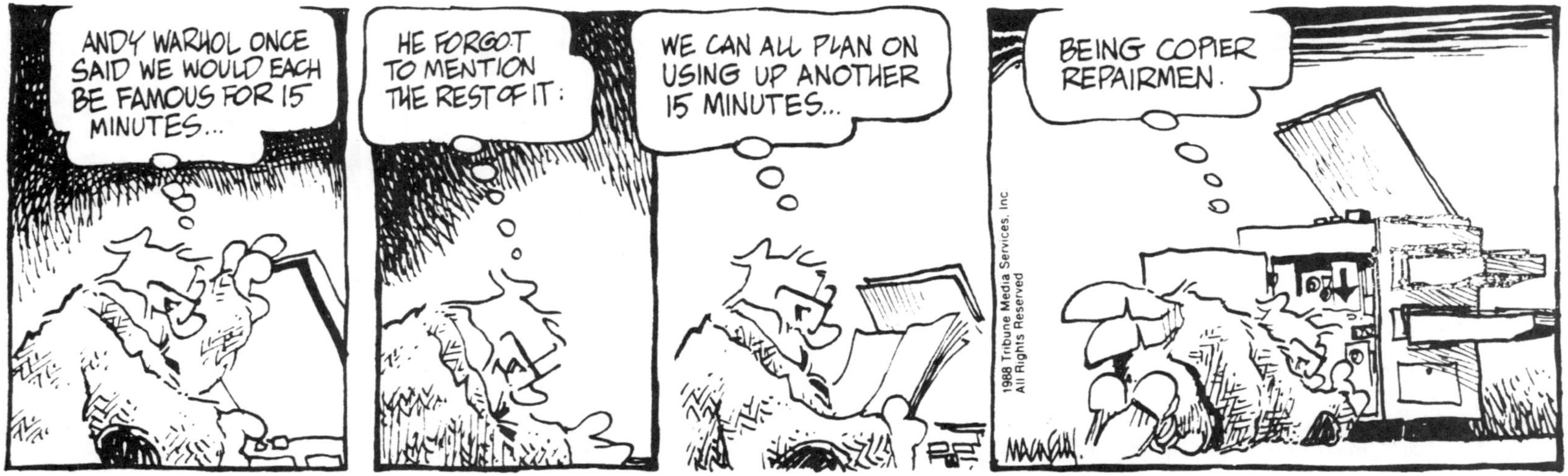
ANDY WARHOL ONCE SAID WE WOULD EACH BE FAMOUS FOR 15 MINUTES...
HE FORGOT TO MENTION THE REST OF IT:
WE CAN ALL PLAN ON USING UP ANOTHER 15 MINUTES...
BEING COPIER REPAIRMEN.
1988 Tribune Media Services, Inc
All Rights Reserved
MACNELLY

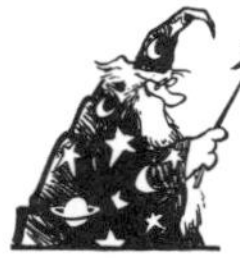

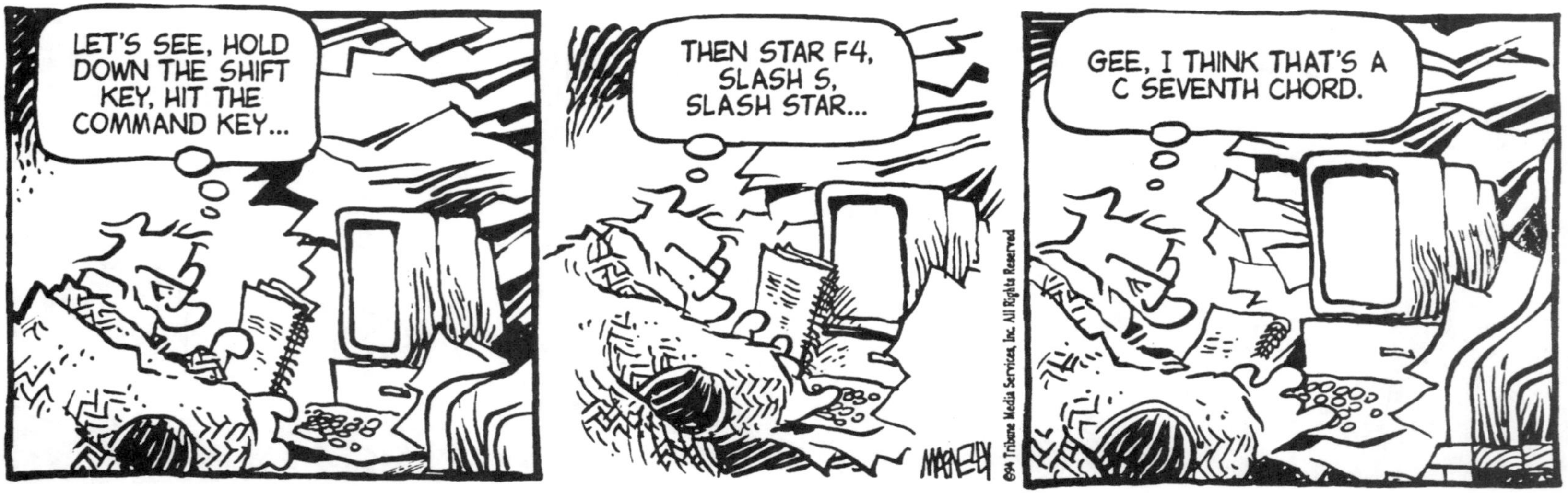
LET'S SEE, HOLD DOWN THE SHIFT KEY, HIT THE COMMAND KEY...
THEN STAR F4, SLASH S, SLASH STAR...
GEE, I THINK THAT'S A C SEVENTH CHORD.
MACNELLY
©94 Tribune Media Services, Inc. All Rights Reserved

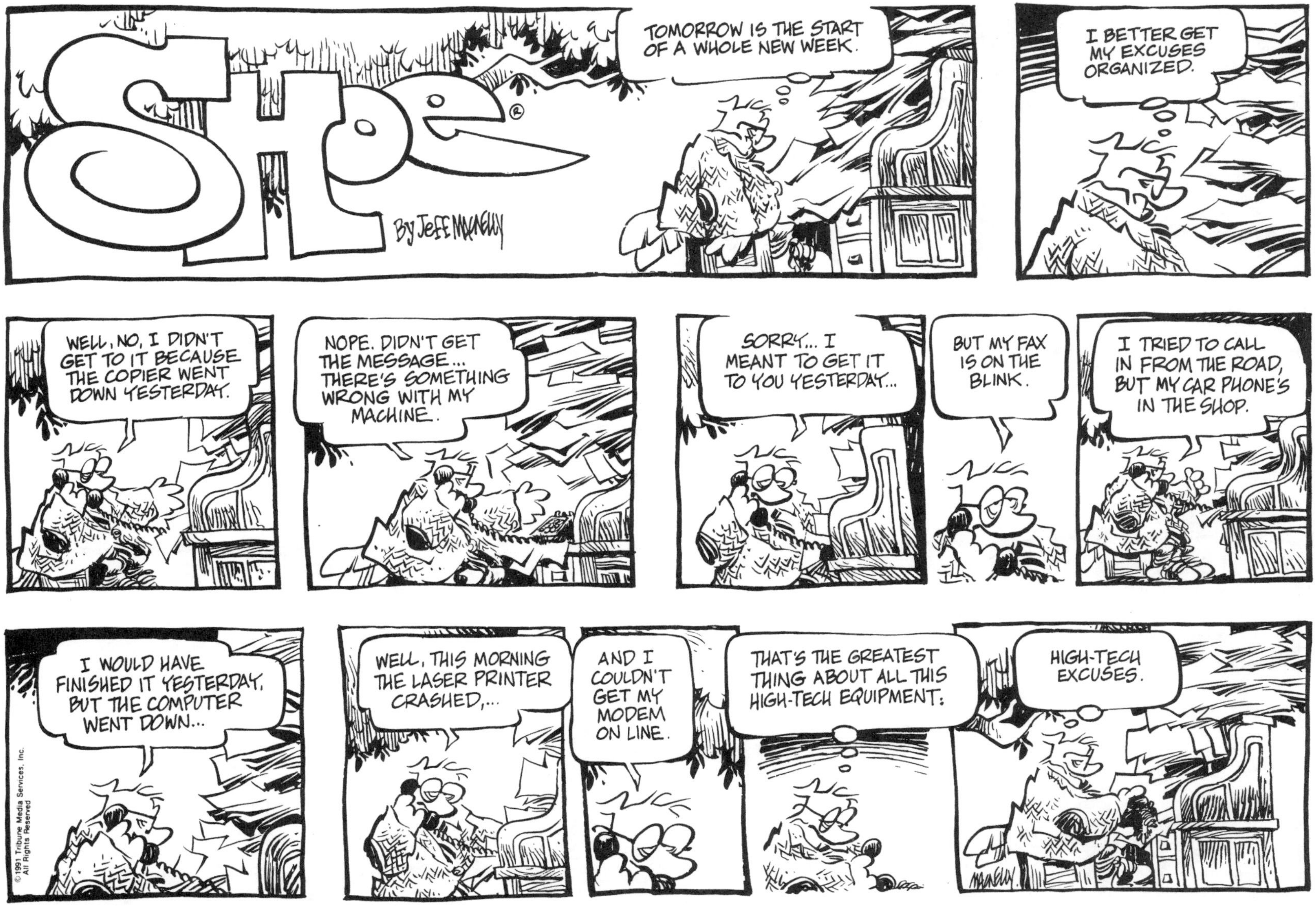
SHOE®
By Jeff MacNelly
TOMORROW IS THE START OF A WHOLE NEW WEEK.
I BETTER GET MY EXCUSES ORGANIZED.
WELL, NO, I DIDN'T GET TO IT BECAUSE THE COPIER WENT DOWN YESTERDAY.
NOPE. DIDN'T GET THE MESSAGE... THERE'S SOMETHING WRONG WITH MY MACHINE.
SORRY... I MEANT TO GET IT TO YOU YESTERDAY...
BUT MY FAX IS ON THE BLINK.
I TRIED TO CALL IN FROM THE ROAD, BUT MY CAR PHONE'S IN THE SHOP.
I WOULD HAVE FINISHED IT YESTERDAY, BUT THE COMPUTER WENT DOWN...
© 1991 Tribune Media Services, Inc. All Rights Reserved
WELL, THIS MORNING THE LASER PRINTER CRASHED,...
AND I COULDN'T GET MY MODEM ON LINE.
THAT'S THE GREATEST THING ABOUT ALL THIS HIGH-TECH EQUIPMENT:
HIGH-TECH EXCUSES.
MACNELLY

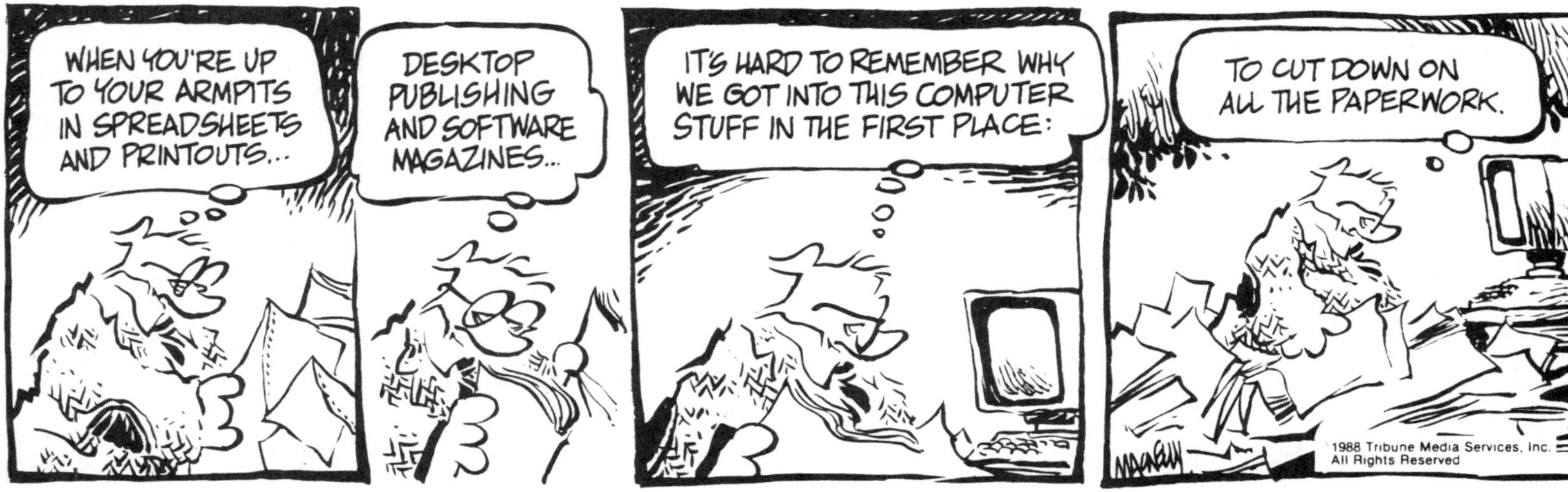
WHEN YOU'RE UP TO YOUR ARMPITS IN SPREADSHEETS AND PRINTOUTS...
DESKTOP PUBLISHING AND SOFTWARE MAGAZINES...
IT'S HARD TO REMEMBER WHY WE GOT INTO THIS COMPUTER STUFF IN THE FIRST PLACE:
TO CUT DOWN ON ALL THE PAPERWORK.
©1988 Tribune Media Services, Inc. All Rights Reserved

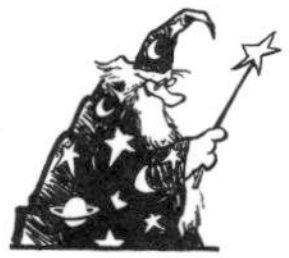

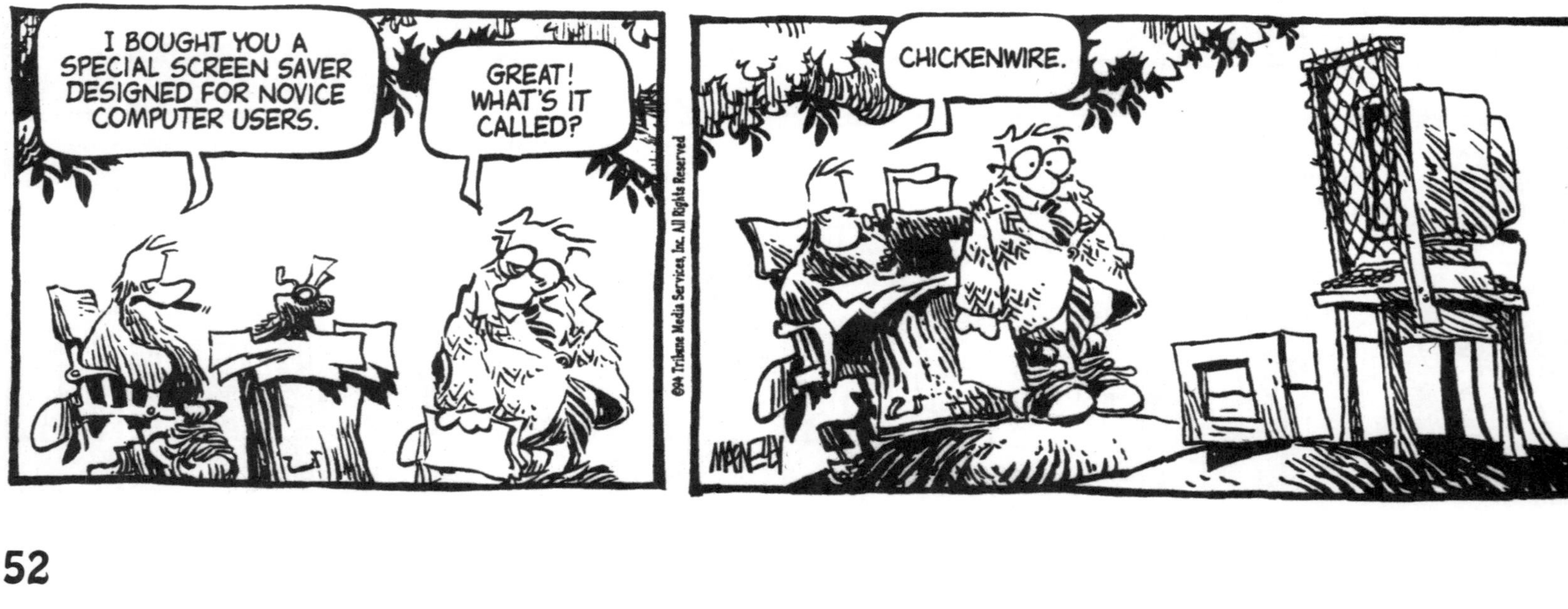
I BOUGHT YOU A SPECIAL SCREEN SAVER DESIGNED FOR NOVICE COMPUTER USERS.
GREAT! WHAT'S IT CALLED?
©94 Tribune Media Services, Inc. All Rights Reserved
CHICKENWIRE.

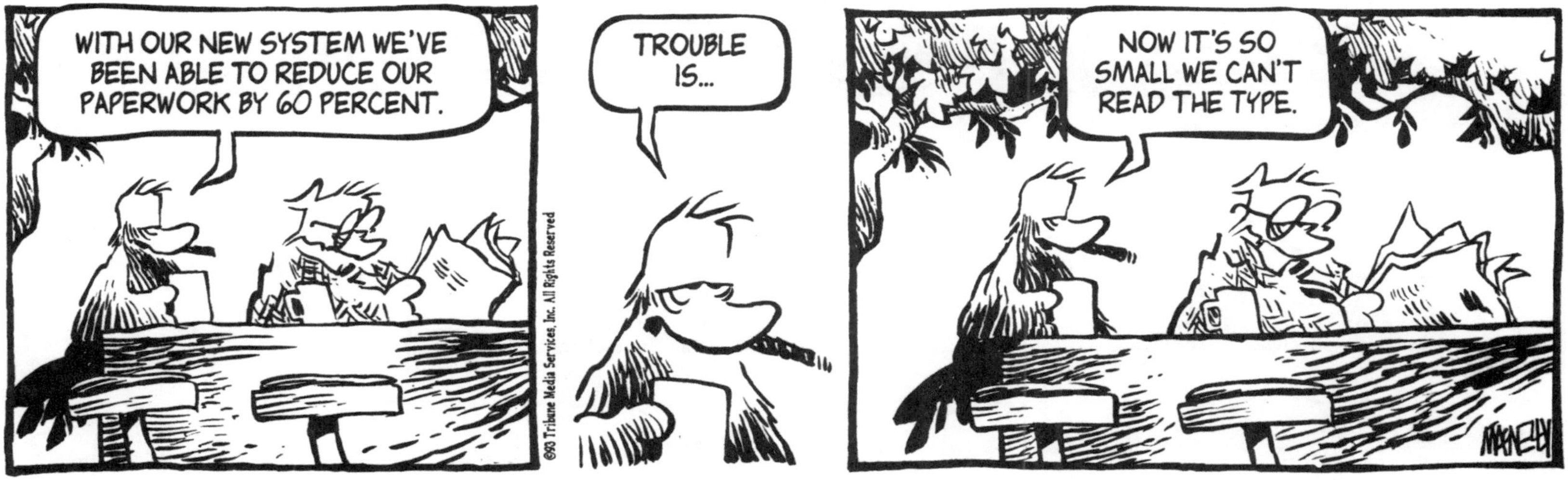
WITH OUR NEW SYSTEM WE'VE BEEN ABLE TO REDUCE OUR PAPERWORK BY 60 PERCENT.
TROUBLE IS...
NOW IT'S SO SMALL WE CAN'T READ THE TYPE.
©93 Tribune Media Services, Inc. All Rights Reserved
MACNELLY

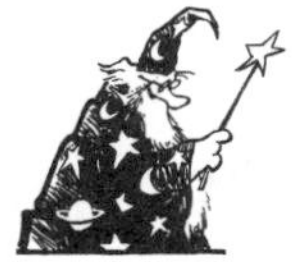

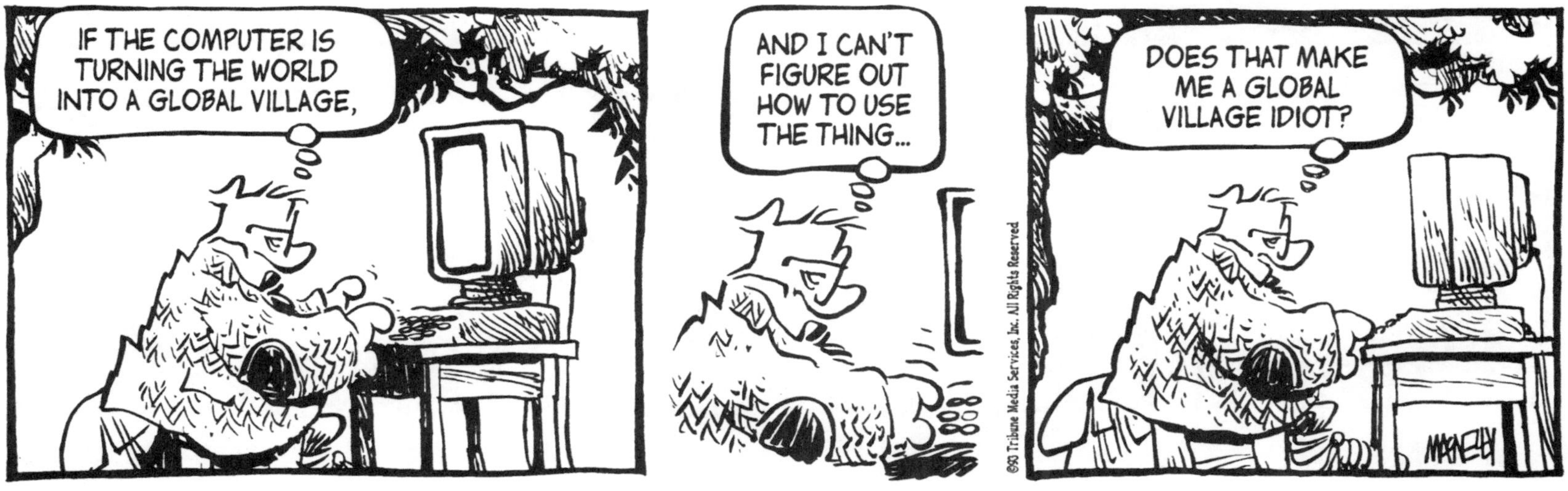
IF THE COMPUTER IS TURNING THE WORLD INTO A GLOBAL VILLAGE,
AND I CAN'T FIGURE OUT HOW TO USE THE THING...
DOES THAT MAKE ME A GLOBAL VILLAGE IDIOT?
©93 Tribune Media Services, Inc. All Rights Reserved
MACNELLY

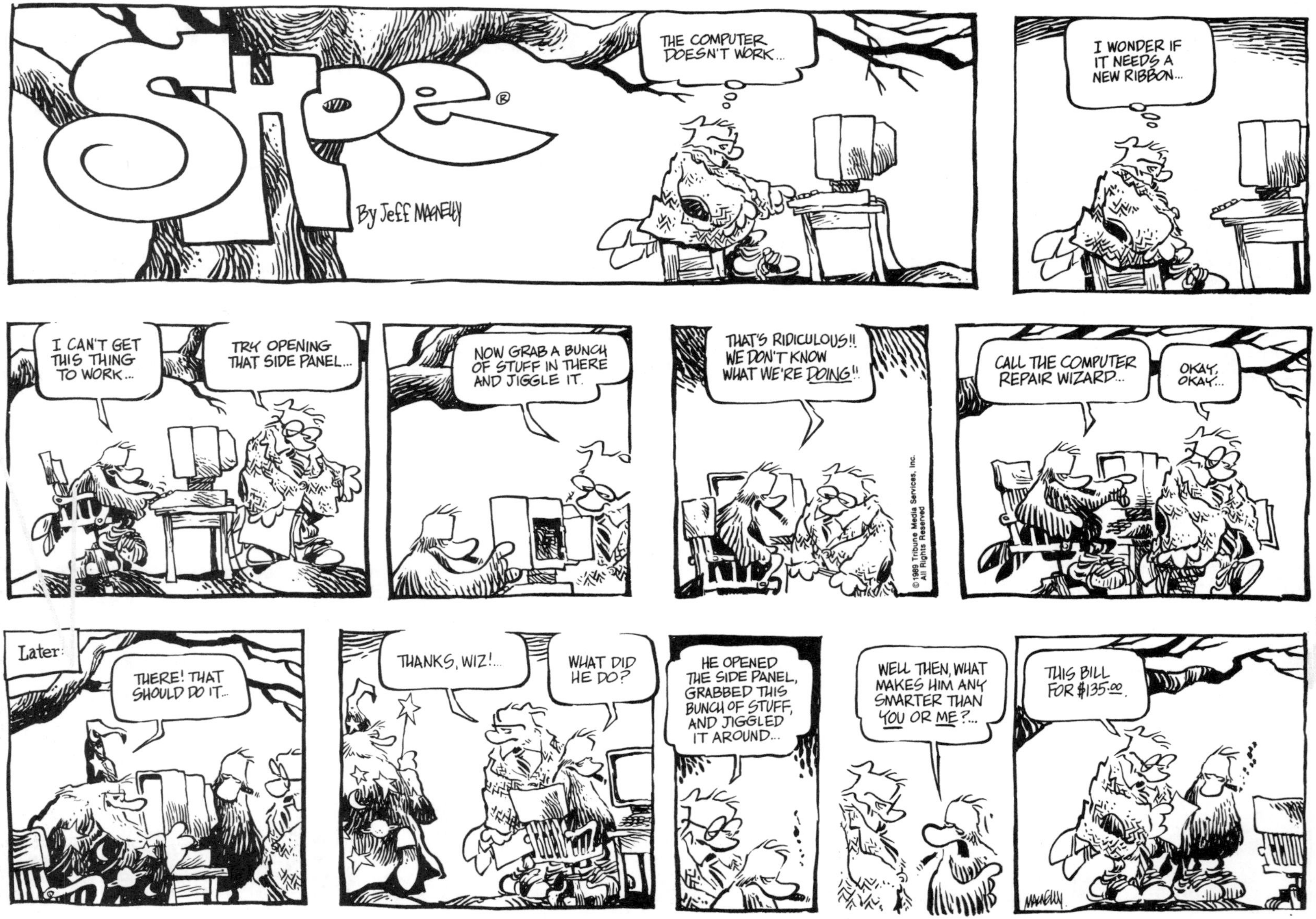
Shoe®
By Jeff MacNelly
THE COMPUTER DOESN'T WORK...
I WONDER IF IT NEEDS A NEW RIBBON...
I CAN'T GET THIS THING TO WORK...
TRY OPENING THAT SIDE PANEL...
NOW GRAB A BUNCH OF STUFF IN THERE AND JIGGLE IT.
THAT'S RIDICULOUS!! WE DON'T KNOW WHAT WE'RE DOING!!
© 1989 Tribune Media Services, Inc. All Rights Reserved
CALL THE COMPUTER REPAIR WIZARD...
OKAY, OKAY...
Later:
THERE! THAT SHOULD DO IT...
THANKS, WIZ!...
WHAT DID HE DO?
HE OPENED THE SIDE PANEL, GRABBED THIS BUNCH OF STUFF, AND JIGGLED IT AROUND...
WELL THEN, WHAT MAKES HIM ANY SMARTER THAN YOU OR ME?...
THIS BILL FOR $135.00.
MACNELLY

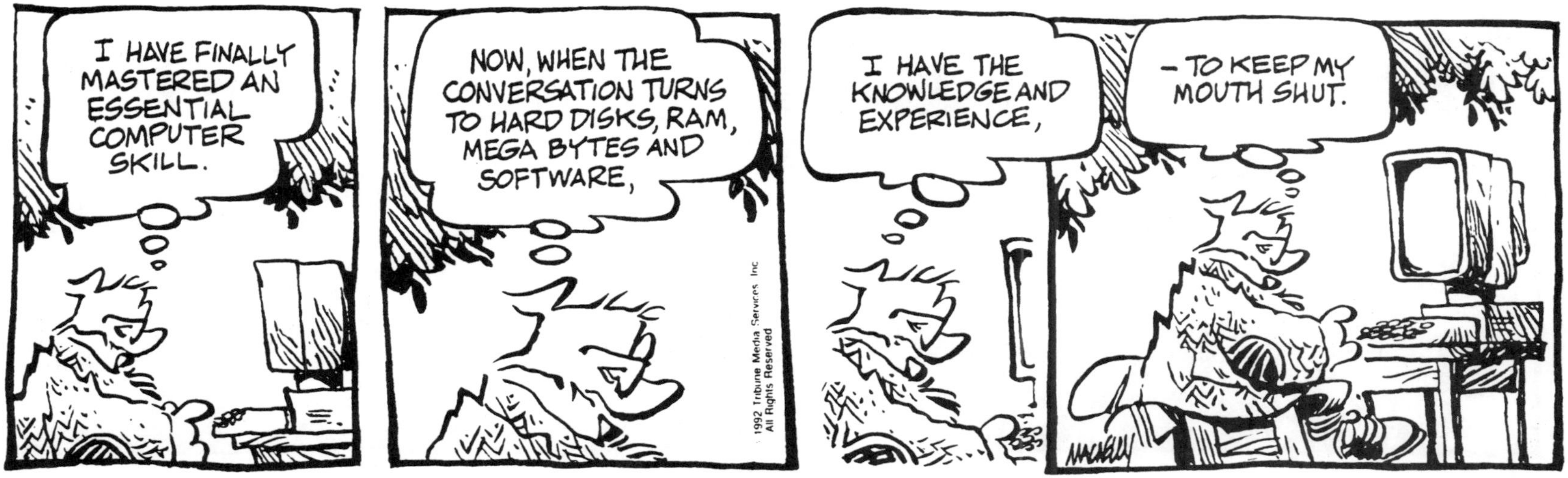
I HAVE FINALLY MASTERED AN ESSENTIAL COMPUTER SKILL.
NOW, WHEN THE CONVERSATION TURNS TO HARD DISKS, RAM, MEGA BYTES AND SOFTWARE,
I HAVE THE KNOWLEDGE AND EXPERIENCE,
– TO KEEP MY MOUTH SHUT.
© 1992 Tribune Media Services, Inc
All Rights Reserved

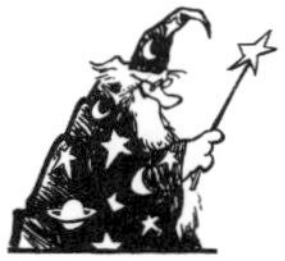

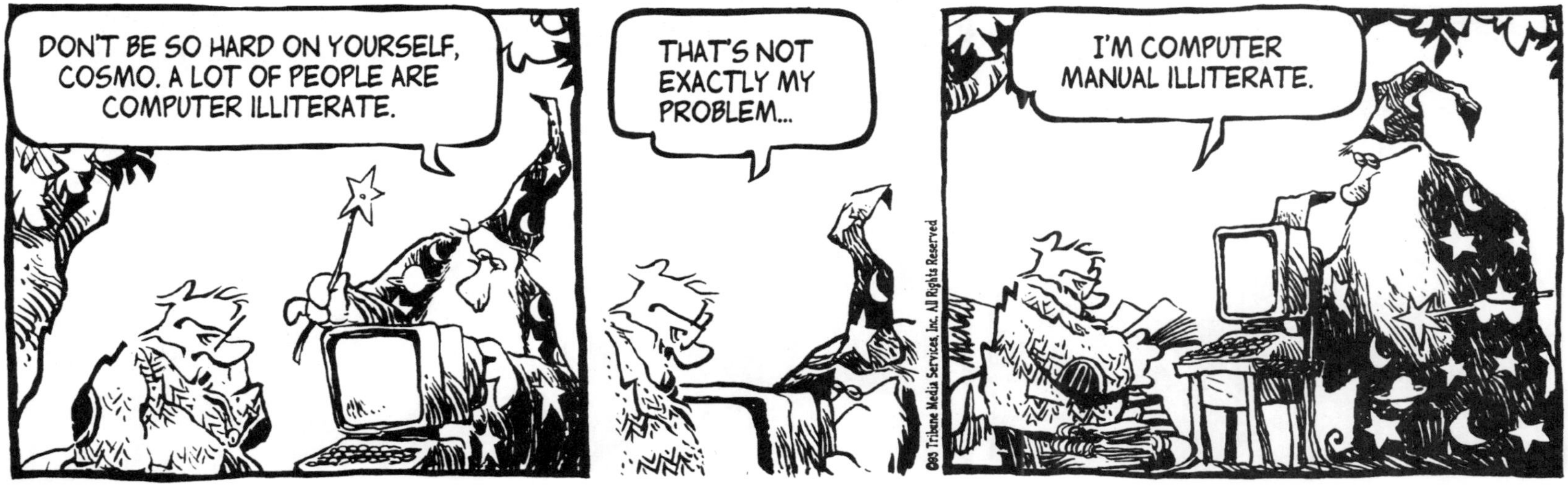
DON'T BE SO HARD ON YOURSELF, COSMO. A LOT OF PEOPLE ARE COMPUTER ILLITERATE.
THAT'S NOT EXACTLY MY PROBLEM...
I'M COMPUTER MANUAL ILLITERATE.
©93 Tribune Media Services, Inc. All Rights Reserved

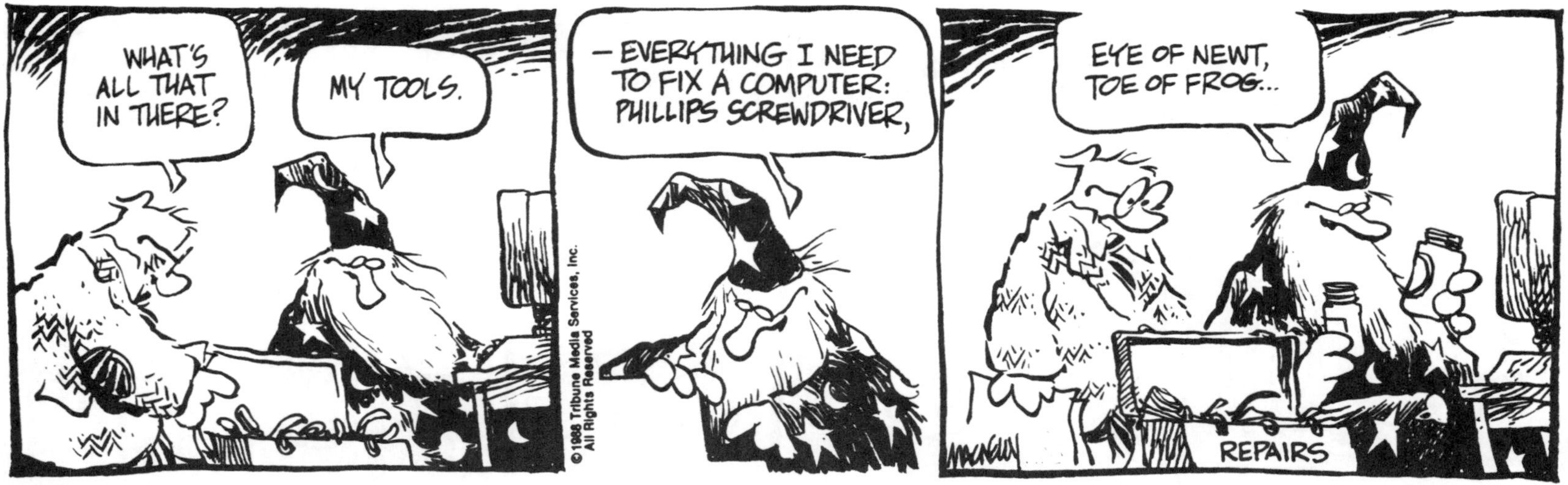
WHAT'S ALL THAT IN THERE?
MY TOOLS.
– EVERYTHING I NEED TO FIX A COMPUTER: PHILLIPS SCREWDRIVER,
EYE OF NEWT, TOE OF FROG...
REPAIRS

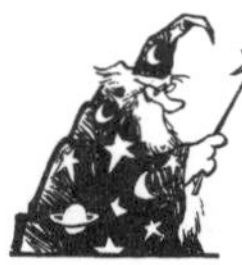

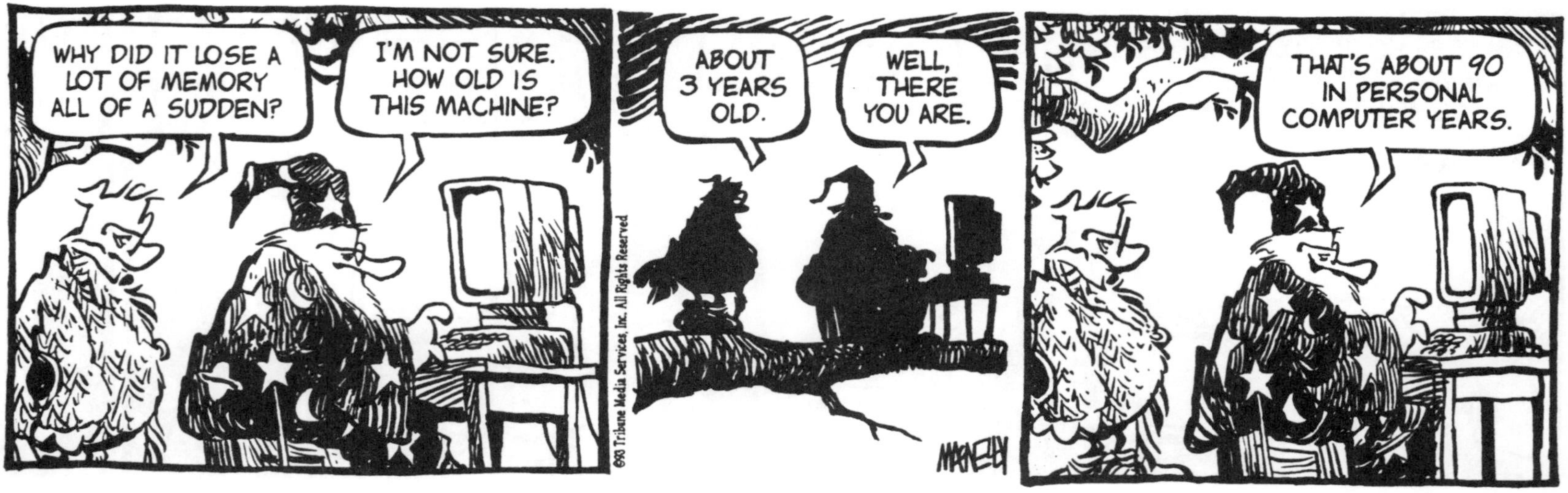
WHY DID IT LOSE A LOT OF MEMORY ALL OF A SUDDEN?
I'M NOT SURE. HOW OLD IS THIS MACHINE?
ABOUT 3 YEARS OLD.
WELL, THERE YOU ARE.
THAT'S ABOUT 90 IN PERSONAL COMPUTER YEARS.

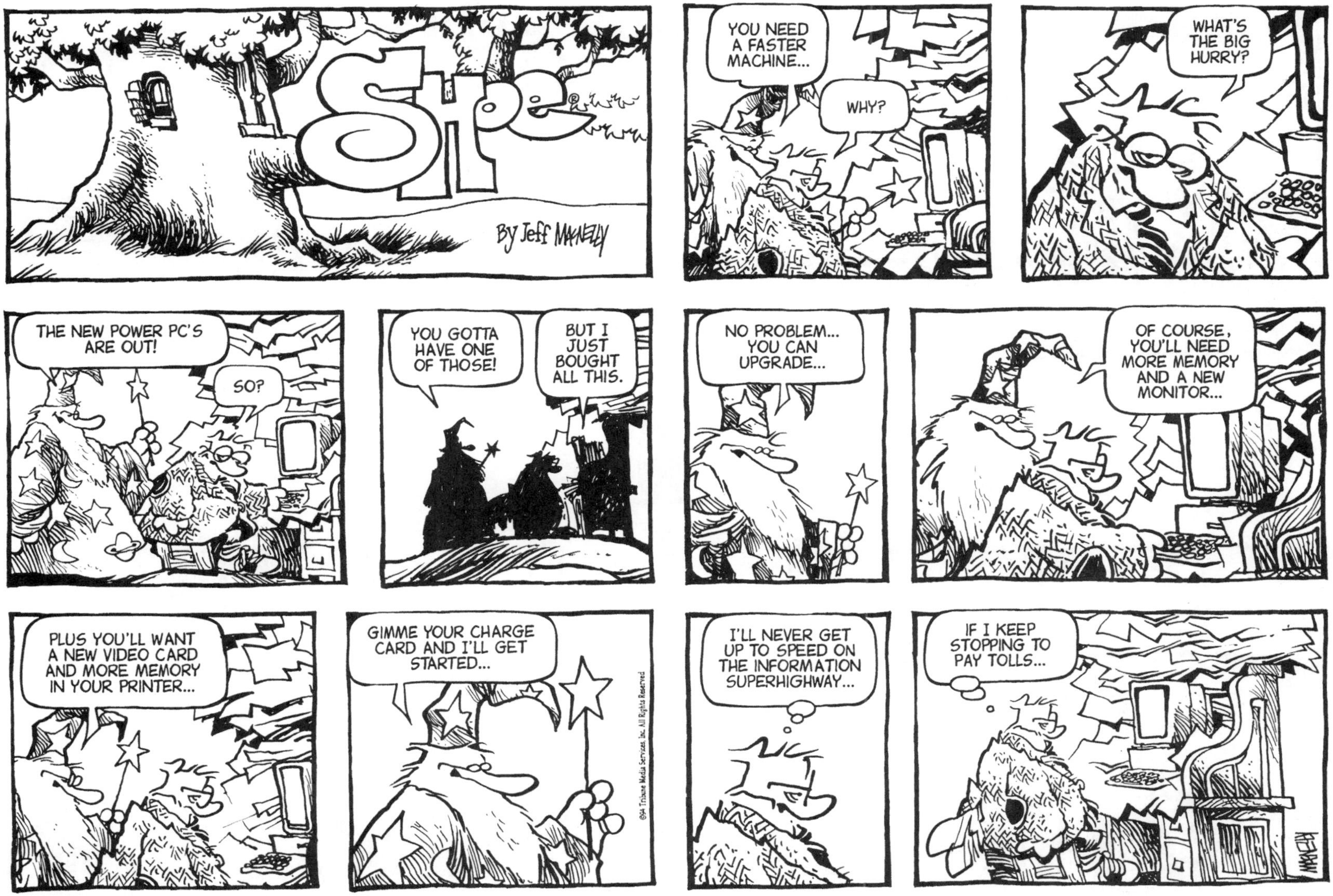
Shoe
By Jeff MacNelly
YOU NEED A FASTER MACHINE...
WHY?
WHAT'S THE BIG HURRY?
THE NEW POWER PC'S ARE OUT!
SO?
YOU GOTTA HAVE ONE OF THOSE!
BUT I JUST BOUGHT ALL THIS.
NO PROBLEM... YOU CAN UPGRADE...
OF COURSE, YOU'LL NEED MORE MEMORY AND A NEW MONITOR...
PLUS YOU'LL WANT A NEW VIDEO CARD AND MORE MEMORY IN YOUR PRINTER...
GIMME YOUR CHARGE CARD AND I'LL GET STARTED...
©94 Tribune Media Services, Inc. All Rights Reserved
I'LL NEVER GET UP TO SPEED ON THE INFORMATION SUPERHIGHWAY...
IF I KEEP STOPPING TO PAY TOLLS...

IS MY JOB SAFE IN THE FACE OF THIS INFORMATION SUPERHIGHWAY?
©94 Tribune Media Services, Inc. All Rights Reserved
WELL, WITH ANY SUPERHIGHWAY...
YOU'VE GOTTA EXPECT SOME ROADKILL.

THIS IS VERY SIMPLE:
FIRST, YOU ACCESS YOUR MAINFRAME.
© 1990 Tribune Media Services, Inc. All Rights Reserved
OR "ON" TO THE COMPUTER ILLITERATE.

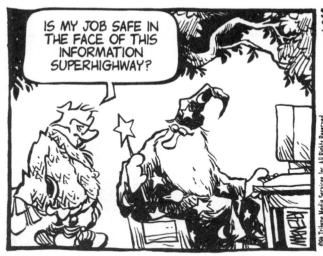

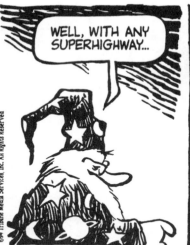

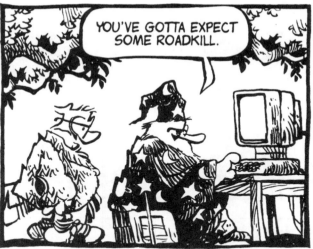

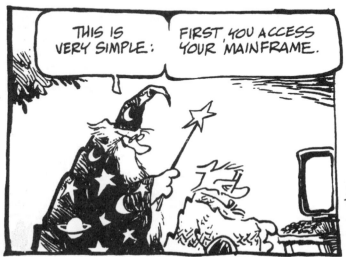

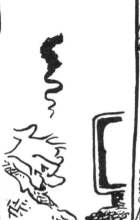

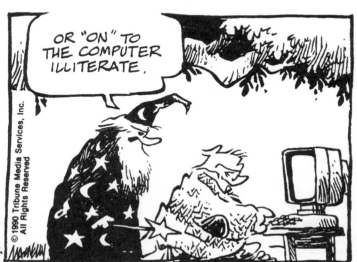

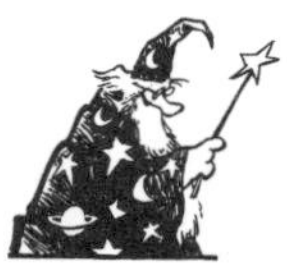

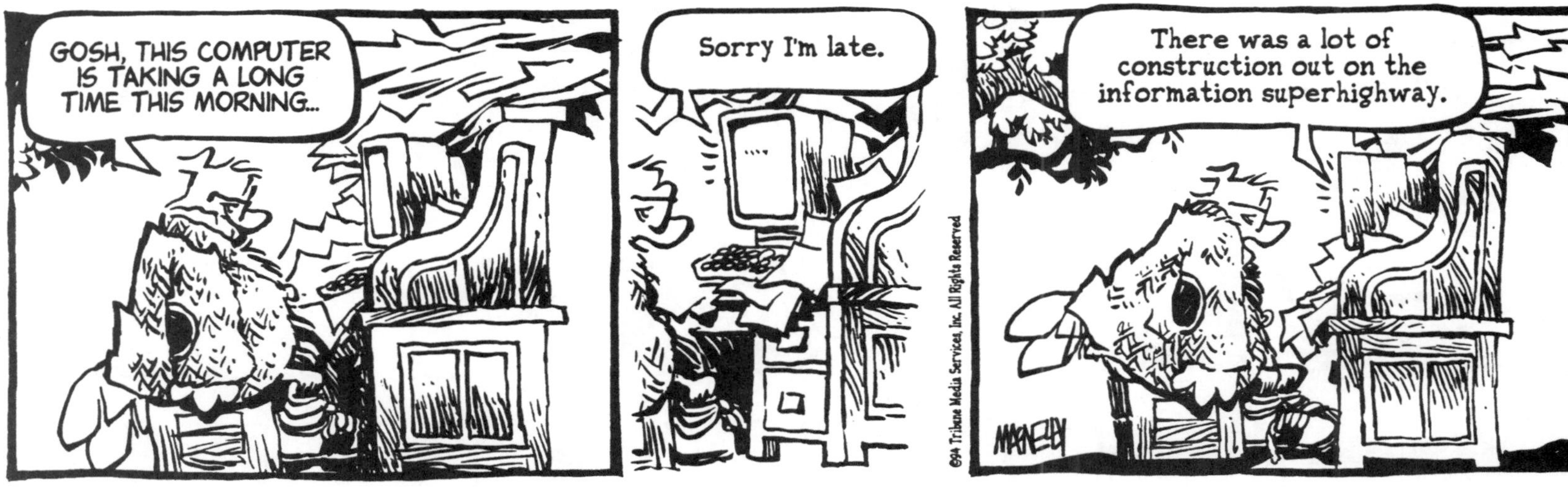
GOSH, THIS COMPUTER IS TAKING A LONG TIME THIS MORNING...
Sorry I'm late.
There was a lot of construction out on the information superhighway.
©94 Tribune Media Services, Inc. All Rights Reserved
MACNELLY

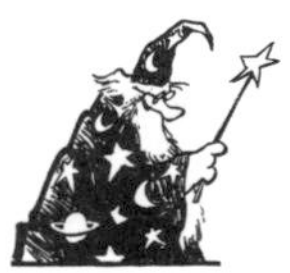

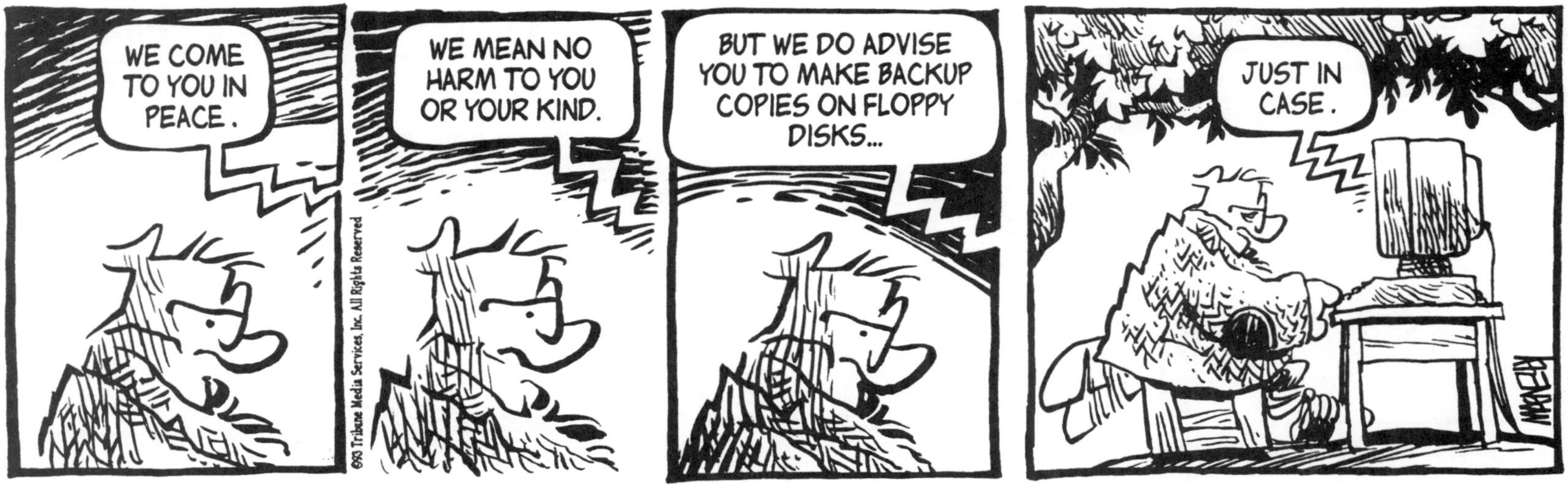
WE COME TO YOU IN PEACE.
WE MEAN NO HARM TO YOU OR YOUR KIND.
BUT WE DO ADVISE YOU TO MAKE BACKUP COPIES ON FLOPPY DISKS...
JUST IN CASE.
©93 Tribune Media Services, Inc. All Rights Reserved
MACNELLY

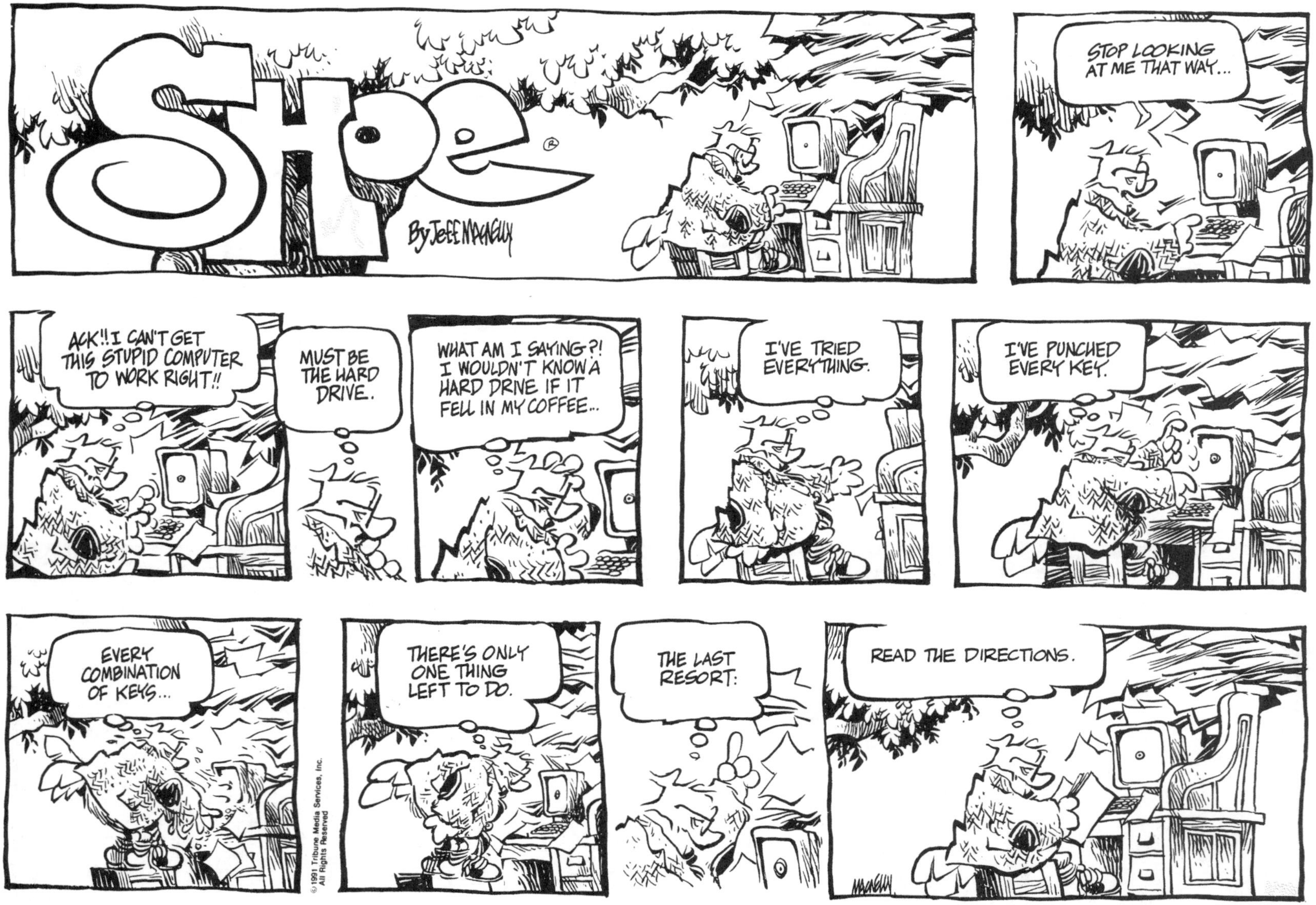
SHOE®
By Jeff MacNelly
STOP LOOKING AT ME THAT WAY...
ACK!! I CAN'T GET THIS STUPID COMPUTER TO WORK RIGHT!!
MUST BE THE HARD DRIVE.
WHAT AM I SAYING?! I WOULDN'T KNOW A HARD DRIVE IF IT FELL IN MY COFFEE...
I'VE TRIED EVERYTHING.
I'VE PUNCHED EVERY KEY.
EVERY COMBINATION OF KEYS...
THERE'S ONLY ONE THING LEFT TO DO.
THE LAST RESORT:
READ THE DIRECTIONS.
MacNelly

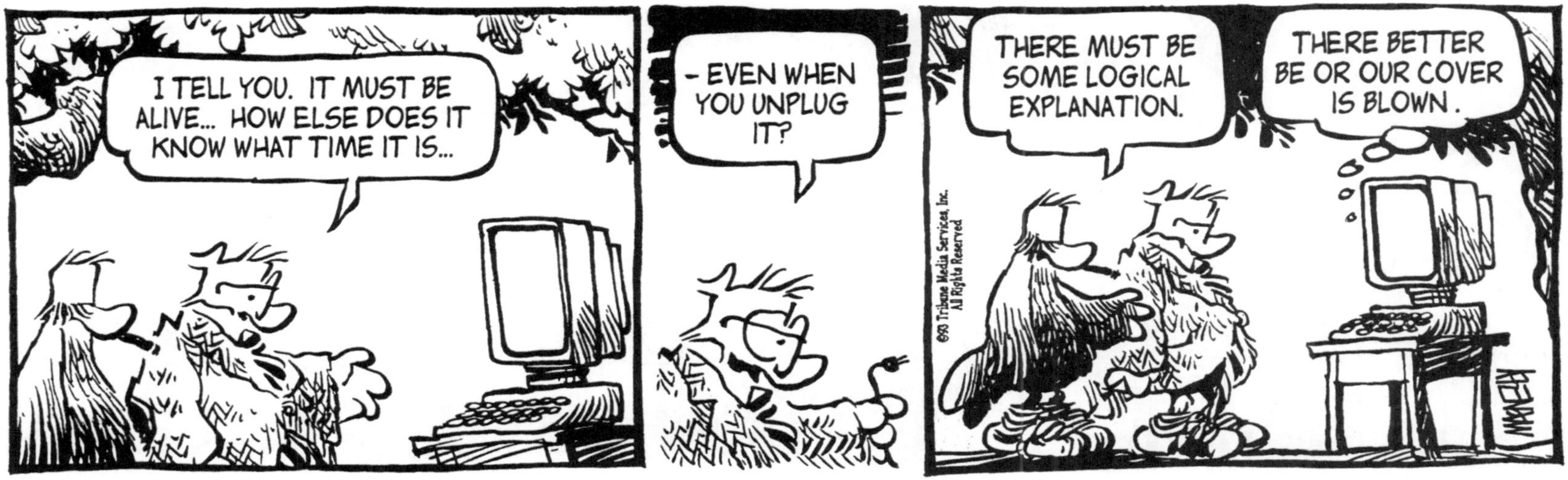
I TELL YOU. IT MUST BE ALIVE... HOW ELSE DOES IT KNOW WHAT TIME IT IS...
- EVEN WHEN YOU UNPLUG IT?
©93 Tribune Media Services, Inc. All Rights Reserved
THERE MUST BE SOME LOGICAL EXPLANATION.
THERE BETTER BE OR OUR COVER IS BLOWN.

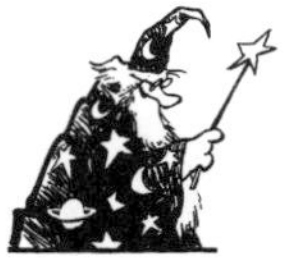

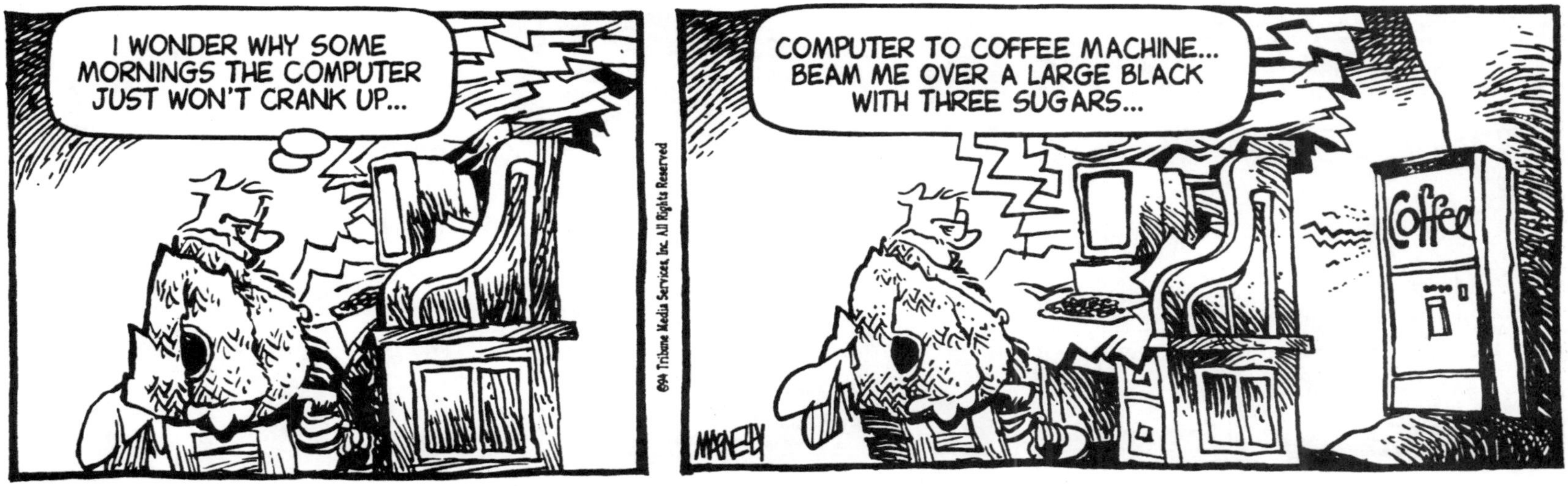
I WONDER WHY SOME MORNINGS THE COMPUTER JUST WON'T CRANK UP...
©94 Tribune Media Services, Inc. All Rights Reserved
COMPUTER TO COFFEE MACHINE... BEAM ME OVER A LARGE BLACK WITH THREE SUGARS...
Coffee

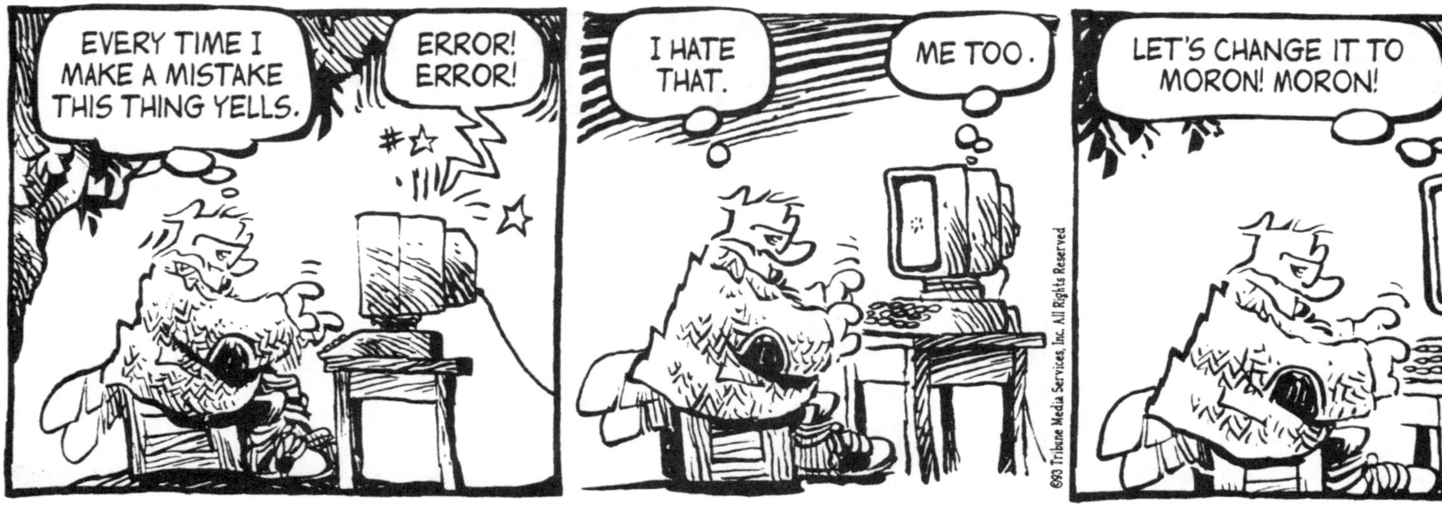
EVERY TIME I MAKE A MISTAKE THIS THING YELLS.
ERROR! ERROR!
I HATE THAT.
ME TOO.
LET'S CHANGE IT TO MORON! MORON!
©93 Tribune Media Services, Inc. All Rights Reserved

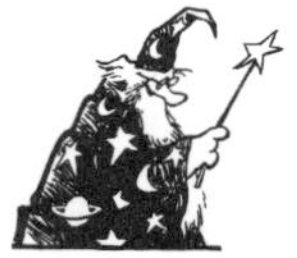

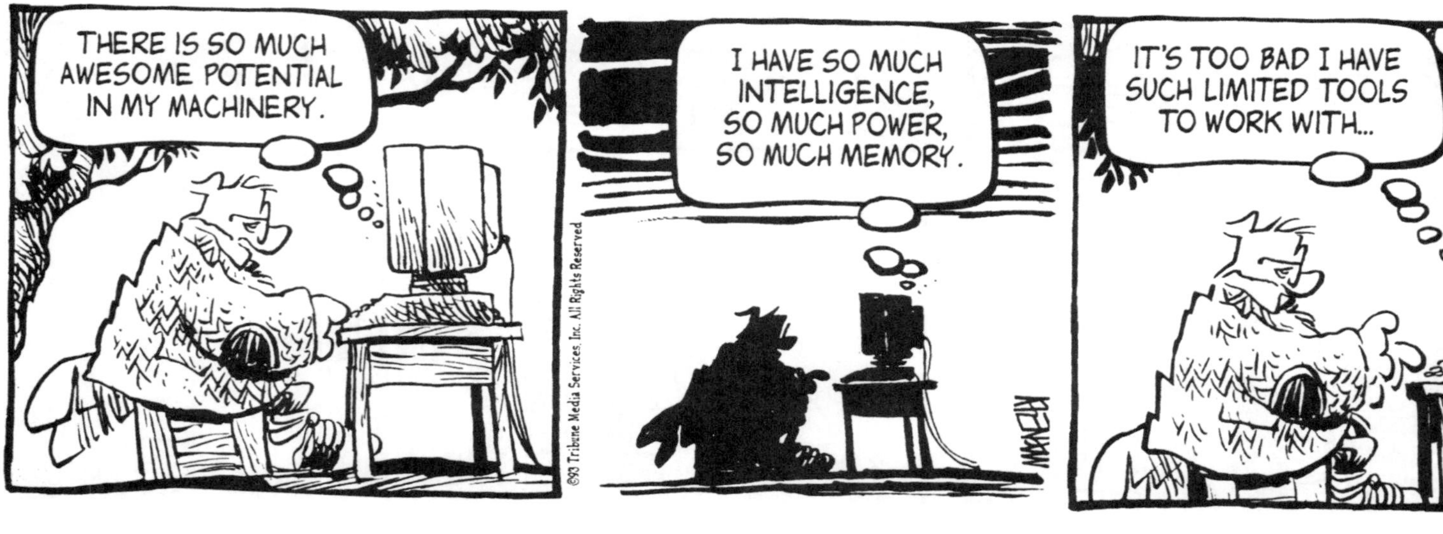
THERE IS SO MUCH AWESOME POTENTIAL IN MY MACHINERY.
I HAVE SO MUCH INTELLIGENCE, SO MUCH POWER, SO MUCH MEMORY.
IT'S TOO BAD I HAVE SUCH LIMITED TOOLS TO WORK WITH...
©93 Tribune Media Services, Inc. All Rights Reserved

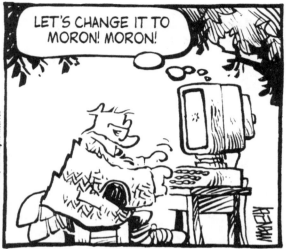

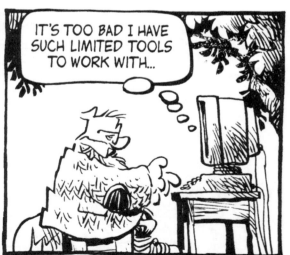

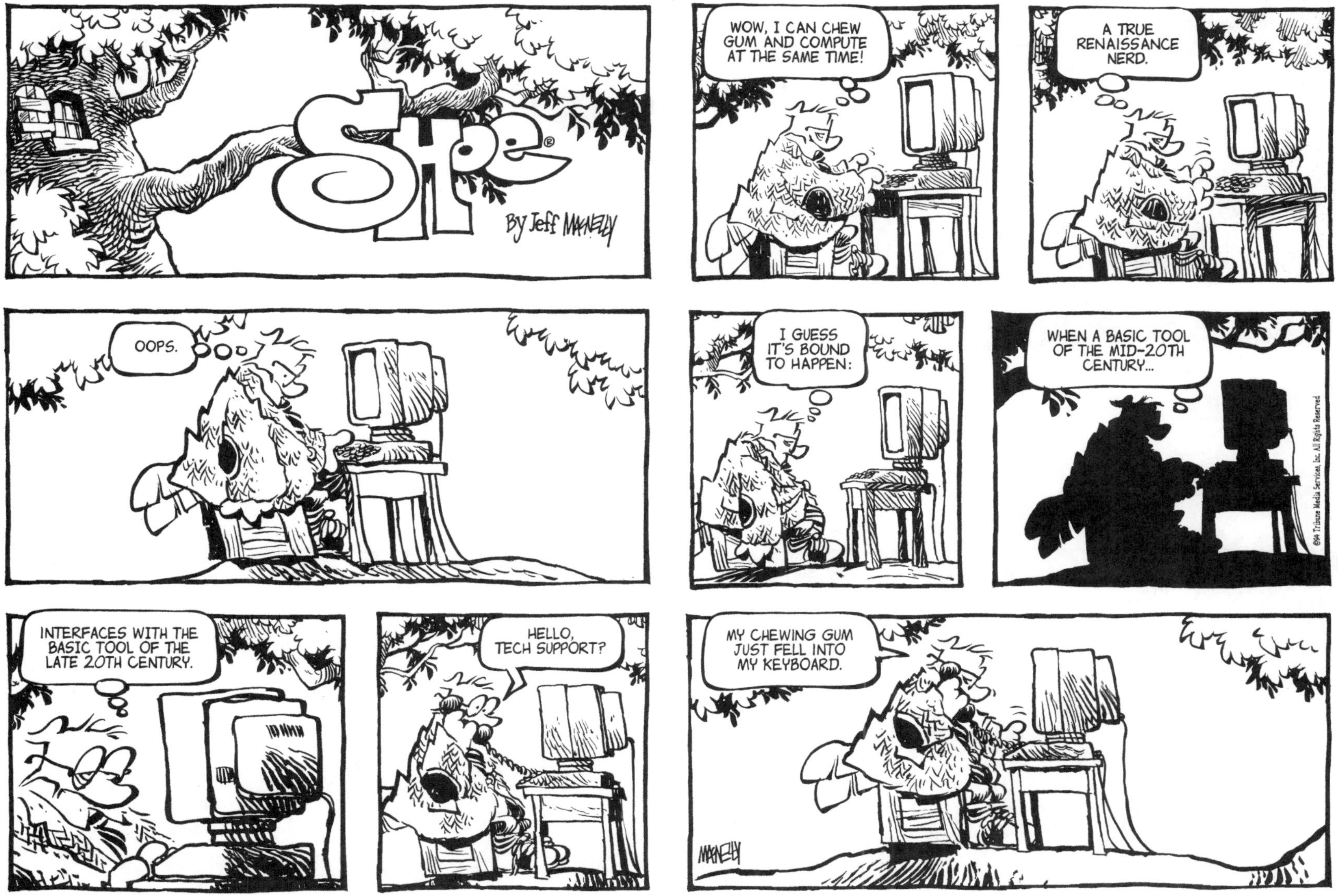
Shoe®
By Jeff MacNelly
WOW, I CAN CHEW GUM AND COMPUTE AT THE SAME TIME!
A TRUE RENAISSANCE NERD.
OOPS.
I GUESS IT'S BOUND TO HAPPEN:
WHEN A BASIC TOOL OF THE MID-20TH CENTURY...
©94 Tribune Media Services, Inc. All Rights Reserved
INTERFACES WITH THE BASIC TOOL OF THE LATE 20TH CENTURY.
HELLO, TECH SUPPORT?
MY CHEWING GUM JUST FELL INTO MY KEYBOARD.
MACNELLY

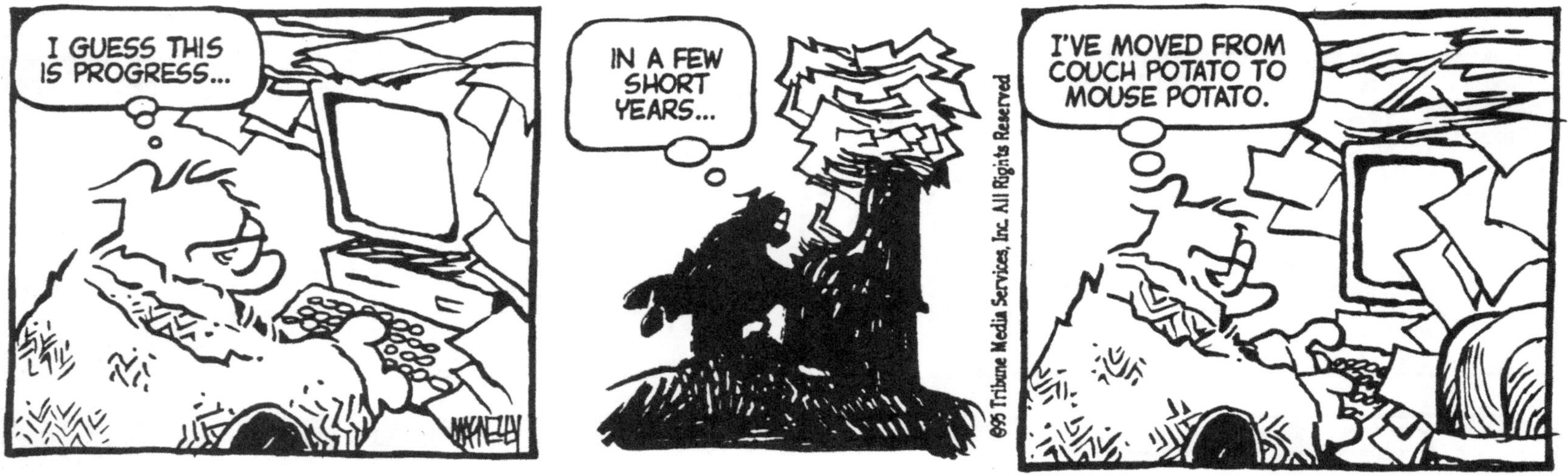
I GUESS THIS IS PROGRESS...
IN A FEW SHORT YEARS...
I'VE MOVED FROM COUCH POTATO TO MOUSE POTATO.
©95 Tribune Media Services, Inc. All Rights Reserved

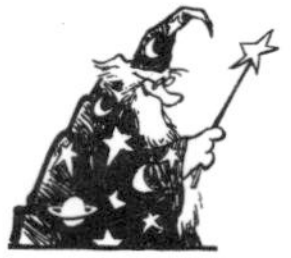

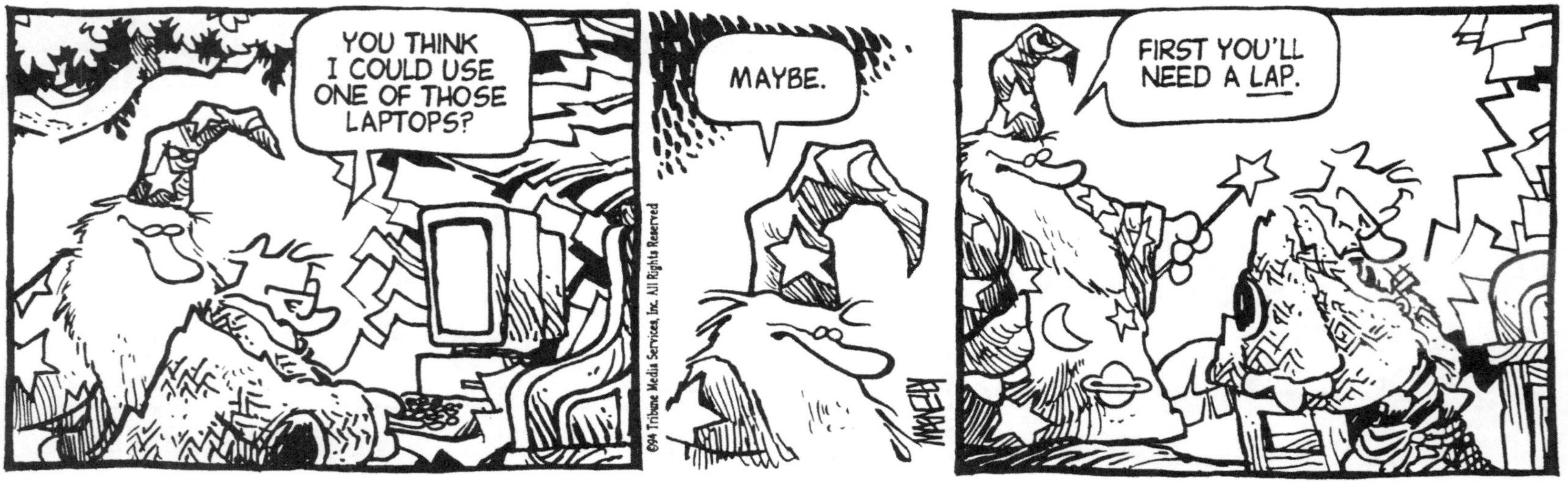
YOU THINK I COULD USE ONE OF THOSE LAPTOPS?
MAYBE.
FIRST YOU'LL NEED A LAP.
©94 Tribune Media Services, Inc. All Rights Reserved

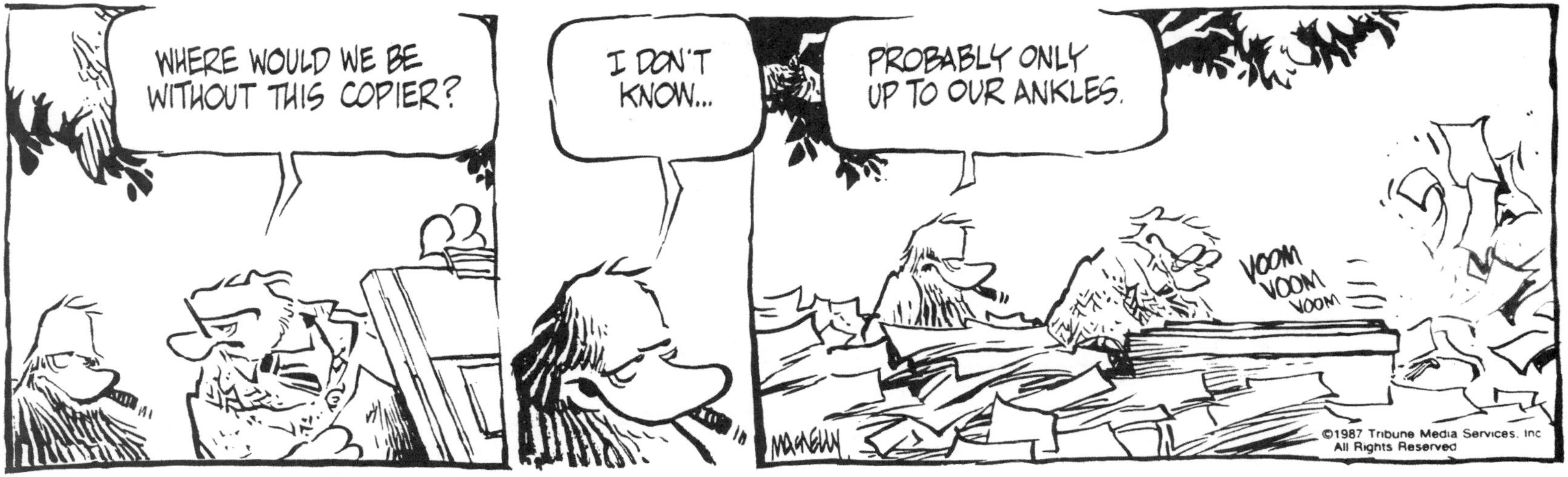
WHERE WOULD WE BE WITHOUT THIS COPIER?
I DON'T KNOW...
PROBABLY ONLY UP TO OUR ANKLES.
VOOM VOOM VOOM
©1987 Tribune Media Services, Inc
All Rights Reserved

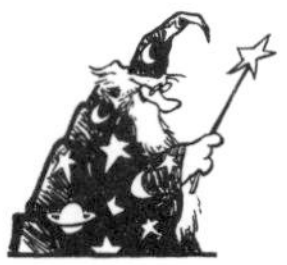

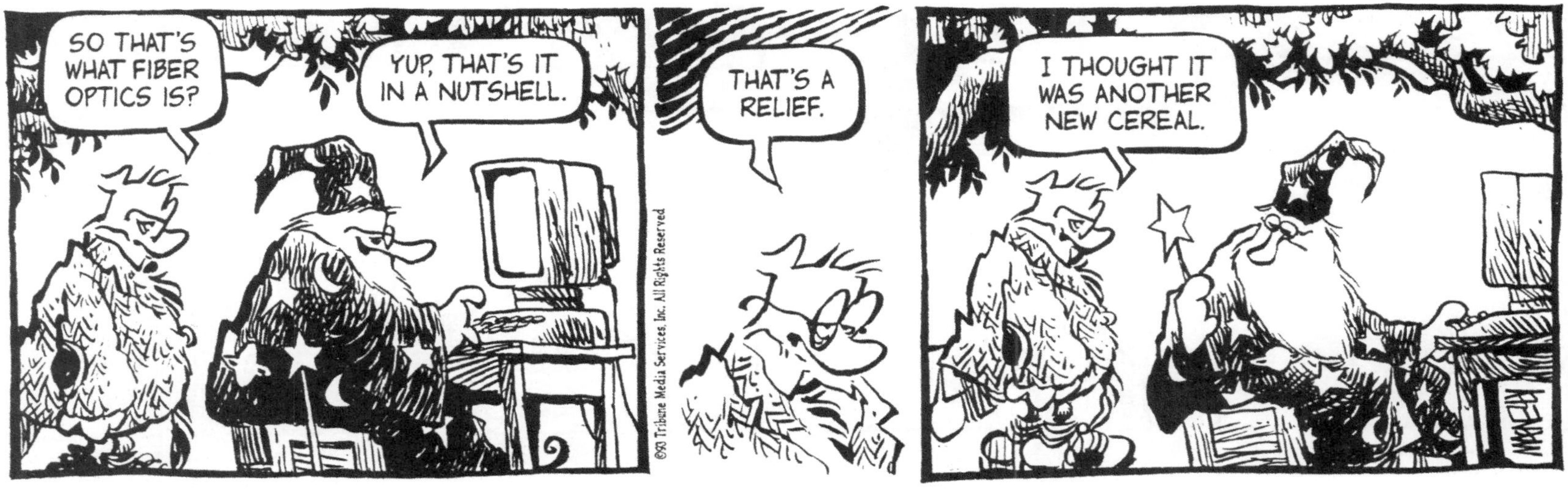
SO THAT'S WHAT FIBER OPTICS IS?
YUP, THAT'S IT IN A NUTSHELL.
©93 Tribune Media Services, Inc. All Rights Reserved
THAT'S A RELIEF.
I THOUGHT IT WAS ANOTHER NEW CEREAL.

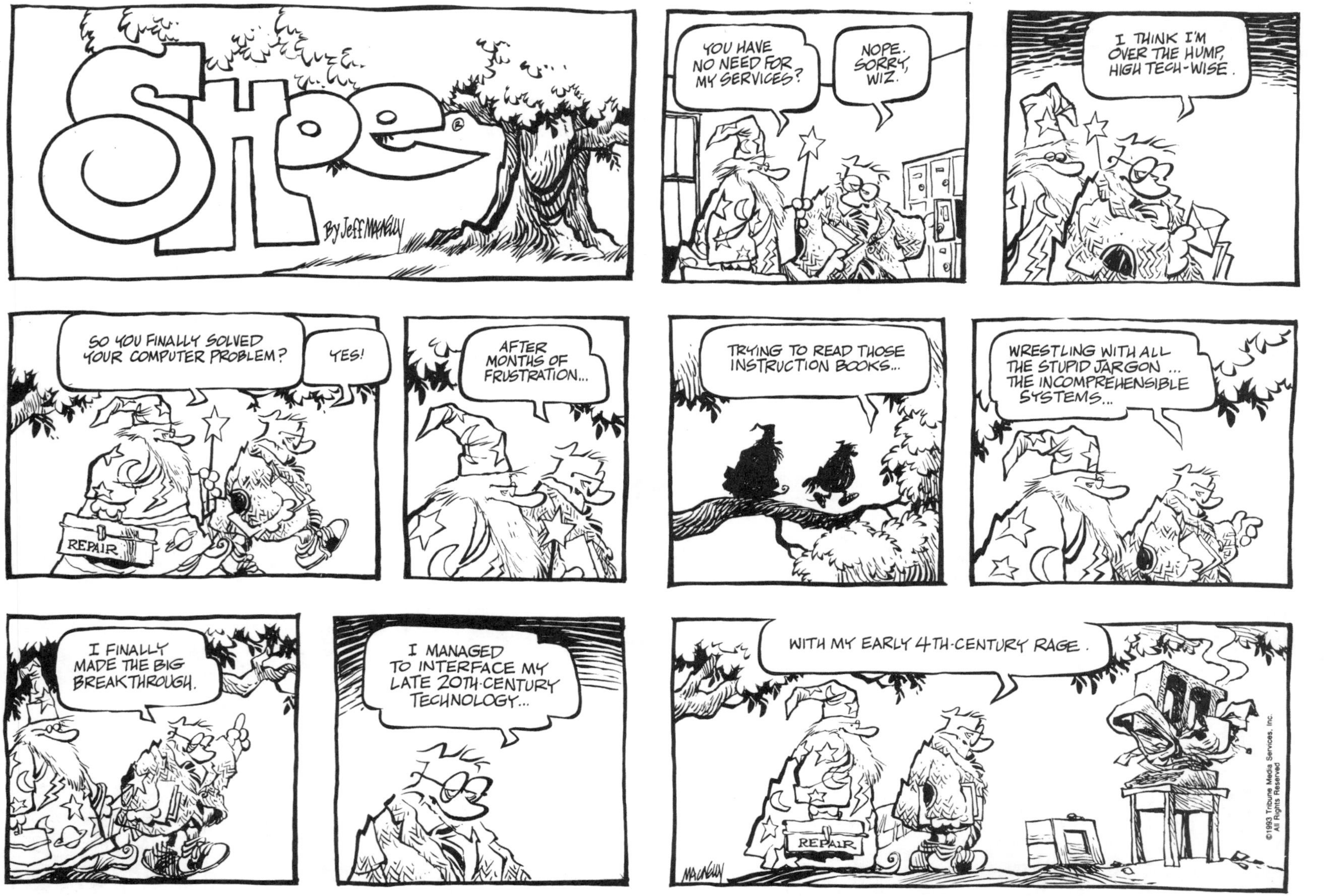
SHOE
By Jeff MacNelly
YOU HAVE NO NEED FOR MY SERVICES?
NOPE. SORRY, WIZ.
I THINK I'M OVER THE HUMP, HIGH TECH-WISE.
SO YOU FINALLY SOLVED YOUR COMPUTER PROBLEM?
YES!
REPAIR
AFTER MONTHS OF FRUSTRATION...
TRYING TO READ THOSE INSTRUCTION BOOKS...
WRESTLING WITH ALL THE STUPID JARGON ... THE INCOMPREHENSIBLE SYSTEMS...
I FINALLY MADE THE BIG BREAKTHROUGH.
I MANAGED TO INTERFACE MY LATE 20TH-CENTURY TECHNOLOGY...
WITH MY EARLY 4TH-CENTURY RAGE.
REPAIR
MACNELLY
©1993 Tribune Media Services, Inc. All Rights Reserved

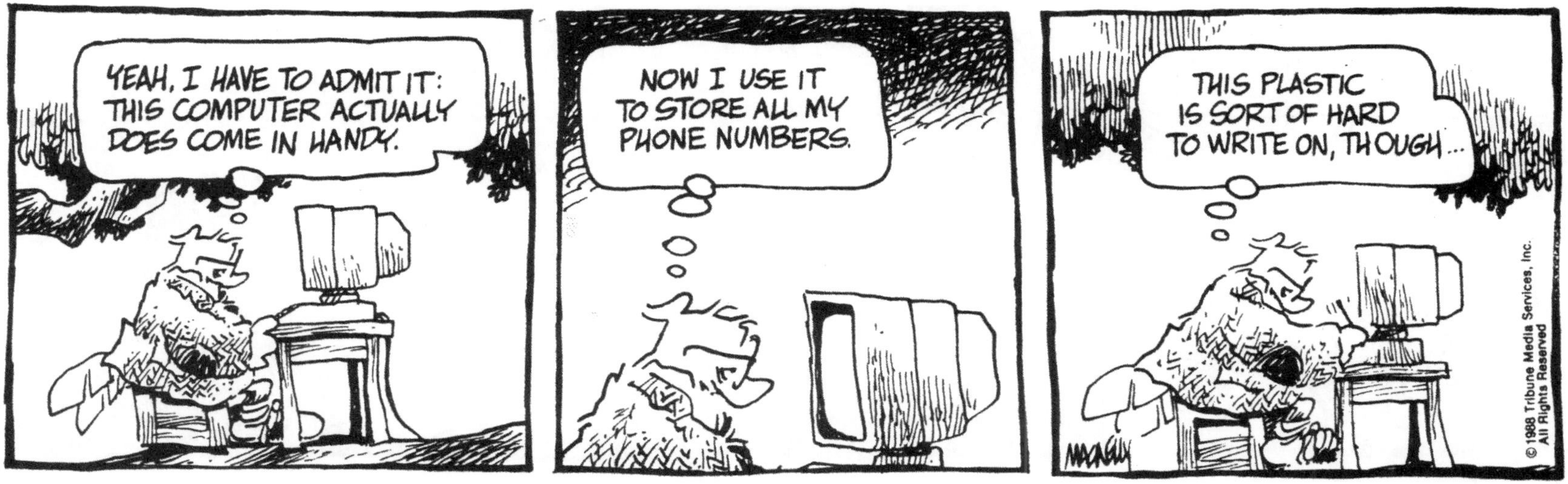
YEAH, I HAVE TO ADMIT IT: THIS COMPUTER ACTUALLY DOES COME IN HANDY.
NOW I USE IT TO STORE ALL MY PHONE NUMBERS.
THIS PLASTIC IS SORT OF HARD TO WRITE ON, THOUGH...
© 1988 Tribune Media Services, Inc. All Rights Reserved

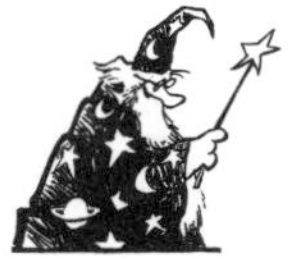

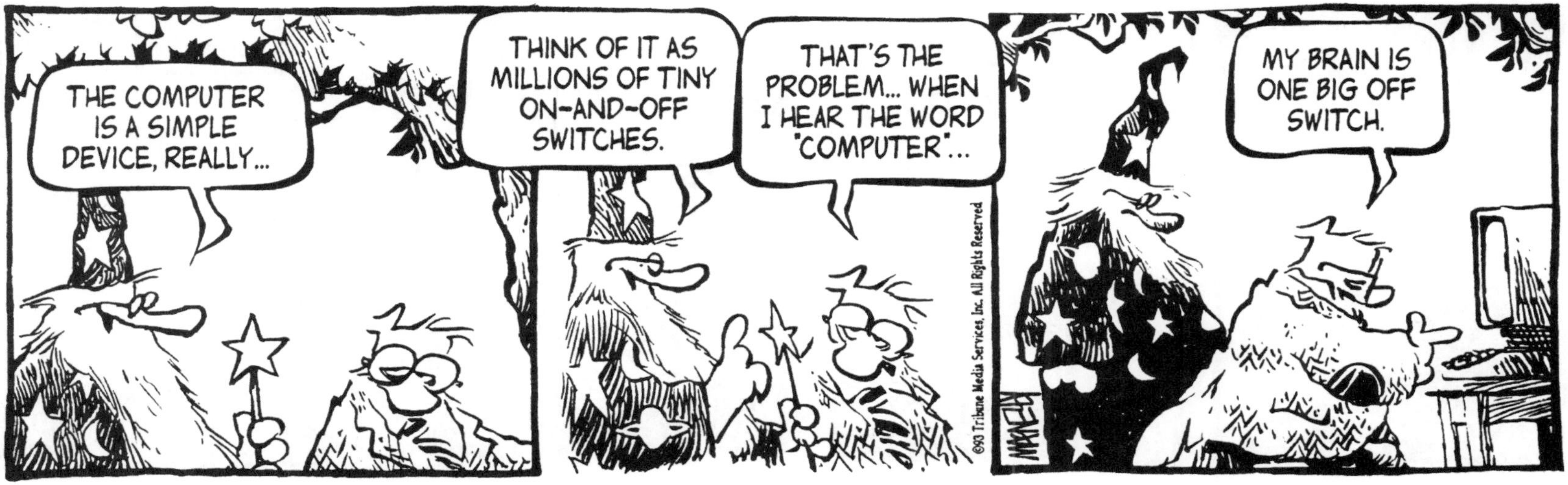
THE COMPUTER IS A SIMPLE DEVICE, REALLY...
THINK OF IT AS MILLIONS OF TINY ON-AND-OFF SWITCHES.
THAT'S THE PROBLEM... WHEN I HEAR THE WORD "COMPUTER"...
MY BRAIN IS ONE BIG OFF SWITCH.
©93 Tribune Media Services, Inc. All Rights Reserved

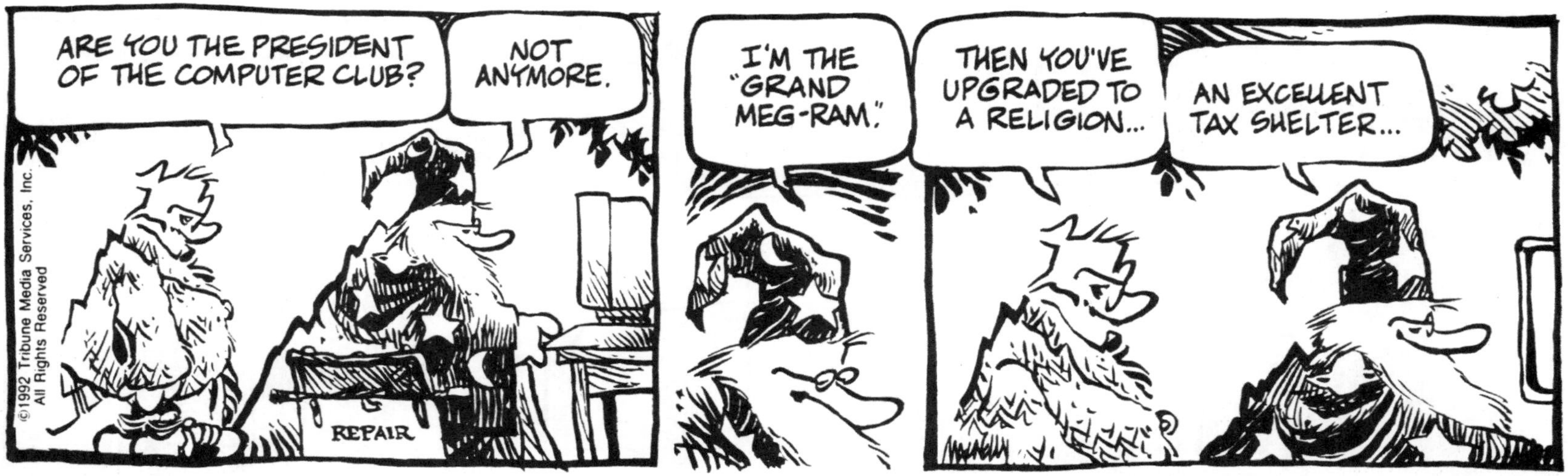
ARE YOU THE PRESIDENT OF THE COMPUTER CLUB?
NOT ANYMORE.
I'M THE "GRAND MEG-RAM."
THEN YOU'VE UPGRADED TO A RELIGION...
AN EXCELLENT TAX SHELTER...
REPAIR
© 1992 Tribune Media Services, Inc. All Rights Reserved

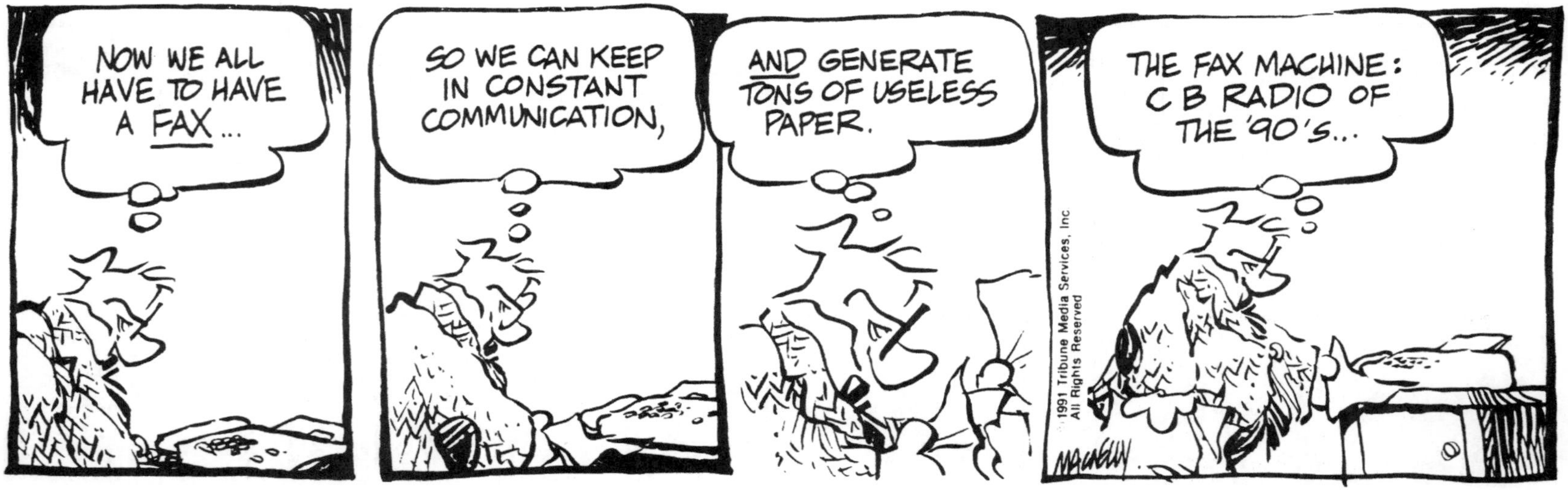
NOW WE ALL HAVE TO HAVE A FAX...
SO WE CAN KEEP IN CONSTANT COMMUNICATION,
AND GENERATE TONS OF USELESS PAPER.
THE FAX MACHINE: C B RADIO OF THE '90's...
© 1991 Tribune Media Services, Inc All Rights Reserved

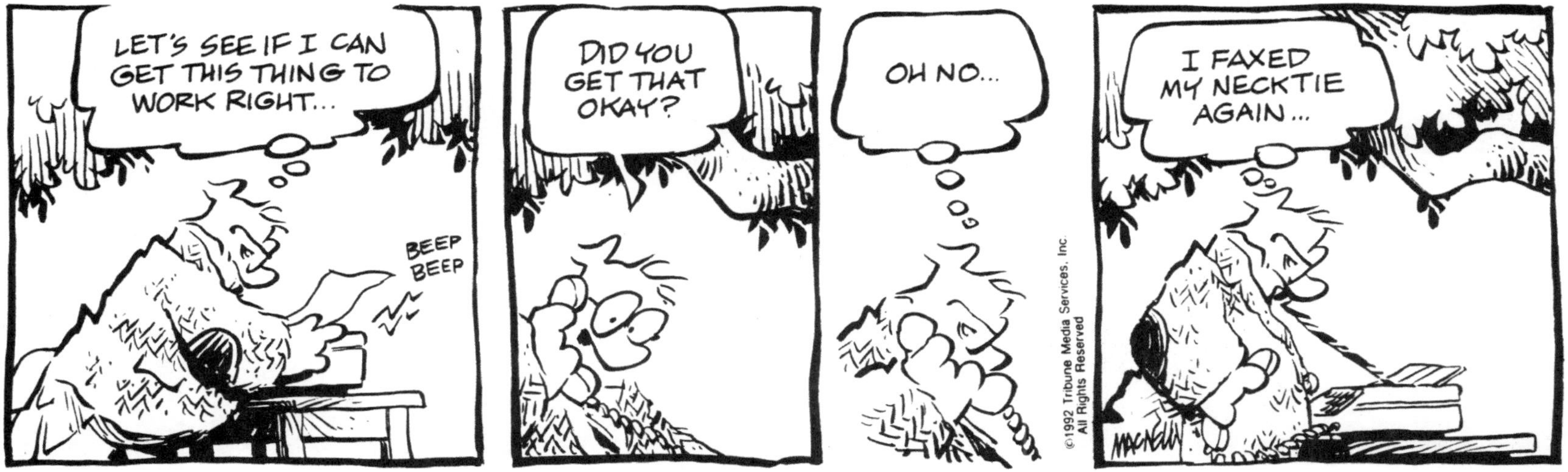
LET'S SEE IF I CAN GET THIS THING TO WORK RIGHT...
BEEP BEEP
DID YOU GET THAT OKAY?
OH NO...
©1992 Tribune Media Services, Inc. All Rights Reserved
I FAXED MY NECKTIE AGAIN...

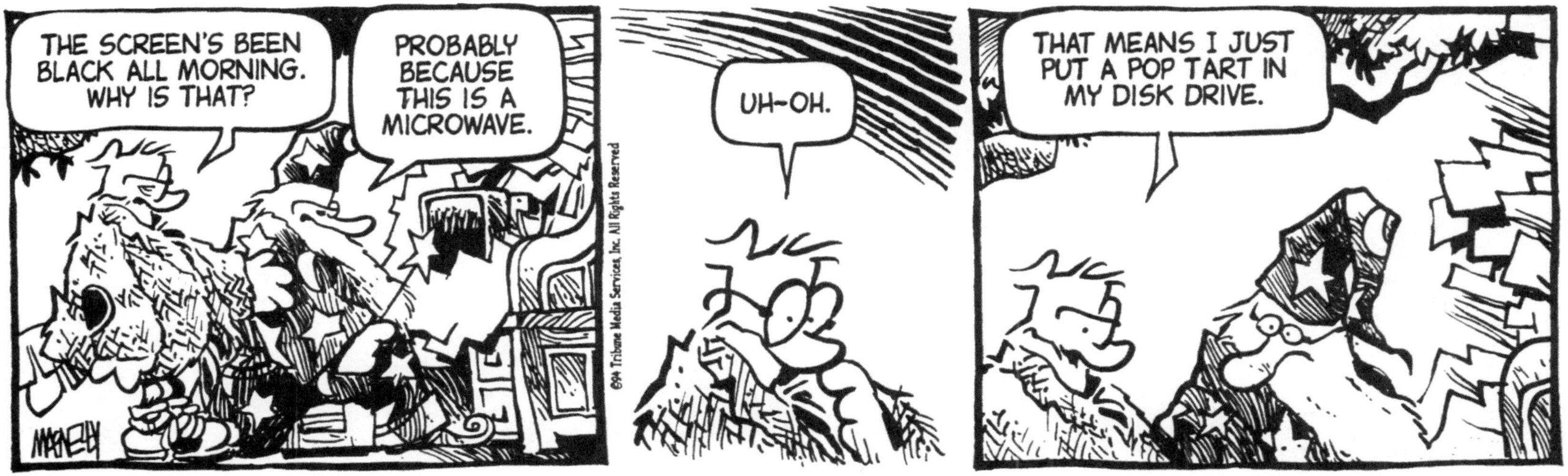
THE SCREEN'S BEEN BLACK ALL MORNING. WHY IS THAT?
PROBABLY BECAUSE THIS IS A MICROWAVE.
©94 Tribune Media Services, Inc. All Rights Reserved
UH-OH.
THAT MEANS I JUST PUT A POP TART IN MY DISK DRIVE.

Chapter Four

Vacations, Sick Leave, and Other Fringe Benefits

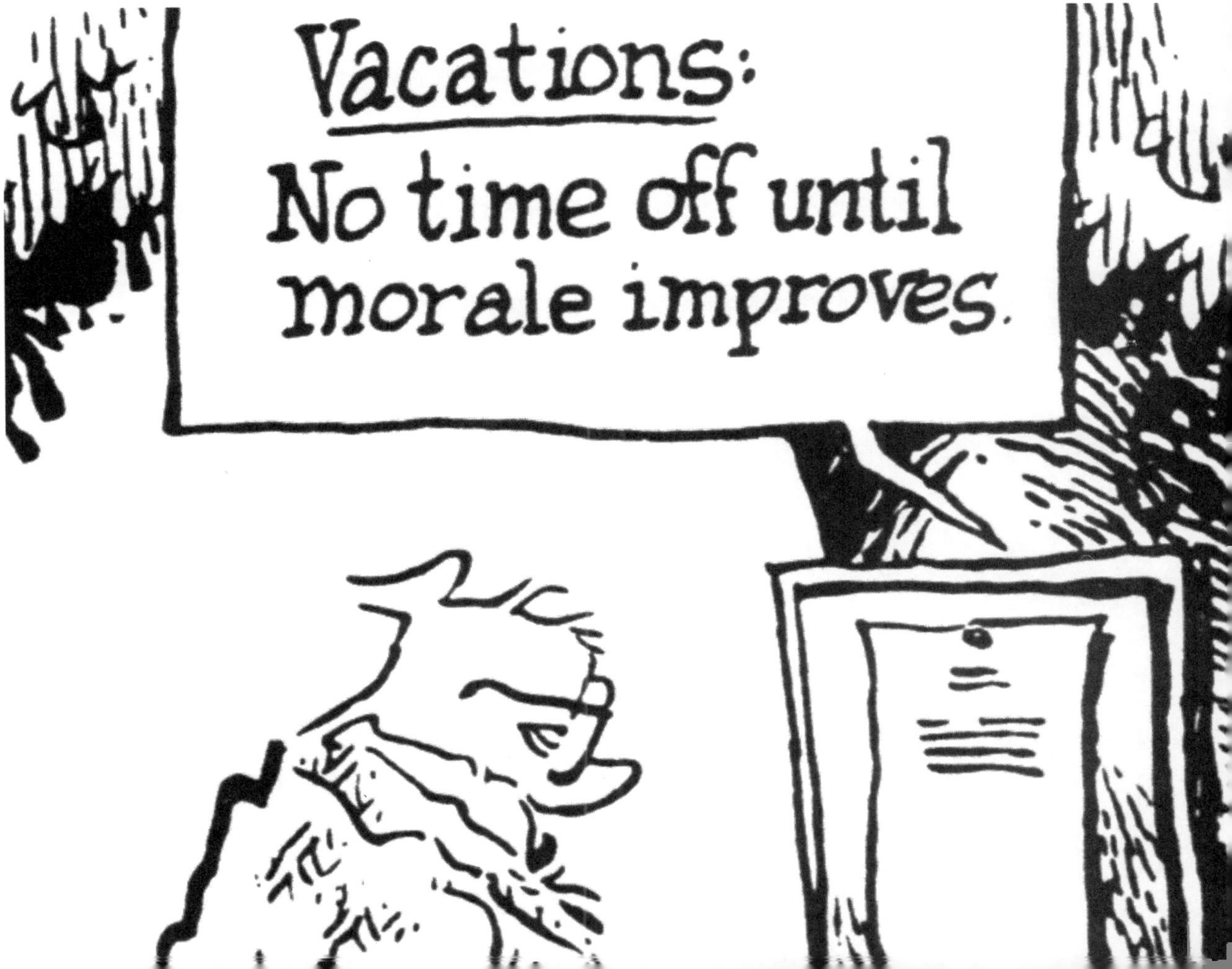
Vacations:
No time off until morale improves.

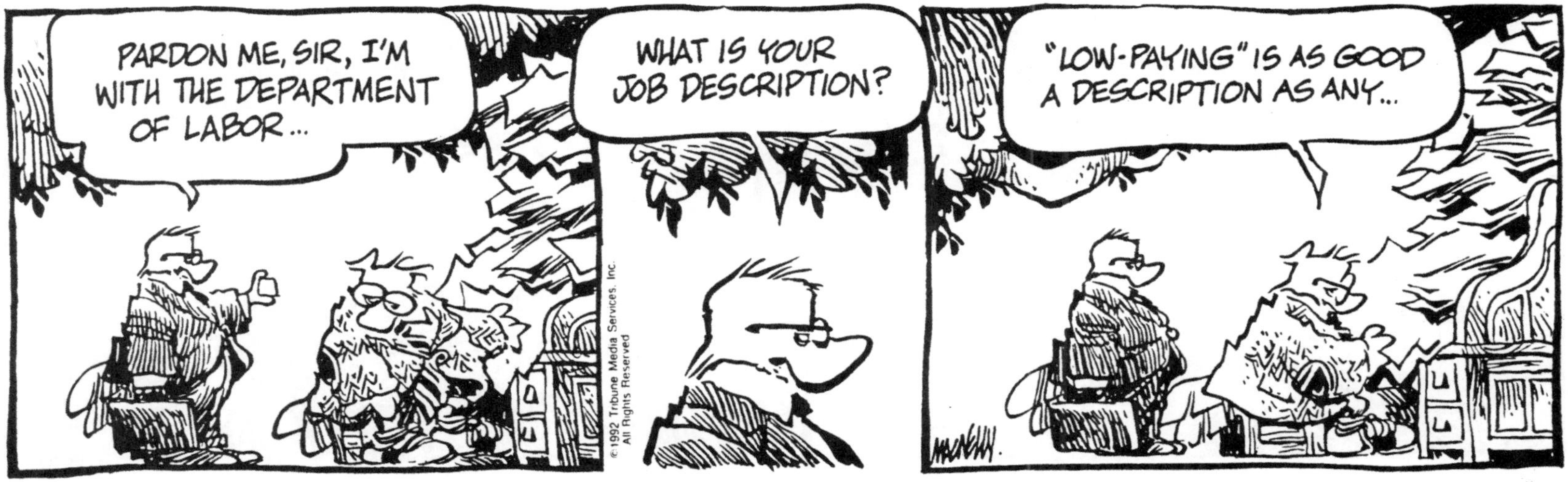
PARDON ME, SIR, I'M WITH THE DEPARTMENT OF LABOR...
WHAT IS YOUR JOB DESCRIPTION?
"LOW-PAYING" IS AS GOOD A DESCRIPTION AS ANY...
© 1992 Tribune Media Services, Inc. All Rights Reserved

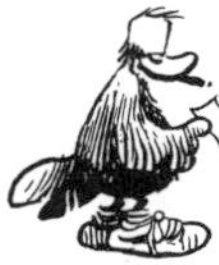

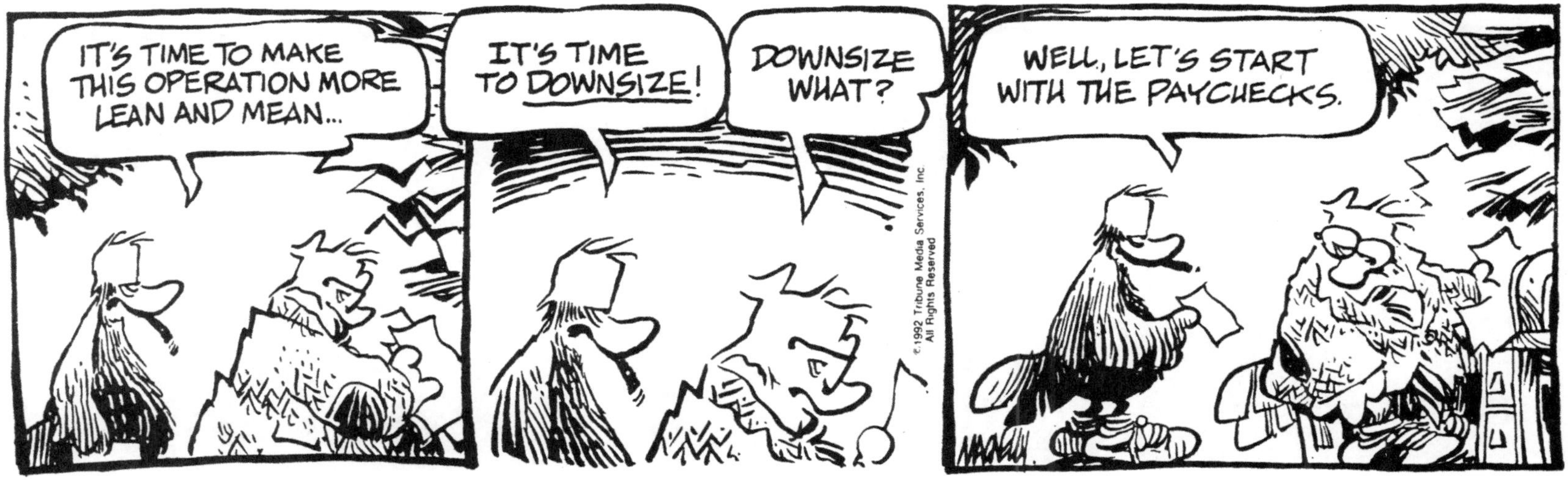
IT'S TIME TO MAKE THIS OPERATION MORE LEAN AND MEAN...
IT'S TIME TO DOWNSIZE!
DOWNSIZE WHAT?
WELL, LET'S START WITH THE PAYCHECKS.
© 1992 Tribune Media Services, Inc. All Rights Reserved

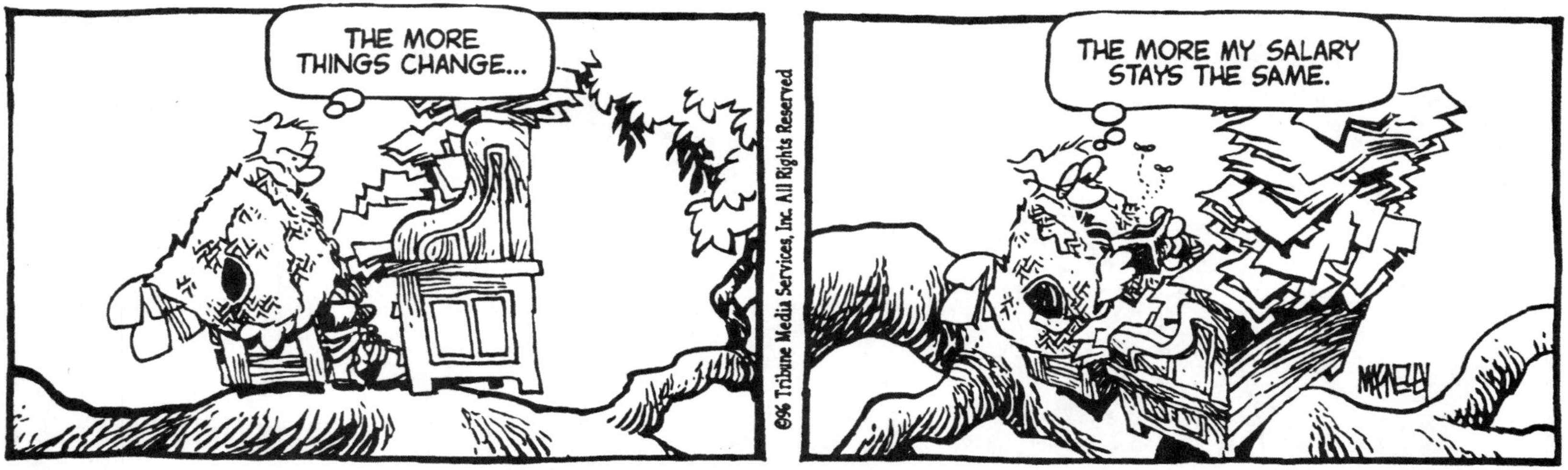
THE MORE THINGS CHANGE...
THE MORE MY SALARY STAYS THE SAME.
©96 Tribune Media Services, Inc. All Rights Reserved

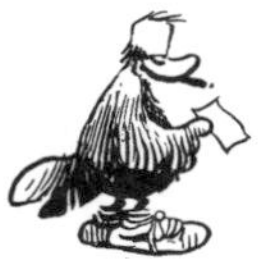

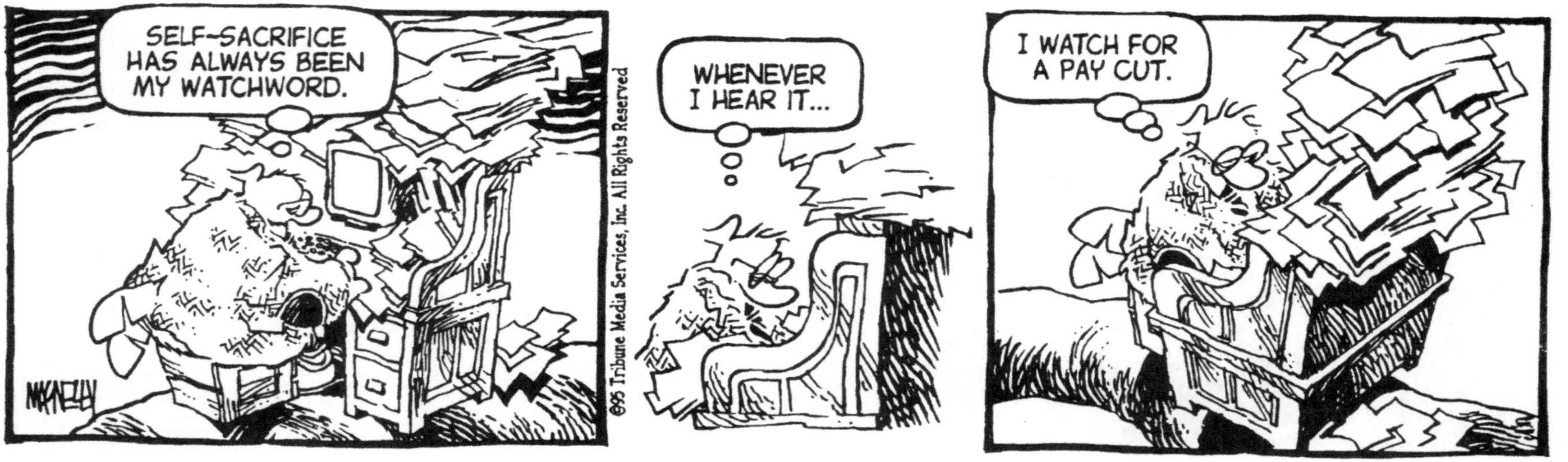
SELF-SACRIFICE HAS ALWAYS BEEN MY WATCHWORD.
WHENEVER I HEAR IT...
I WATCH FOR A PAY CUT.
©95 Tribune Media Services, Inc. All Rights Reserved

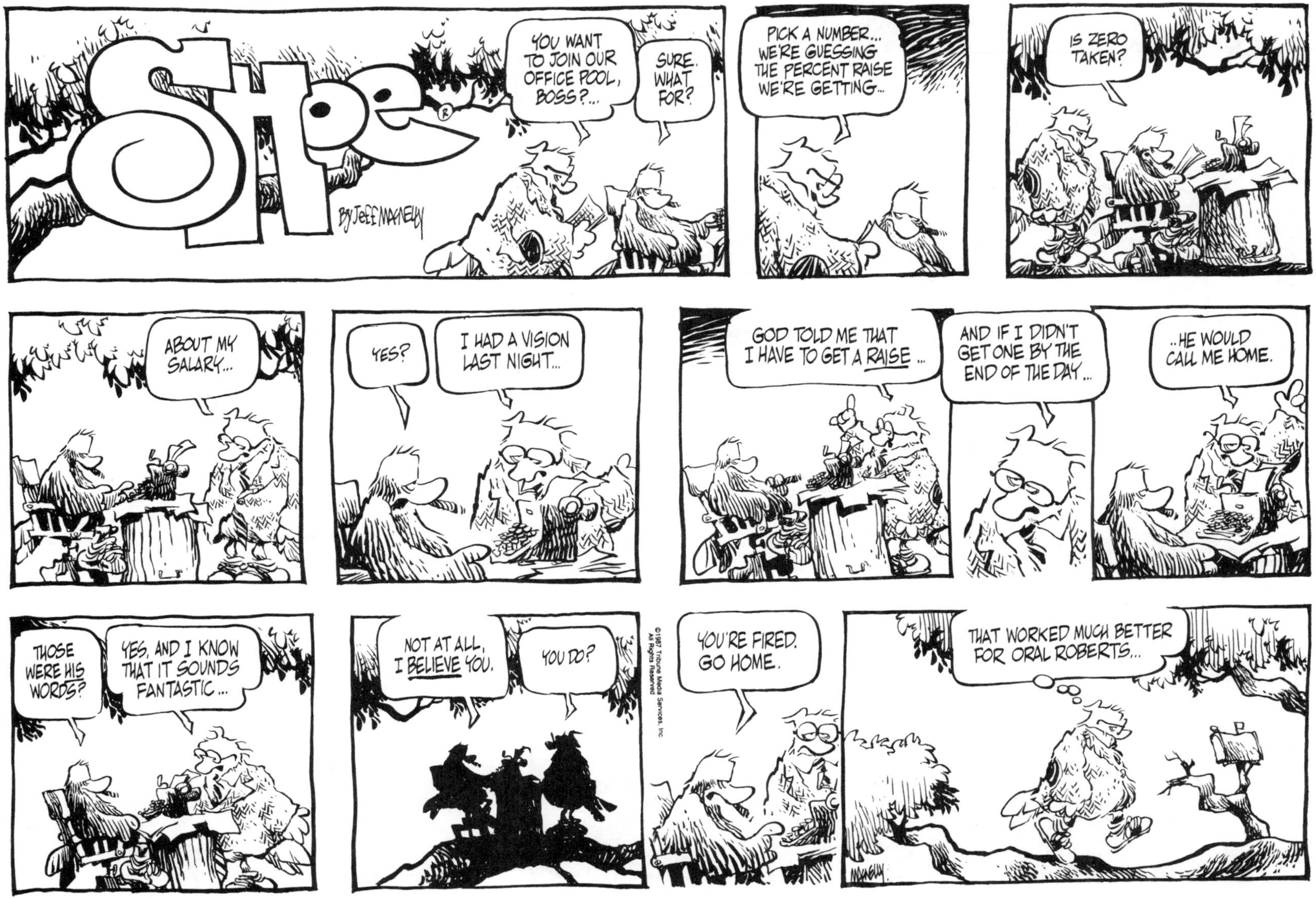
SHOE®
By Jeff MacNelly
YOU WANT TO JOIN OUR OFFICE POOL, BOSS?...
SURE. WHAT FOR?
PICK A NUMBER... WE'RE GUESSING THE PERCENT RAISE WE'RE GETTING...
IS ZERO TAKEN?
ABOUT MY SALARY...
YES?
I HAD A VISION LAST NIGHT...
GOD TOLD ME THAT I HAVE TO GET A RAISE ...
AND IF I DIDN'T GET ONE BY THE END OF THE DAY...
..HE WOULD CALL ME HOME.
THOSE WERE HIS WORDS?
YES, AND I KNOW THAT IT SOUNDS FANTASTIC ...
NOT AT ALL, I BELIEVE YOU.
YOU DO?
© 1987 Tribune Media Services, Inc. All Rights Reserved
YOU'RE FIRED. GO HOME.
THAT WORKED MUCH BETTER FOR ORAL ROBERTS...
MACNELLY

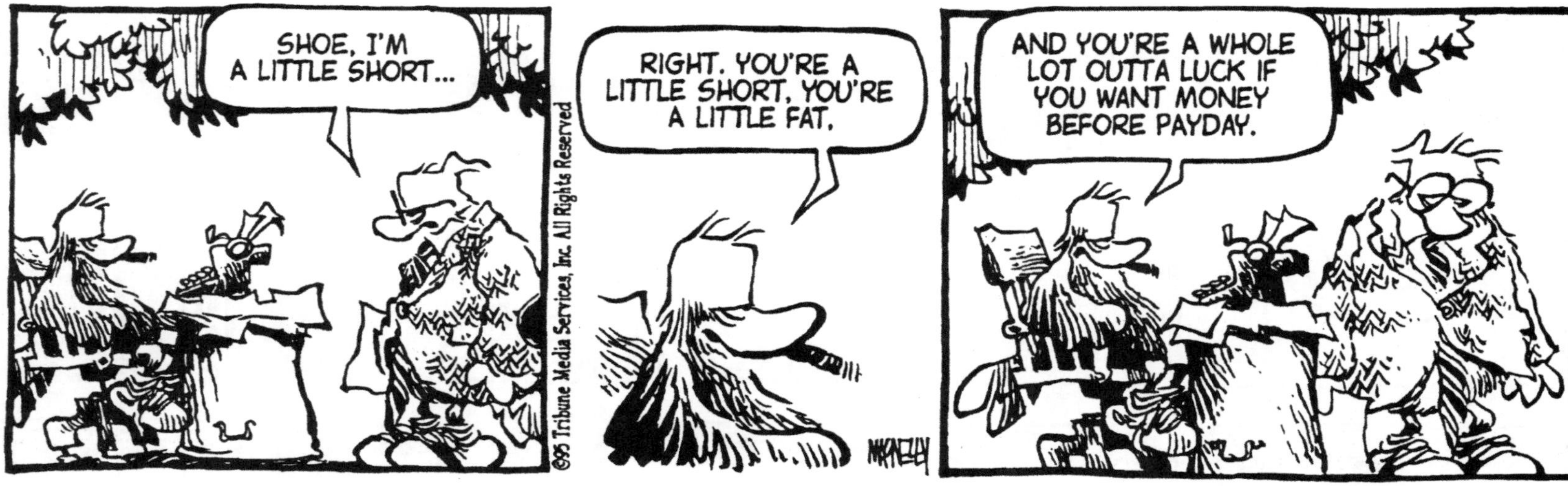
SHOE, I'M A LITTLE SHORT...
©95 Tribune Media Services, Inc. All Rights Reserved
RIGHT. YOU'RE A LITTLE SHORT, YOU'RE A LITTLE FAT.
AND YOU'RE A WHOLE LOT OUTTA LUCK IF YOU WANT MONEY BEFORE PAYDAY.

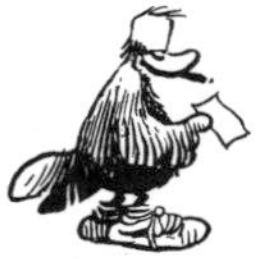

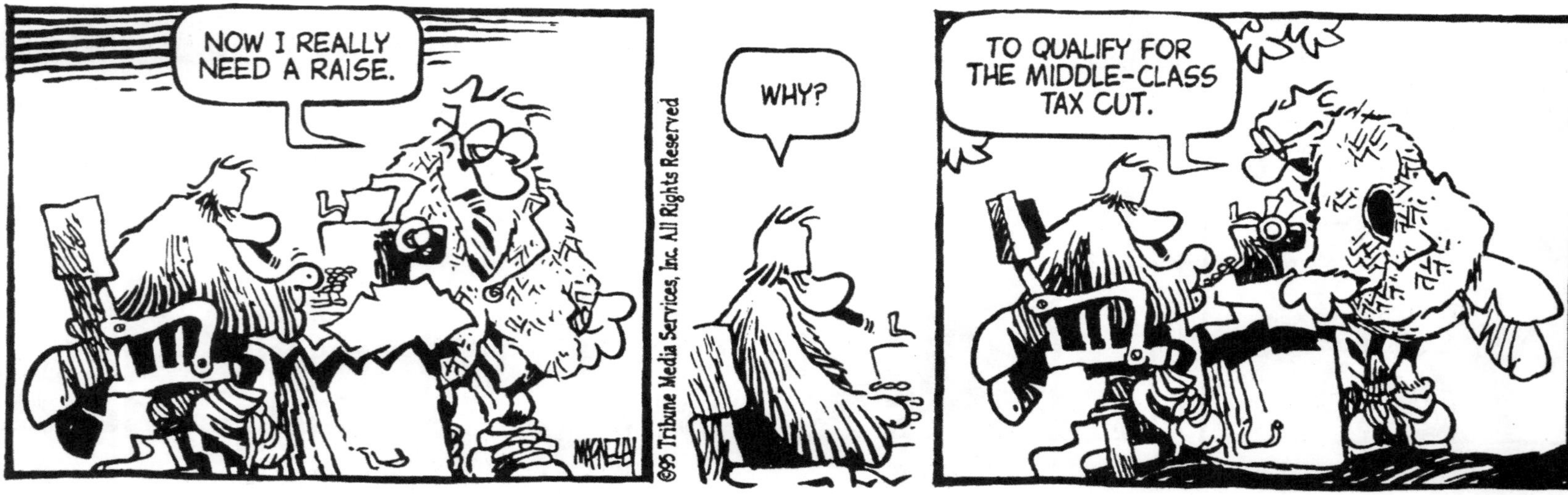
NOW I REALLY NEED A RAISE.
©95 Tribune Media Services, Inc. All Rights Reserved
WHY?
TO QUALIFY FOR THE MIDDLE-CLASS TAX CUT.

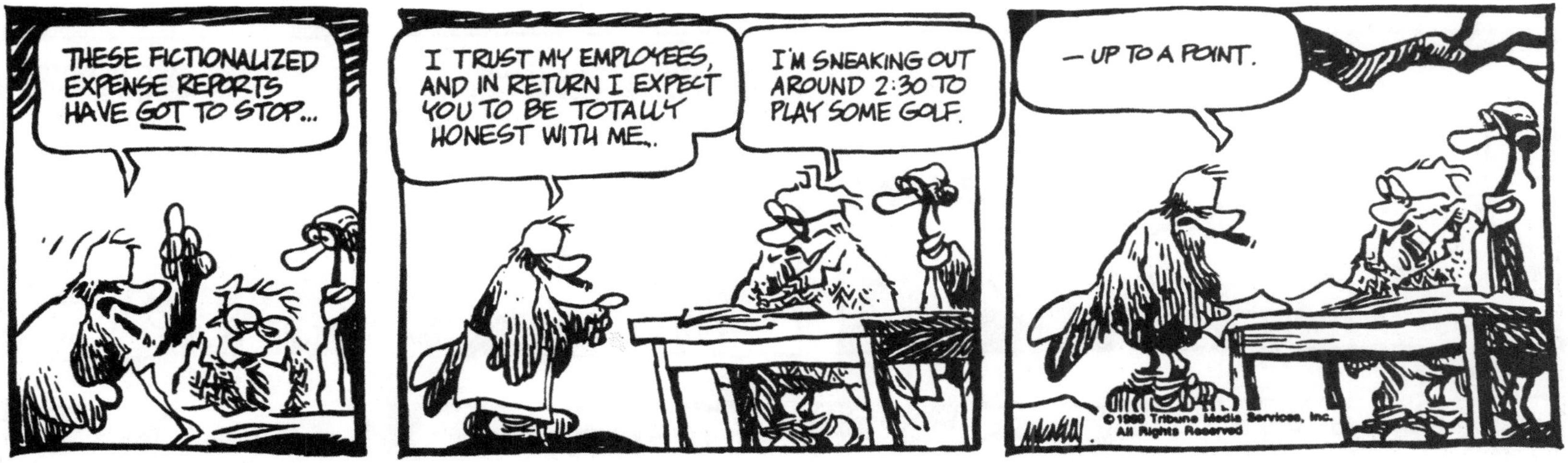
THESE FICTIONALIZED EXPENSE REPORTS HAVE GOT TO STOP...
I TRUST MY EMPLOYEES, AND IN RETURN I EXPECT YOU TO BE TOTALLY HONEST WITH ME..
I'M SNEAKING OUT AROUND 2:30 TO PLAY SOME GOLF.
— UP TO A POINT.
© 1988 Tribune Media Services, Inc. All Rights Reserved

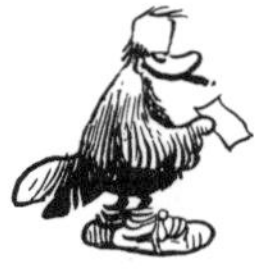

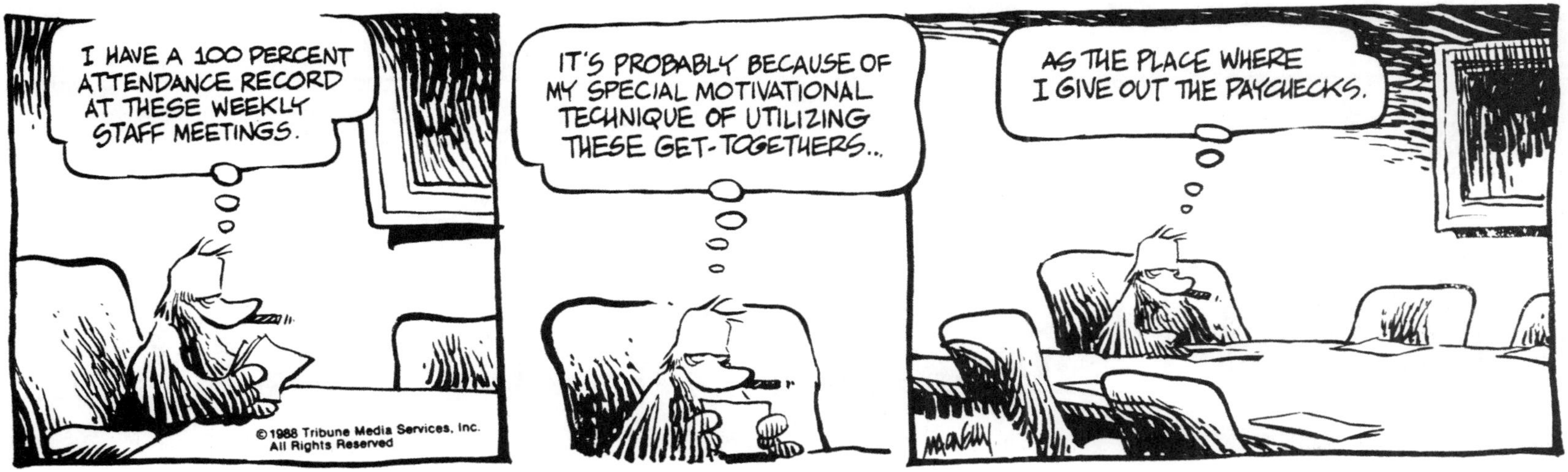
I HAVE A 100 PERCENT ATTENDANCE RECORD AT THESE WEEKLY STAFF MEETINGS.
© 1988 Tribune Media Services, Inc. All Rights Reserved
IT'S PROBABLY BECAUSE OF MY SPECIAL MOTIVATIONAL TECHNIQUE OF UTILIZING THESE GET-TOGETHERS...
AS THE PLACE WHERE I GIVE OUT THE PAYCHECKS.

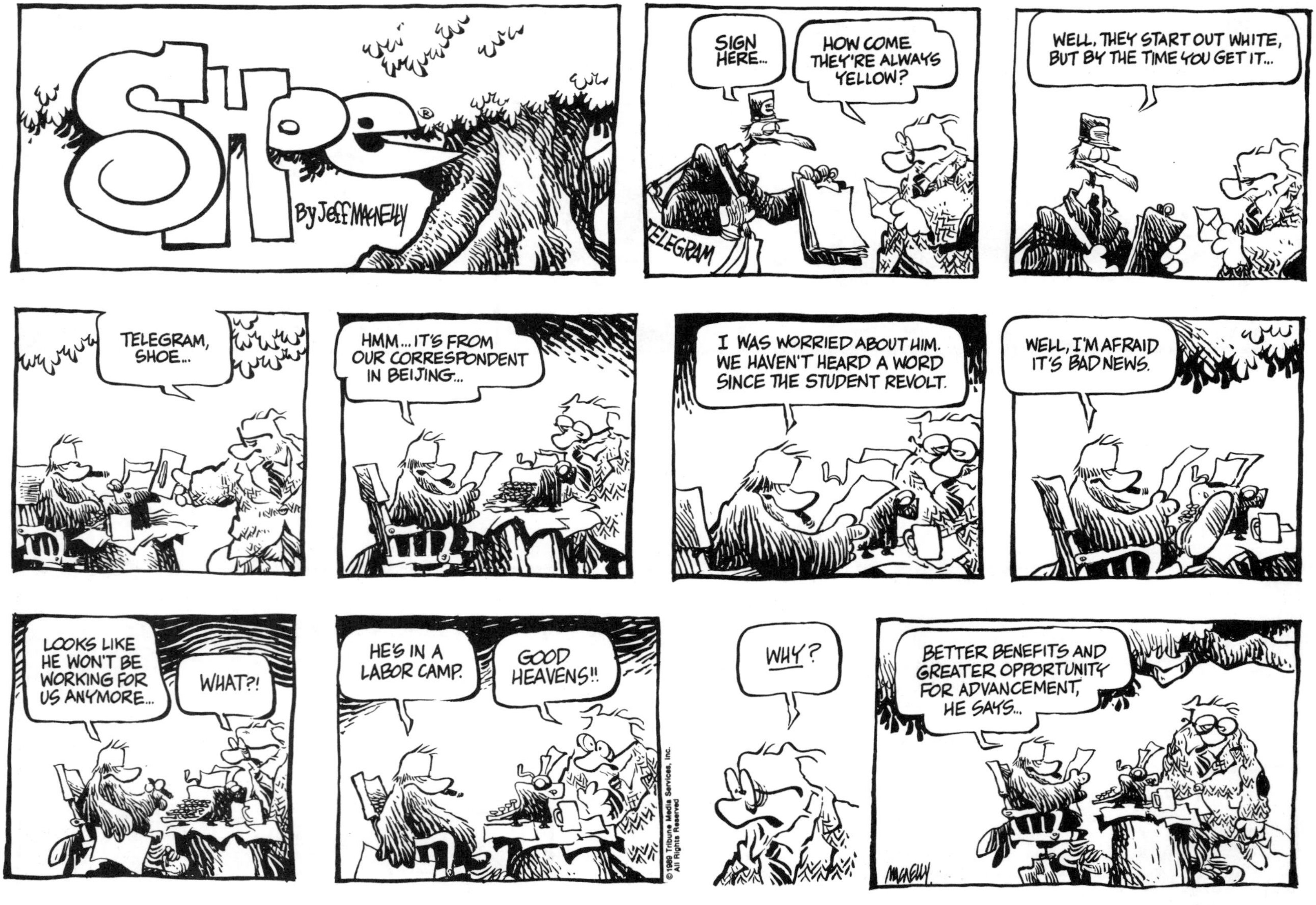
SHOE®
By Jeff MacNelly
SIGN HERE...
HOW COME THEY'RE ALWAYS YELLOW?
TELEGRAM
WELL, THEY START OUT WHITE, BUT BY THE TIME YOU GET IT...
TELEGRAM, SHOE...
HMM... IT'S FROM OUR CORRESPONDENT IN BEIJING...
I WAS WORRIED ABOUT HIM. WE HAVEN'T HEARD A WORD SINCE THE STUDENT REVOLT.
WELL, I'M AFRAID IT'S BAD NEWS.
LOOKS LIKE HE WON'T BE WORKING FOR US ANYMORE...
WHAT?!
HE'S IN A LABOR CAMP.
GOOD HEAVENS!!
© 1989 Tribune Media Services, Inc. All Rights Reserved
WHY?
BETTER BENEFITS AND GREATER OPPORTUNITY FOR ADVANCEMENT, HE SAYS...
MACNELLY

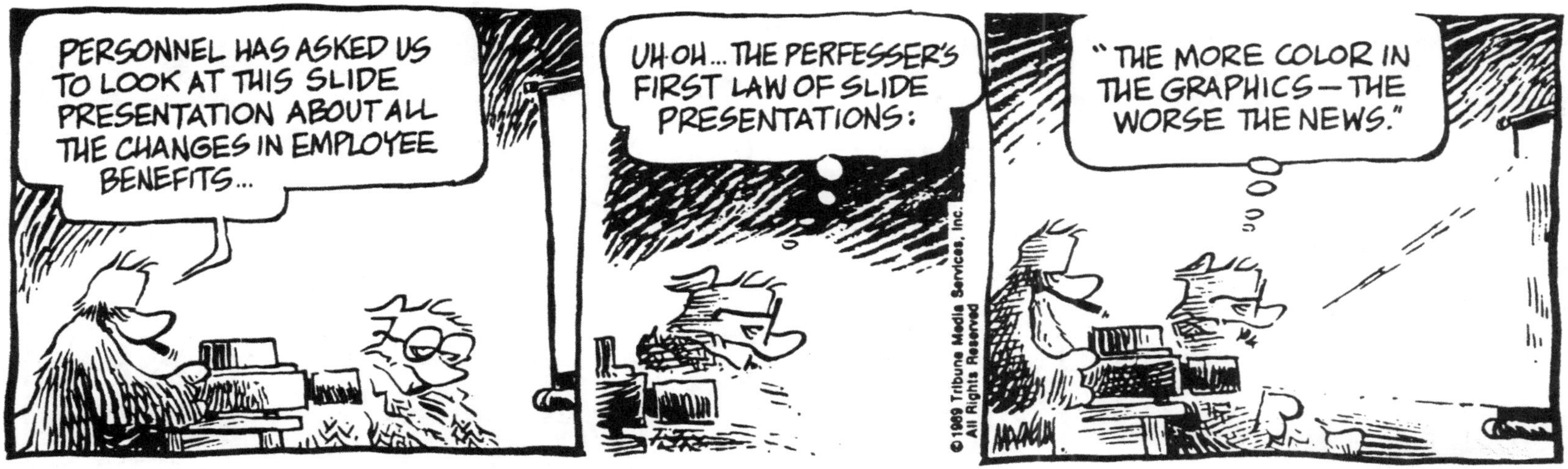
PERSONNEL HAS ASKED US TO LOOK AT THIS SLIDE PRESENTATION ABOUT ALL THE CHANGES IN EMPLOYEE BENEFITS...
UH-OH... THE PERFESSER'S FIRST LAW OF SLIDE PRESENTATIONS:
"THE MORE COLOR IN THE GRAPHICS—THE WORSE THE NEWS."
© 1989 Tribune Media Services, Inc. All Rights Reserved

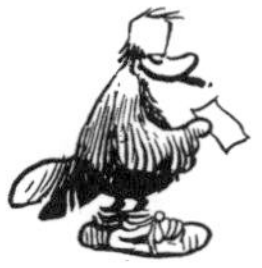

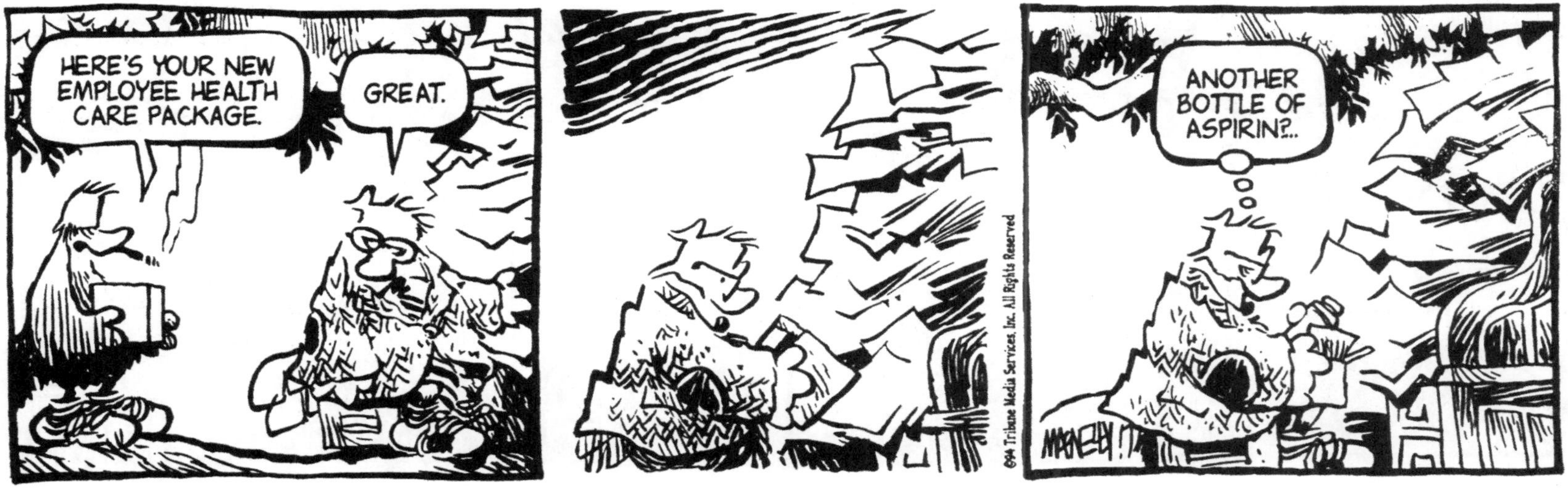
HERE'S YOUR NEW EMPLOYEE HEALTH CARE PACKAGE.
GREAT.
©94 Tribune Media Services, Inc. All Rights Reserved
ANOTHER BOTTLE OF ASPIRIN?..

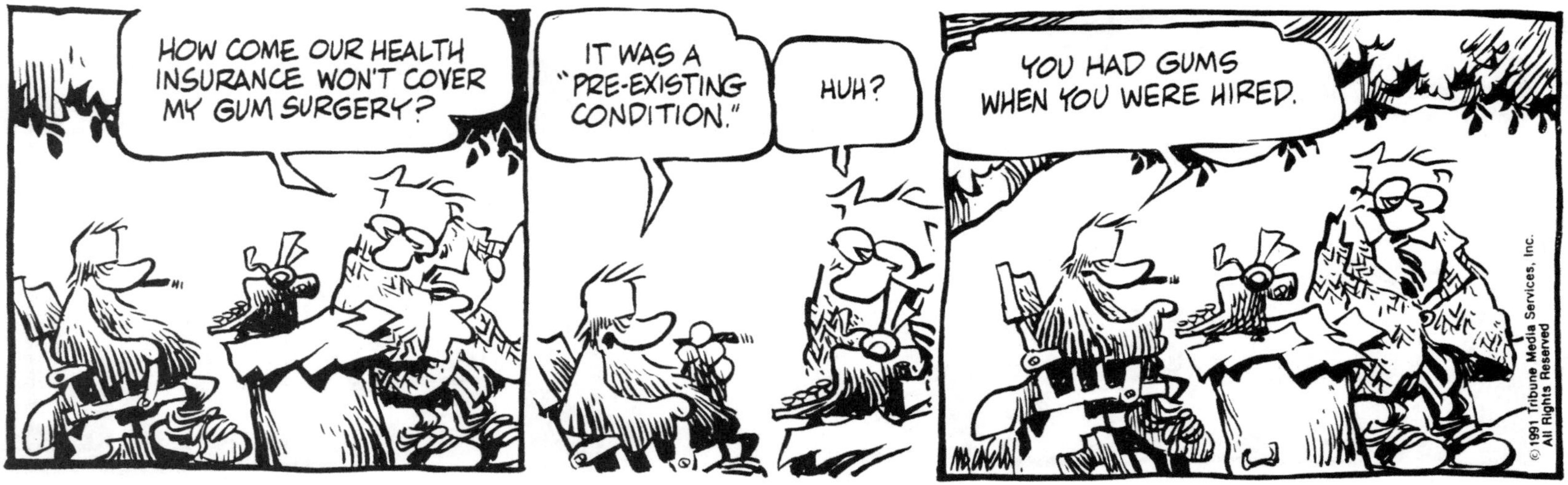
HOW COME OUR HEALTH INSURANCE WON'T COVER MY GUM SURGERY?
IT WAS A "PRE-EXISTING CONDITION."
HUH?
YOU HAD GUMS WHEN YOU WERE HIRED.
© 1991 Tribune Media Services, Inc. All Rights Reserved

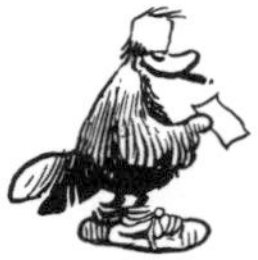

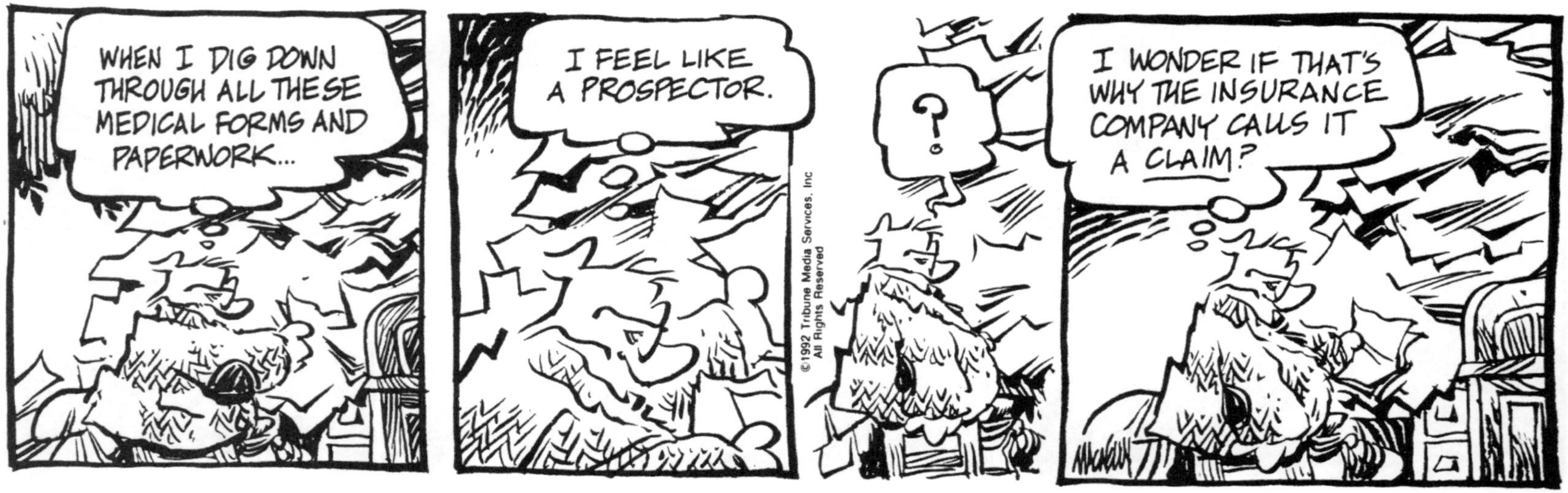
WHEN I DIG DOWN THROUGH ALL THESE MEDICAL FORMS AND PAPERWORK...
I FEEL LIKE A PROSPECTOR.
© 1992 Tribune Media Services, Inc All Rights Reserved
?
I WONDER IF THAT'S WHY THE INSURANCE COMPANY CALLS IT A CLAIM?

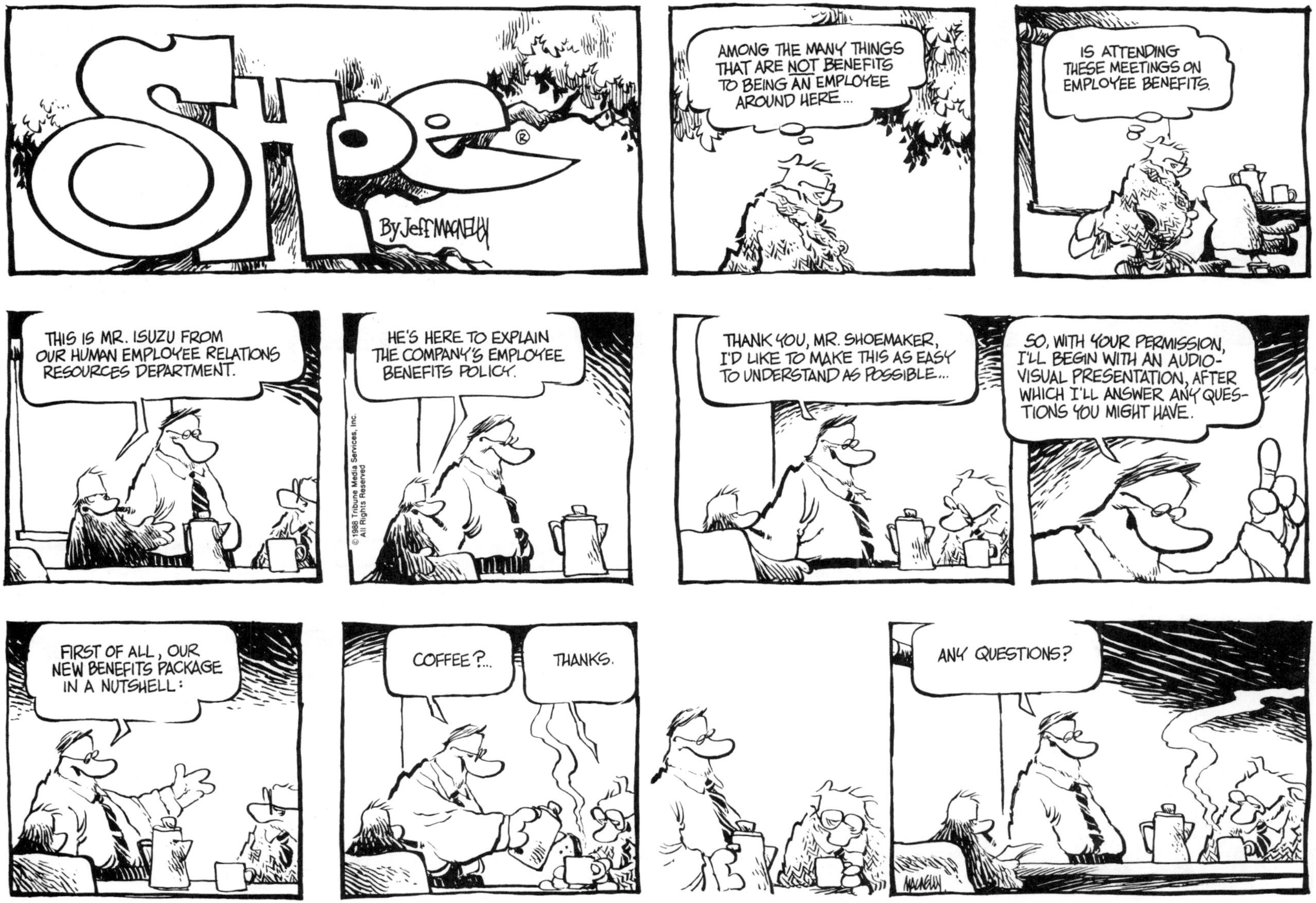
SHOE®
By Jeff MACNELLY
AMONG THE MANY THINGS THAT ARE NOT BENEFITS TO BEING AN EMPLOYEE AROUND HERE...
IS ATTENDING THESE MEETINGS ON EMPLOYEE BENEFITS.
THIS IS MR. ISUZU FROM OUR HUMAN EMPLOYEE RELATIONS RESOURCES DEPARTMENT.
HE'S HERE TO EXPLAIN THE COMPANY'S EMPLOYEE BENEFITS POLICY.
© 1988 Tribune Media Services, Inc. All Rights Reserved
THANK YOU, MR. SHOEMAKER, I'D LIKE TO MAKE THIS AS EASY TO UNDERSTAND AS POSSIBLE...
SO, WITH YOUR PERMISSION, I'LL BEGIN WITH AN AUDIO-VISUAL PRESENTATION, AFTER WHICH I'LL ANSWER ANY QUESTIONS YOU MIGHT HAVE.
FIRST OF ALL, OUR NEW BENEFITS PACKAGE IN A NUTSHELL:
COFFEE?...
THANKS.
ANY QUESTIONS?
MACNELLY

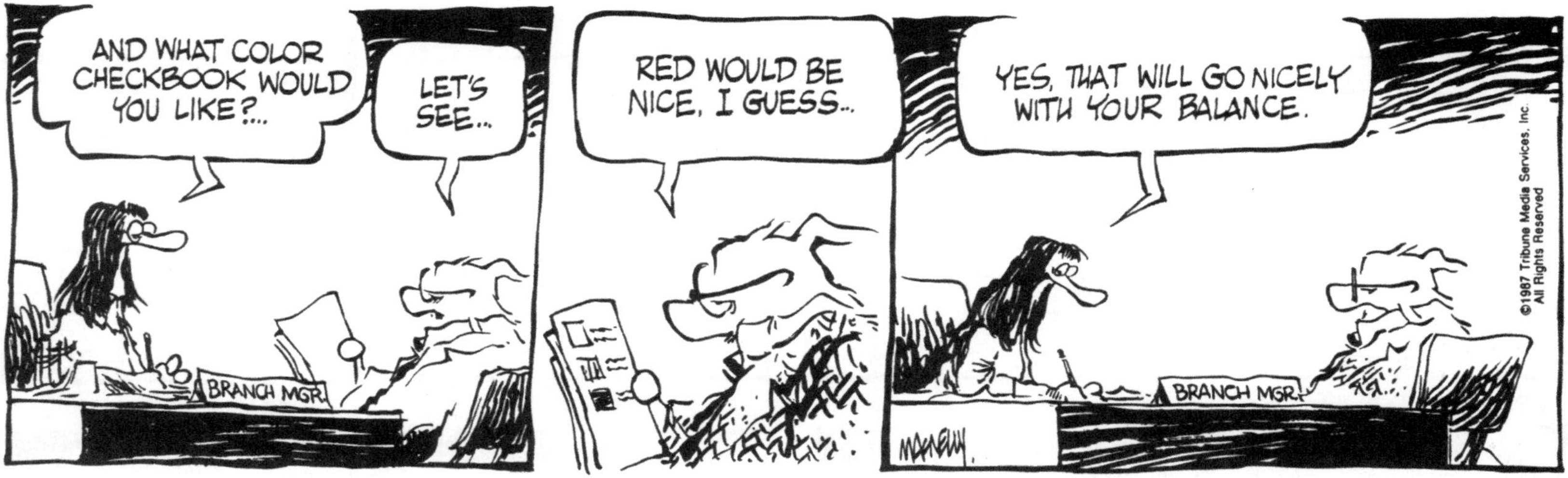
AND WHAT COLOR CHECKBOOK WOULD YOU LIKE?...
LET'S SEE...
BRANCH MGR.
RED WOULD BE NICE, I GUESS...
YES, THAT WILL GO NICELY WITH YOUR BALANCE.
BRANCH MGR.
©1987 Tribune Media Services, Inc. All Rights Reserved

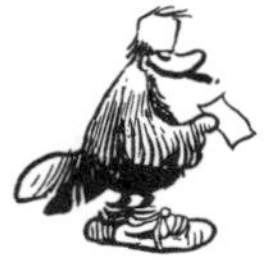

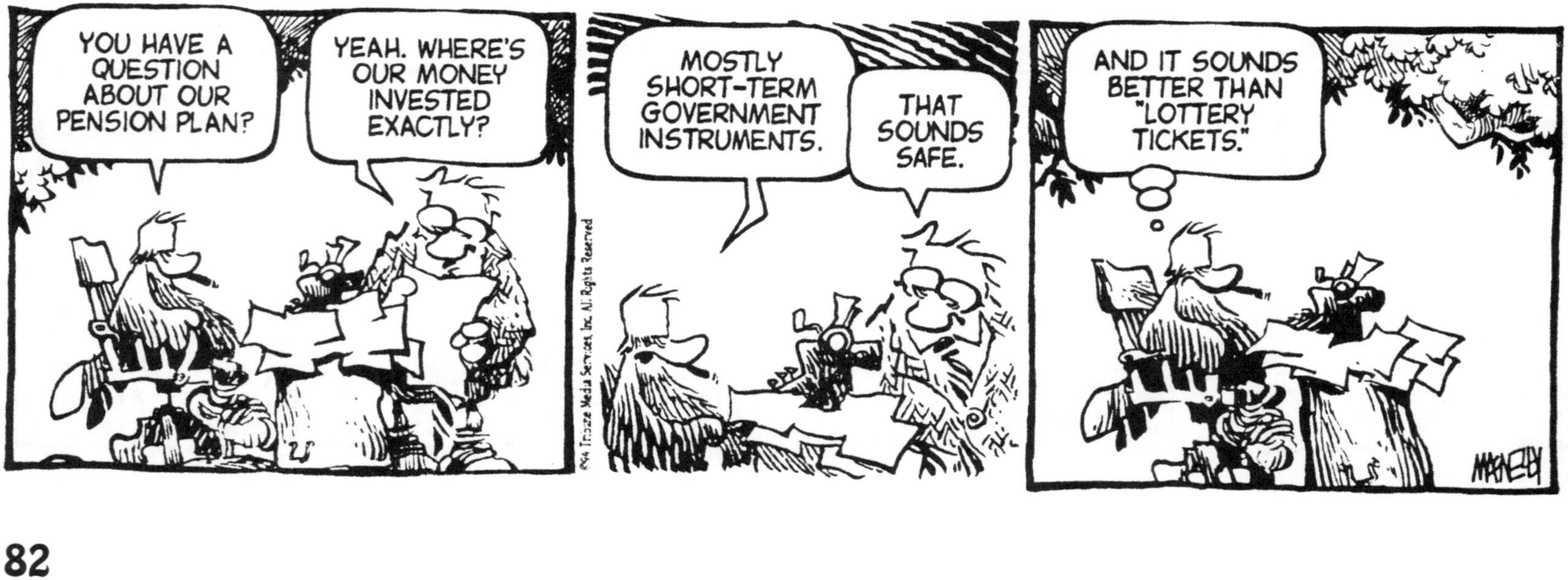
YOU HAVE A QUESTION ABOUT OUR PENSION PLAN?
YEAH. WHERE'S OUR MONEY INVESTED EXACTLY?
MOSTLY SHORT-TERM GOVERNMENT INSTRUMENTS.
THAT SOUNDS SAFE.
AND IT SOUNDS BETTER THAN "LOTTERY TICKETS."

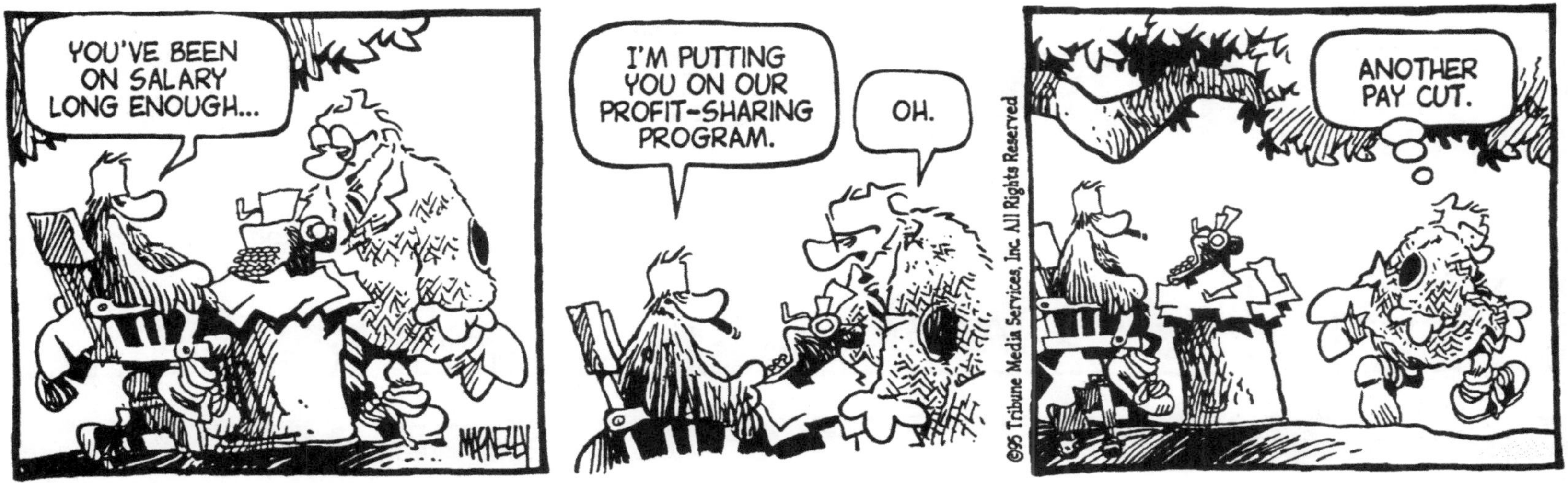
YOU'VE BEEN ON SALARY LONG ENOUGH...
I'M PUTTING YOU ON OUR PROFIT-SHARING PROGRAM.
OH.
©95 Tribune Media Services, Inc. All Rights Reserved
ANOTHER PAY CUT.

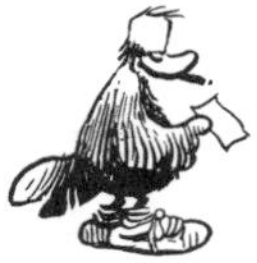

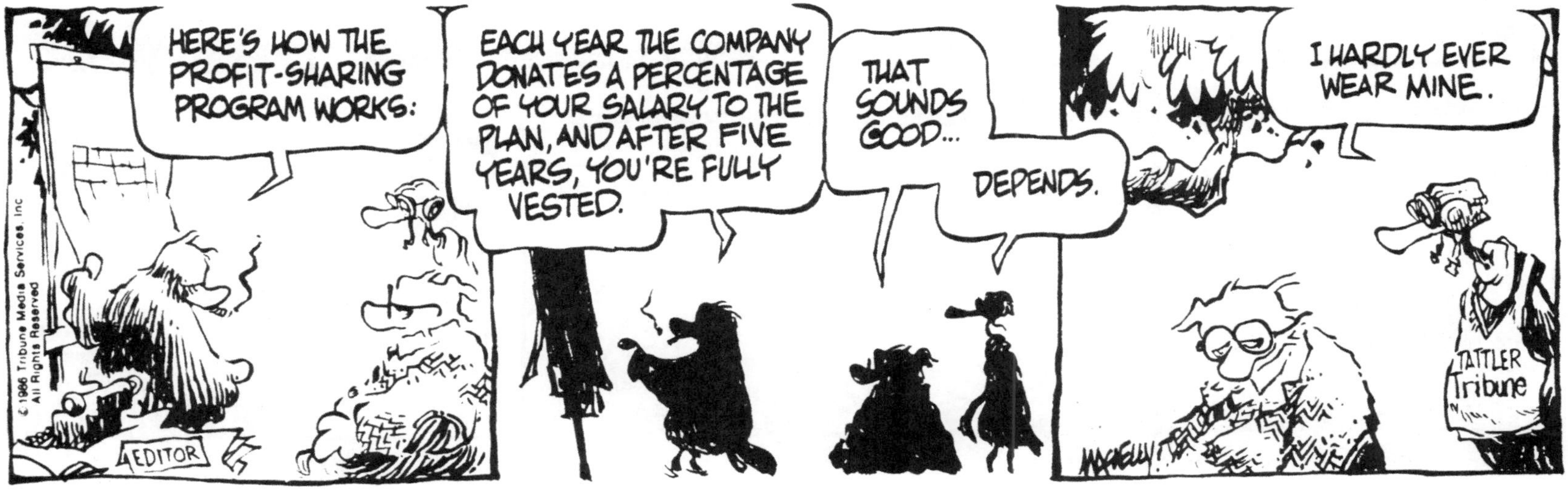
HERE'S HOW THE PROFIT-SHARING PROGRAM WORKS:
© 1986 Tribune Media Services, Inc All Rights Reserved
EDITOR
EACH YEAR THE COMPANY DONATES A PERCENTAGE OF YOUR SALARY TO THE PLAN, AND AFTER FIVE YEARS, YOU'RE FULLY VESTED.
THAT SOUNDS GOOD...
DEPENDS.
I HARDLY EVER WEAR MINE.
TATTLER Tribune

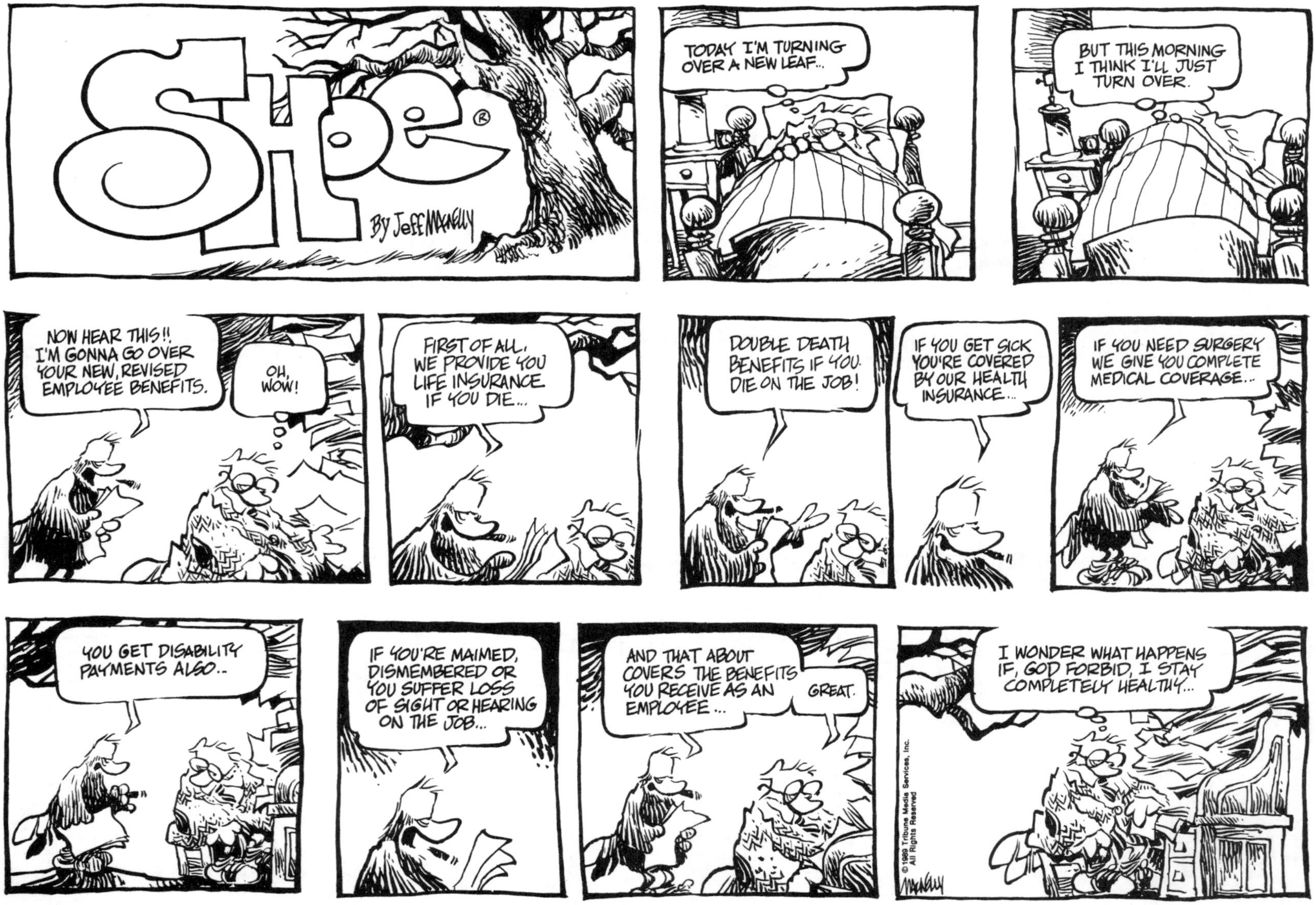
Shoe®
By Jeff MacNelly
TODAY I'M TURNING OVER A NEW LEAF...
BUT THIS MORNING I THINK I'LL JUST TURN OVER.
NOW HEAR THIS!! I'M GONNA GO OVER YOUR NEW, REVISED EMPLOYEE BENEFITS.
OH, WOW!
FIRST OF ALL, WE PROVIDE YOU LIFE INSURANCE IF YOU DIE...
DOUBLE DEATH BENEFITS IF YOU DIE ON THE JOB!
IF YOU GET SICK YOU'RE COVERED BY OUR HEALTH INSURANCE...
IF YOU NEED SURGERY WE GIVE YOU COMPLETE MEDICAL COVERAGE...
YOU GET DISABILITY PAYMENTS ALSO..
IF YOU'RE MAIMED, DISMEMBERED OR YOU SUFFER LOSS OF SIGHT OR HEARING ON THE JOB...
AND THAT ABOUT COVERS THE BENEFITS YOU RECEIVE AS AN EMPLOYEE...
GREAT.
© 1989 Tribune Media Services, Inc. All Rights Reserved
MacNelly
I WONDER WHAT HAPPENS IF, GOD FORBID, I STAY COMPLETELY HEALTHY...

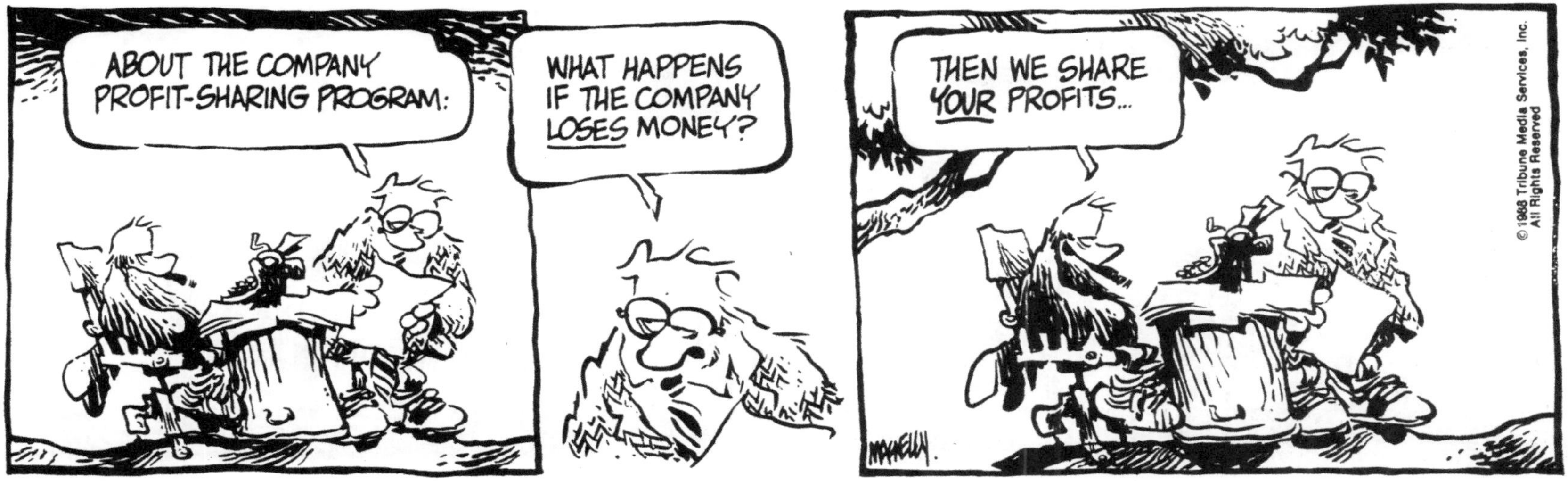
ABOUT THE COMPANY PROFIT-SHARING PROGRAM:
WHAT HAPPENS IF THE COMPANY LOSES MONEY?
THEN WE SHARE YOUR PROFITS...
© 1988 Tribune Media Services, Inc. All Rights Reserved
MACNELLY

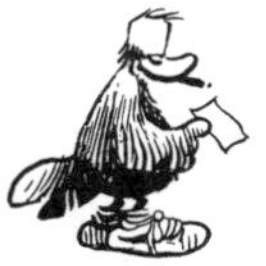

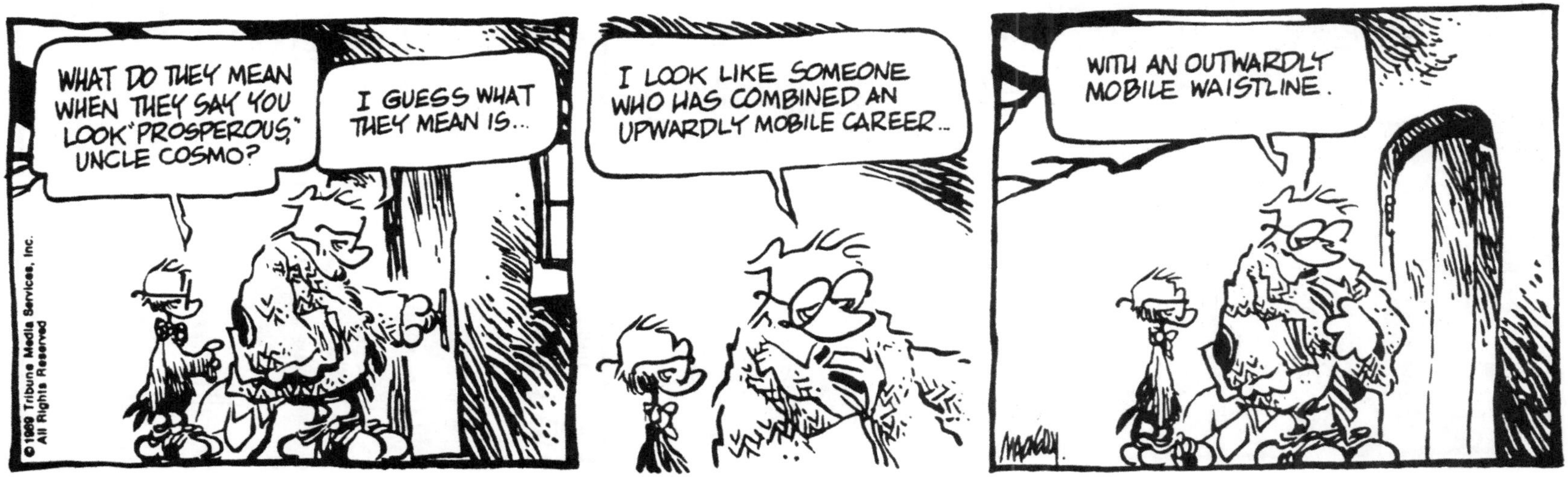
WHAT DO THEY MEAN WHEN THEY SAY YOU LOOK "PROSPEROUS," UNCLE COSMO?
I GUESS WHAT THEY MEAN IS...
I LOOK LIKE SOMEONE WHO HAS COMBINED AN UPWARDLY MOBILE CAREER...
WITH AN OUTWARDLY MOBILE WAISTLINE.
© 1989 Tribune Media Services, Inc. All Rights Reserved
MACNELLY

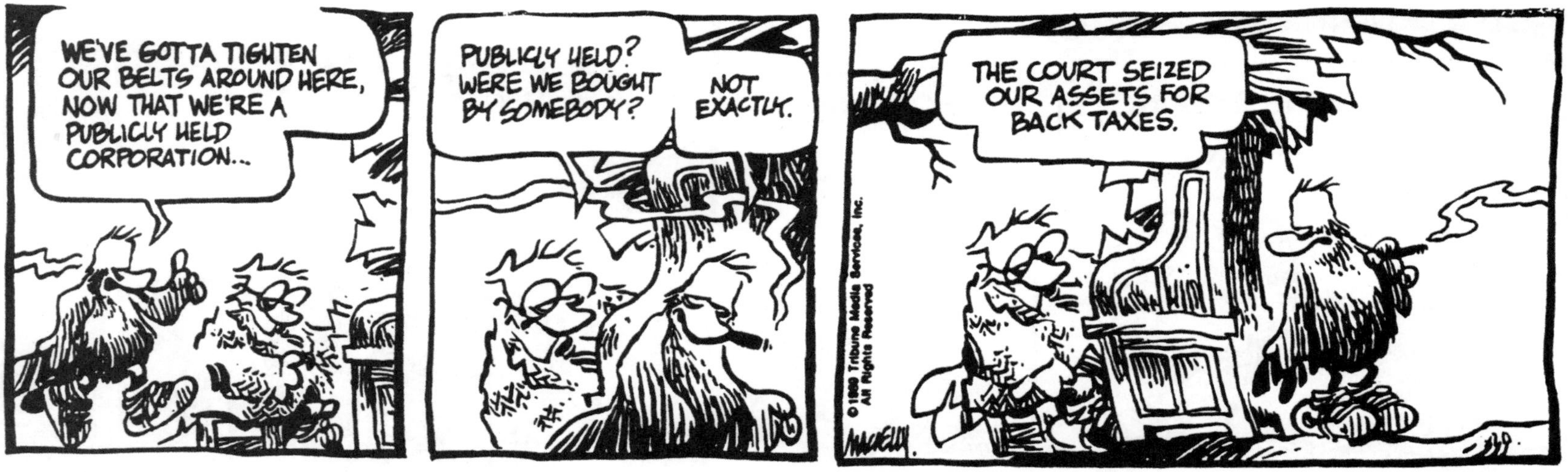
WE'VE GOTTA TIGHTEN OUR BELTS AROUND HERE, NOW THAT WE'RE A PUBLICLY HELD CORPORATION...
PUBLICLY HELD? WERE WE BOUGHT BY SOMEBODY?
NOT EXACTLY.
THE COURT SEIZED OUR ASSETS FOR BACK TAXES.
Tribune Media Services, Inc. All Rights Reserved
MACNELLY

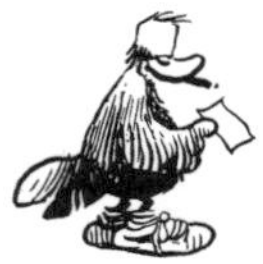

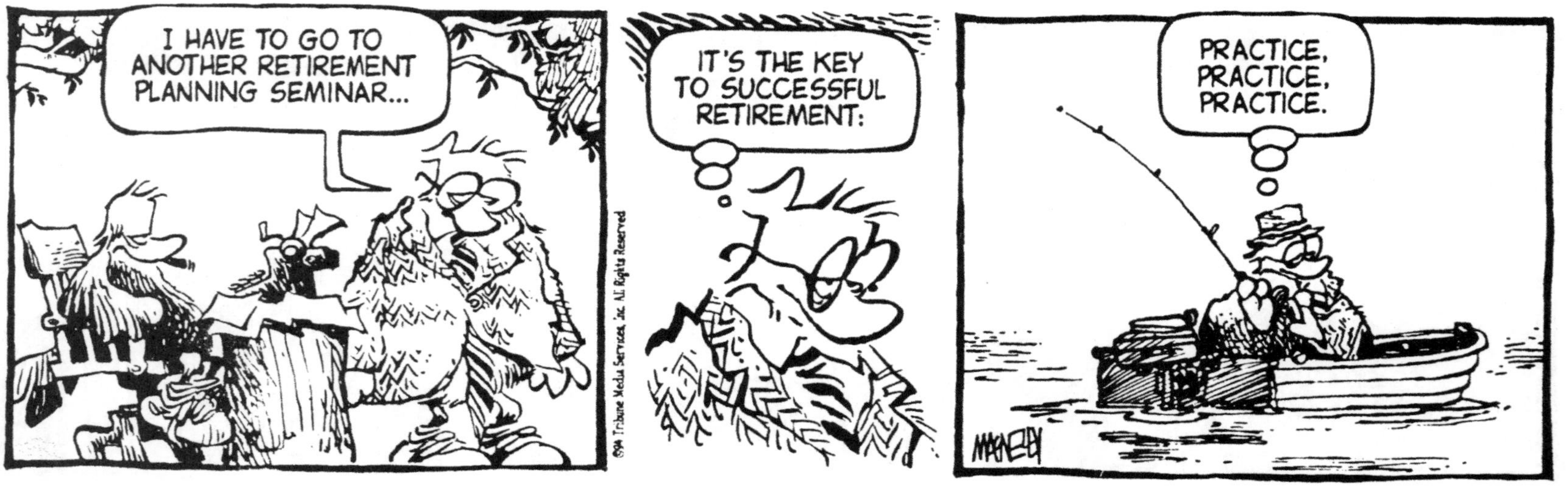
I HAVE TO GO TO ANOTHER RETIREMENT PLANNING SEMINAR...
©1994 Tribune Media Services, Inc. All Rights Reserved
IT'S THE KEY TO SUCCESSFUL RETIREMENT:
PRACTICE, PRACTICE, PRACTICE.
MACNELLY

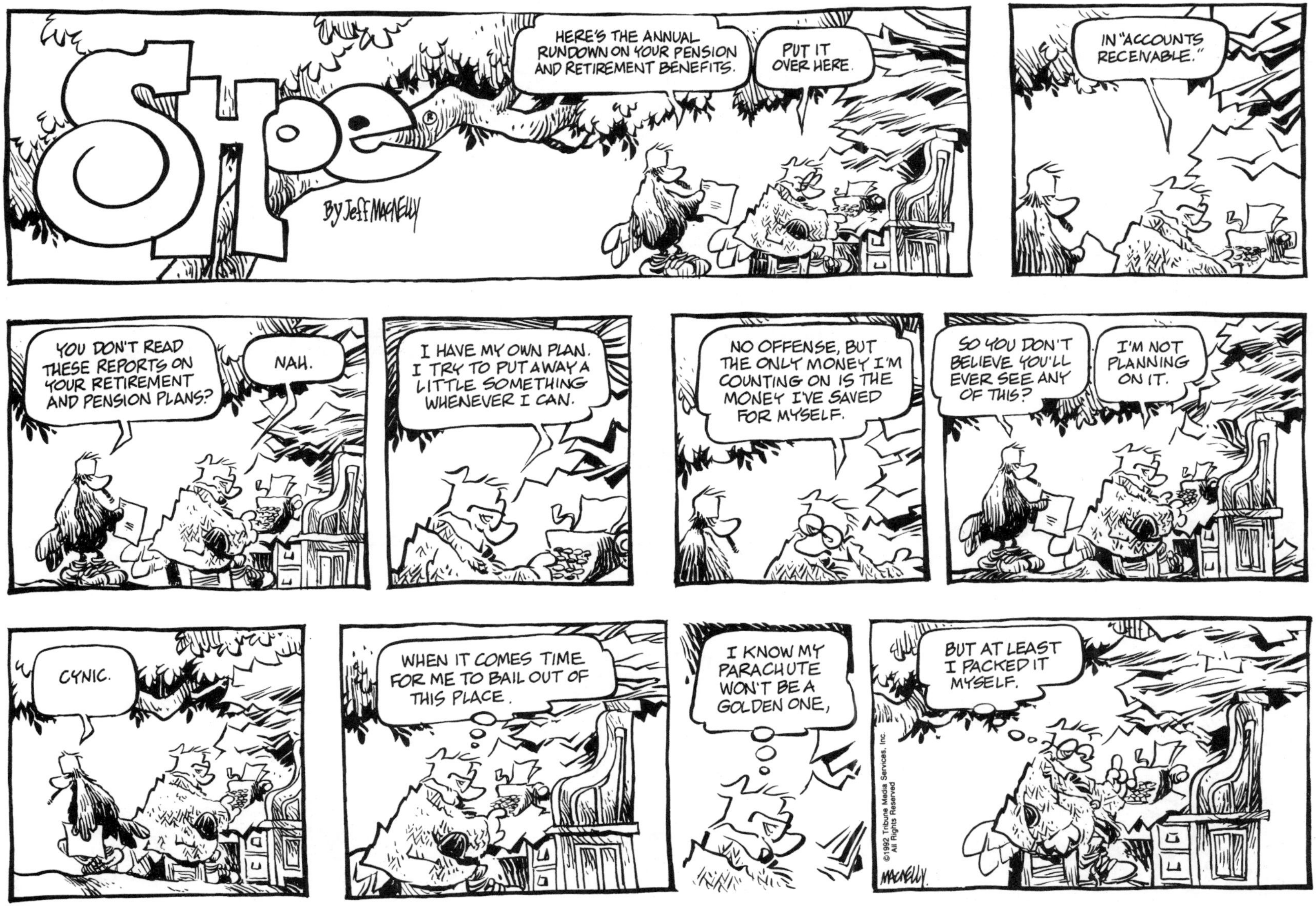
Shoe
By Jeff MacNelly
HERE'S THE ANNUAL RUNDOWN ON YOUR PENSION AND RETIREMENT BENEFITS.
PUT IT OVER HERE.
IN "ACCOUNTS RECEIVABLE."
YOU DON'T READ THESE REPORTS ON YOUR RETIREMENT AND PENSION PLANS?
NAH.
I HAVE MY OWN PLAN. I TRY TO PUT AWAY A LITTLE SOMETHING WHENEVER I CAN.
NO OFFENSE, BUT THE ONLY MONEY I'M COUNTING ON IS THE MONEY I'VE SAVED FOR MYSELF.
SO YOU DON'T BELIEVE YOU'LL EVER SEE ANY OF THIS?
I'M NOT PLANNING ON IT.
CYNIC.
WHEN IT COMES TIME FOR ME TO BAIL OUT OF THIS PLACE,
I KNOW MY PARACHUTE WON'T BE A GOLDEN ONE,
BUT AT LEAST I PACKED IT MYSELF.
©1992 Tribune Media Services, Inc. All Rights Reserved
MACNELLY

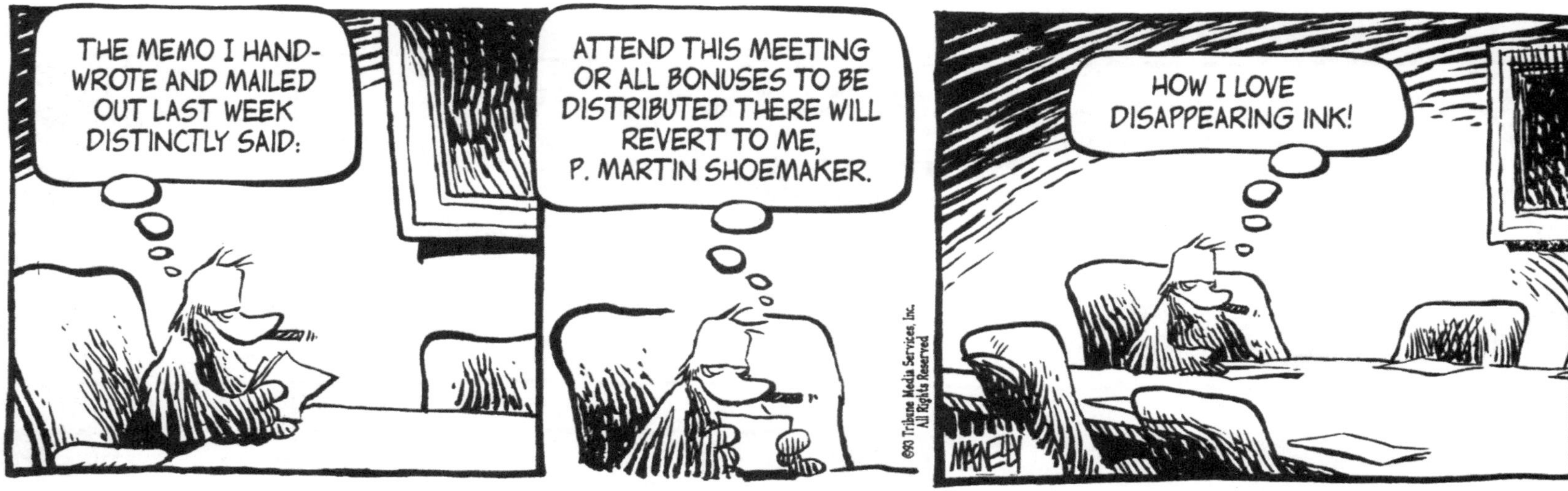
THE MEMO I HAND-WROTE AND MAILED OUT LAST WEEK DISTINCTLY SAID:
ATTEND THIS MEETING OR ALL BONUSES TO BE DISTRIBUTED THERE WILL REVERT TO ME, P. MARTIN SHOEMAKER.
©93 Tribune Media Services, Inc. All Rights Reserved
HOW I LOVE DISAPPEARING INK!
MACNELLY

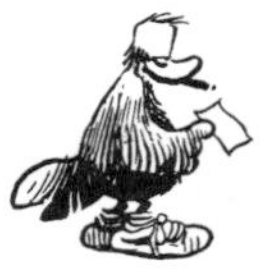

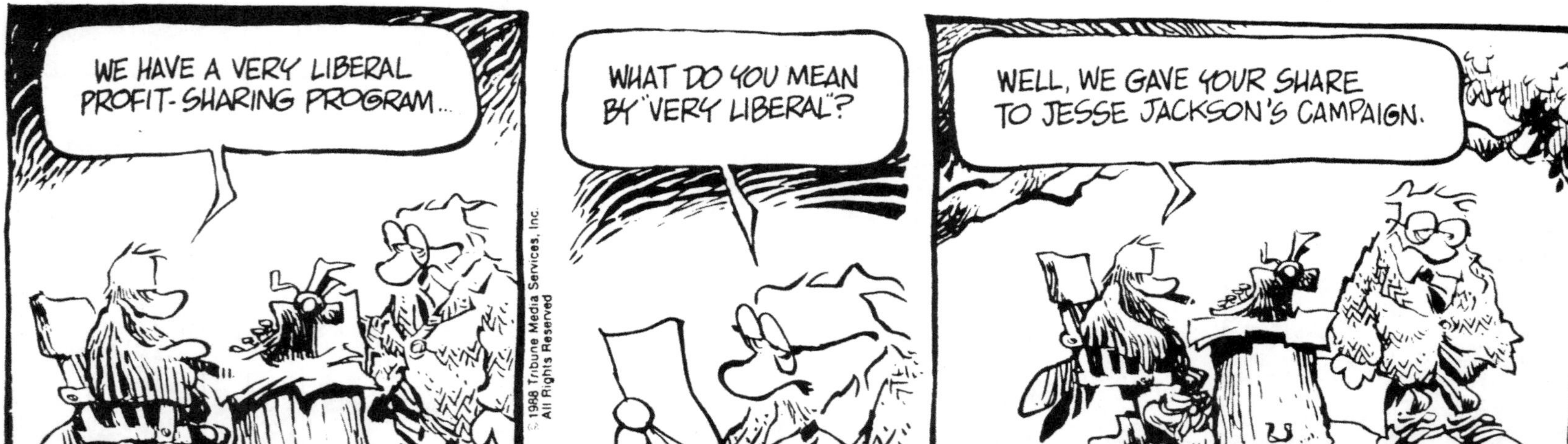
WE HAVE A VERY LIBERAL PROFIT-SHARING PROGRAM...
© 1988 Tribune Media Services, Inc. All Rights Reserved
WHAT DO YOU MEAN BY "VERY LIBERAL"?
WELL, WE GAVE YOUR SHARE TO JESSE JACKSON'S CAMPAIGN.
MACNELLY

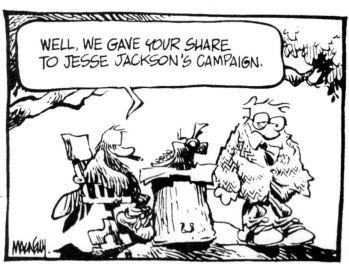

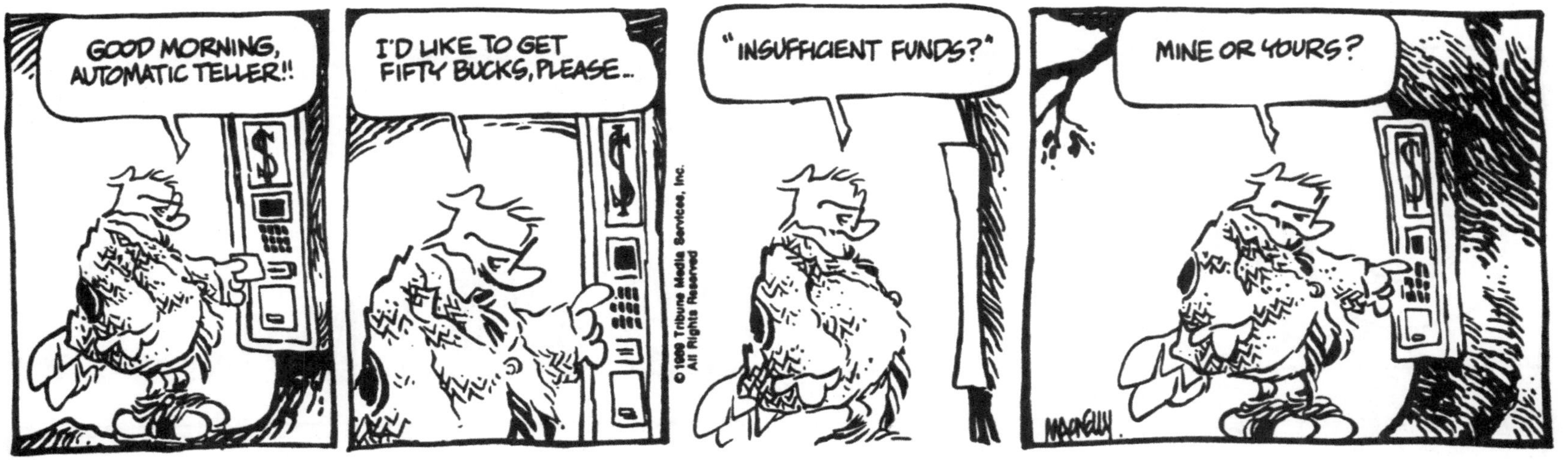
GOOD MORNING, AUTOMATIC TELLER!!
I'D LIKE TO GET FIFTY BUCKS, PLEASE..
"INSUFFICIENT FUNDS?"
MINE OR YOURS?
© 1988 Tribune Media Services, Inc. All Rights Reserved

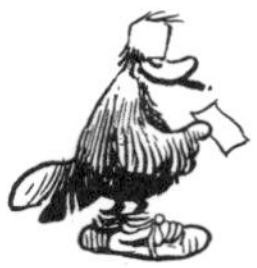

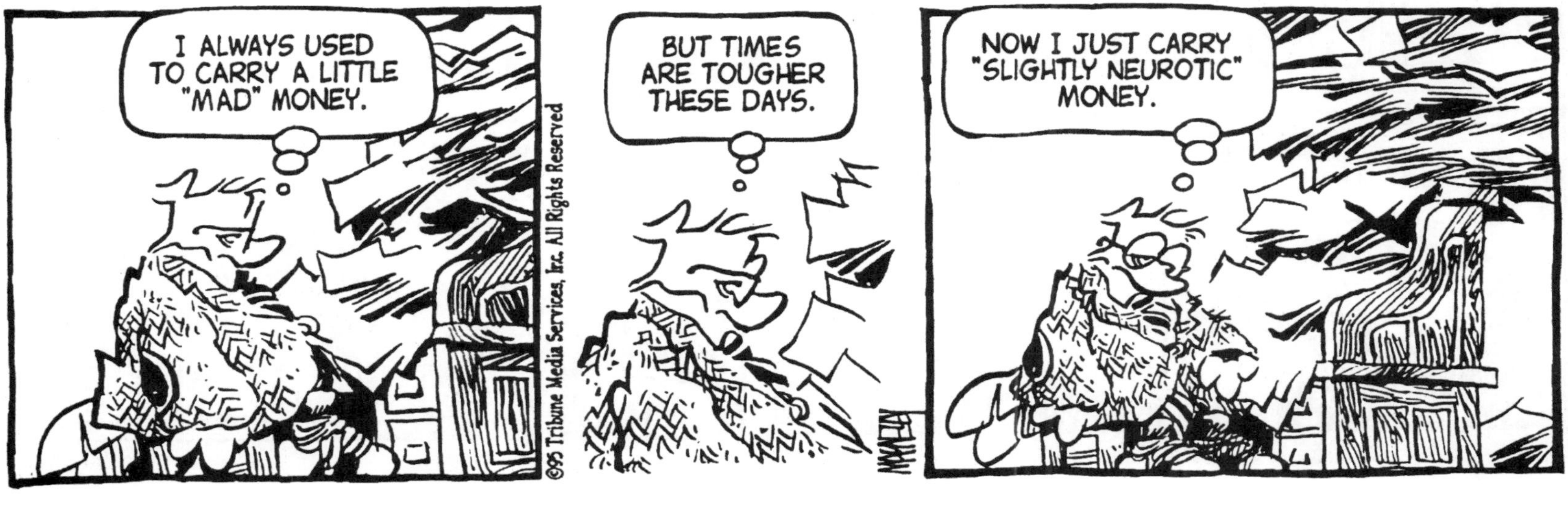
I ALWAYS USED TO CARRY A LITTLE "MAD" MONEY.
BUT TIMES ARE TOUGHER THESE DAYS.
NOW I JUST CARRY "SLIGHTLY NEUROTIC" MONEY.
©93 Tribune Media Services, Inc. All Rights Reserved

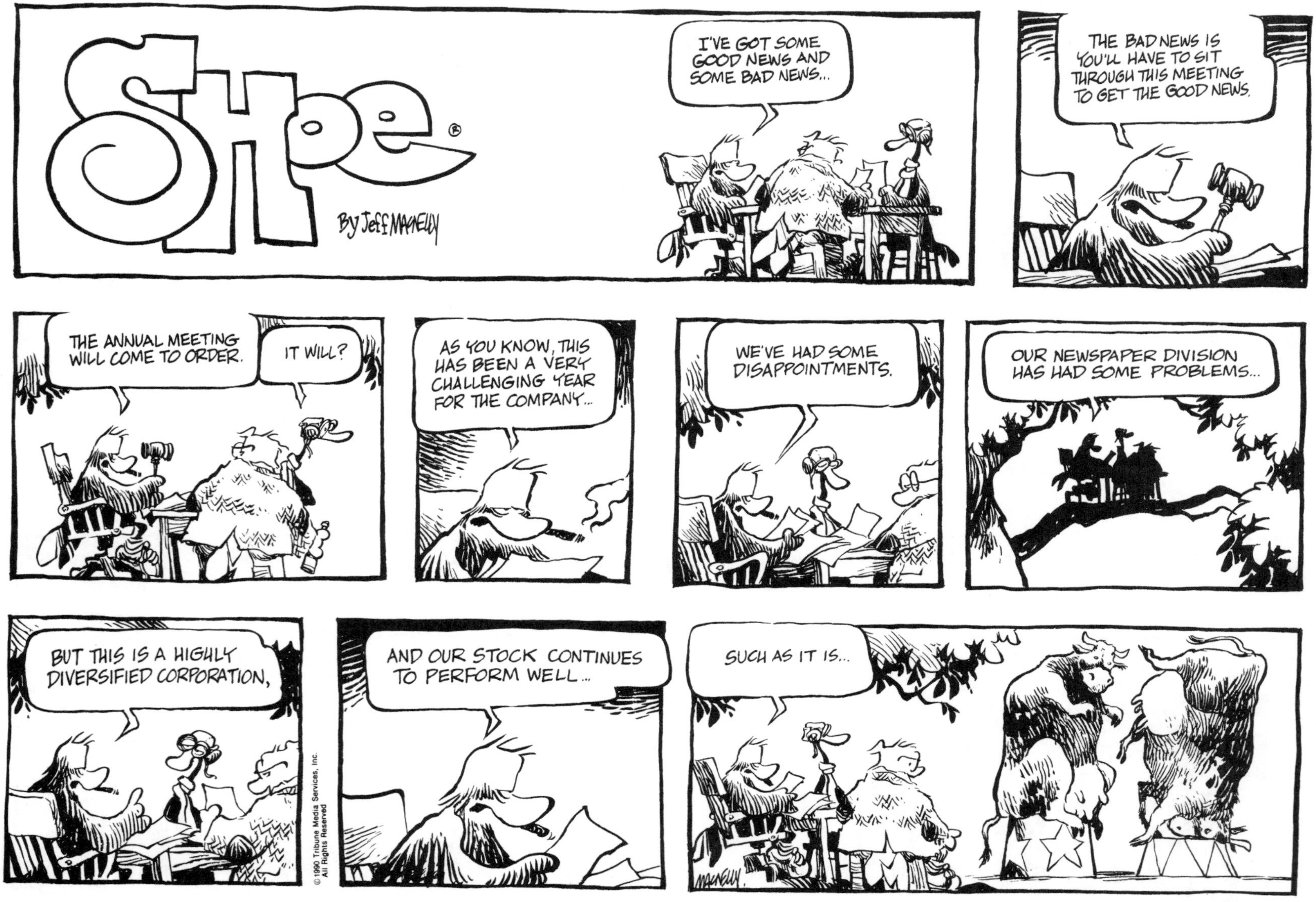

SHOE®
By Jeff MacNelly
I'VE GOT SOME GOOD NEWS AND SOME BAD NEWS...
THE BAD NEWS IS YOU'LL HAVE TO SIT THROUGH THIS MEETING TO GET THE GOOD NEWS.
THE ANNUAL MEETING WILL COME TO ORDER.
IT WILL?
AS YOU KNOW, THIS HAS BEEN A VERY CHALLENGING YEAR FOR THE COMPANY...
WE'VE HAD SOME DISAPPOINTMENTS.
OUR NEWSPAPER DIVISION HAS HAD SOME PROBLEMS...
BUT THIS IS A HIGHLY DIVERSIFIED CORPORATION,
AND OUR STOCK CONTINUES TO PERFORM WELL...
SUCH AS IT IS...
MACNELLY

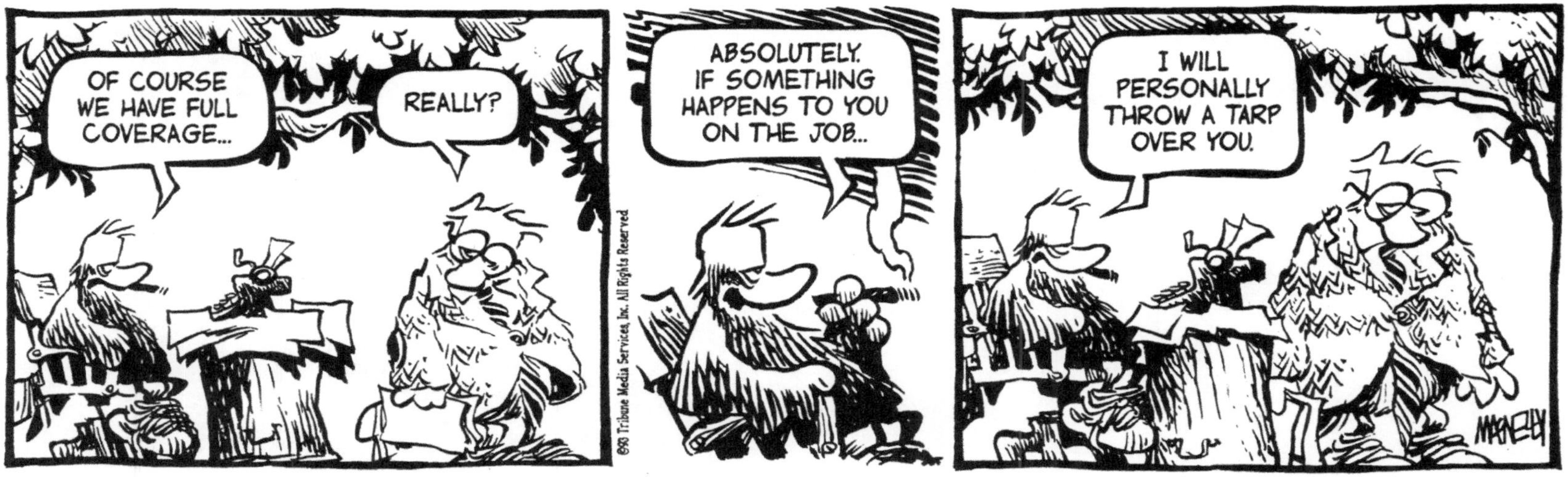
OF COURSE WE HAVE FULL COVERAGE...
REALLY?
ABSOLUTELY. IF SOMETHING HAPPENS TO YOU ON THE JOB...
I WILL PERSONALLY THROW A TARP OVER YOU.
©90 Tribune Media Services, Inc. All Rights Reserved
MACNELLY

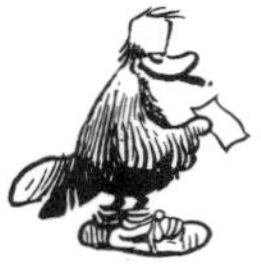

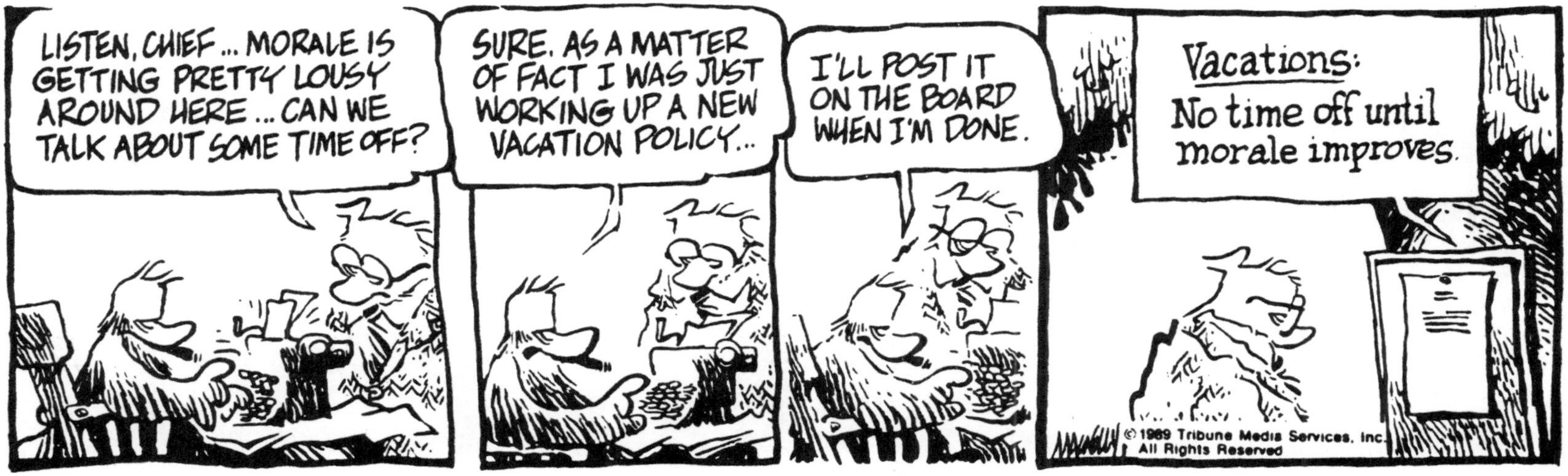
LISTEN, CHIEF ... MORALE IS GETTING PRETTY LOUSY AROUND HERE ... CAN WE TALK ABOUT SOME TIME OFF?
SURE. AS A MATTER OF FACT I WAS JUST WORKING UP A NEW VACATION POLICY...
I'LL POST IT ON THE BOARD WHEN I'M DONE.
Vacations:
No time off until morale improves.
MACNELLY
© 1989 Tribune Media Services, Inc. All Rights Reserved

Chapter Five

It's Lonely at the Top

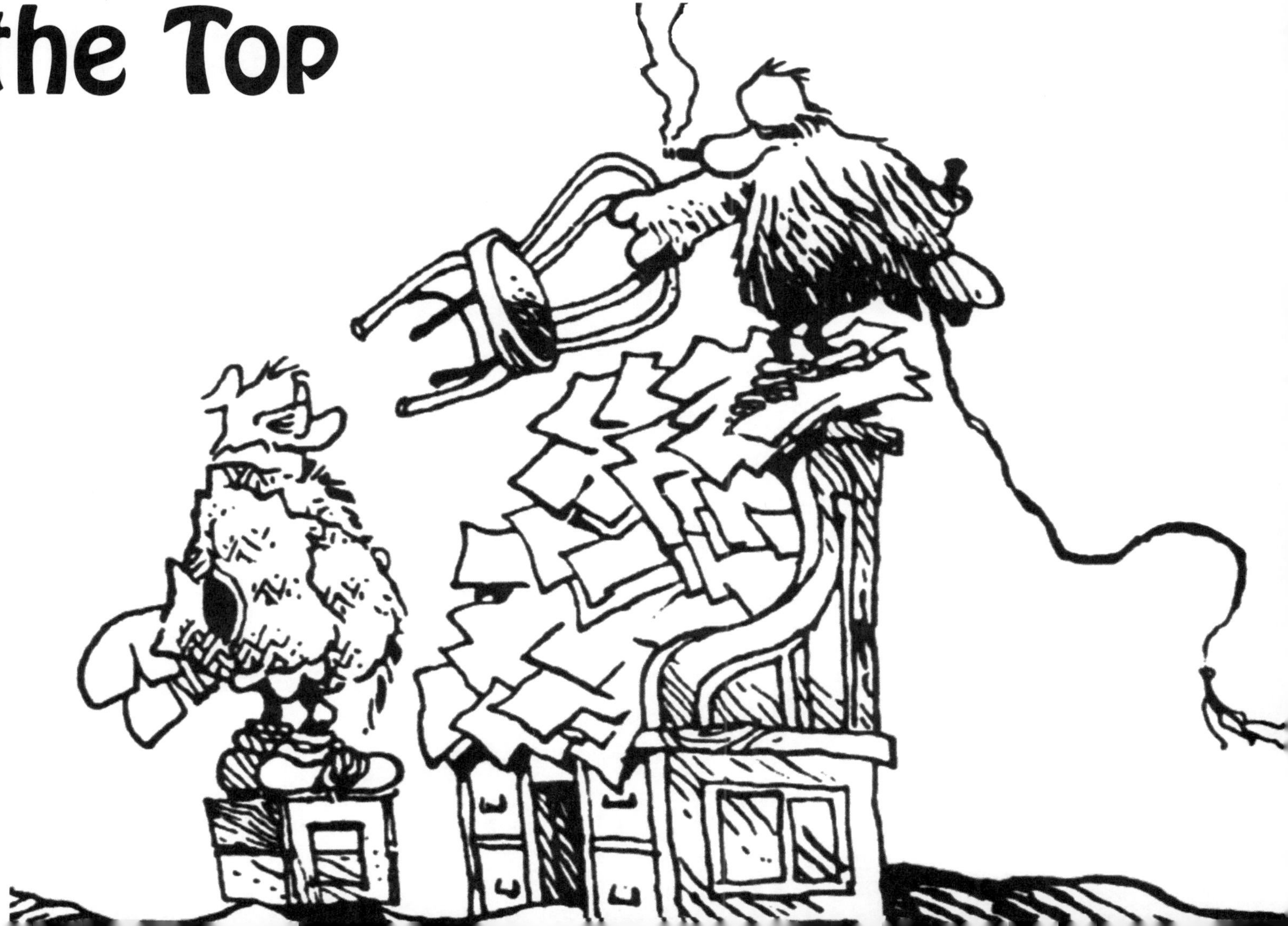

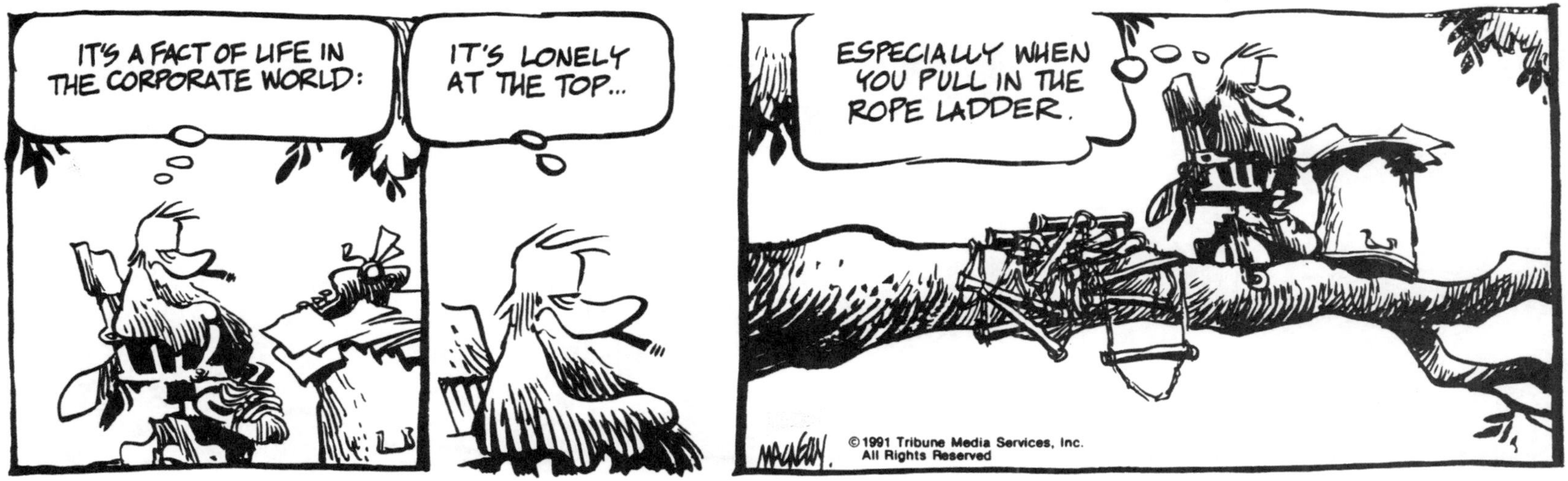
IT'S A FACT OF LIFE IN THE CORPORATE WORLD:
IT'S LONELY AT THE TOP...
ESPECIALLY WHEN YOU PULL IN THE ROPE LADDER.
MACNELLY
© 1991 Tribune Media Services, Inc. All Rights Reserved

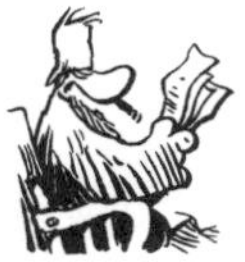

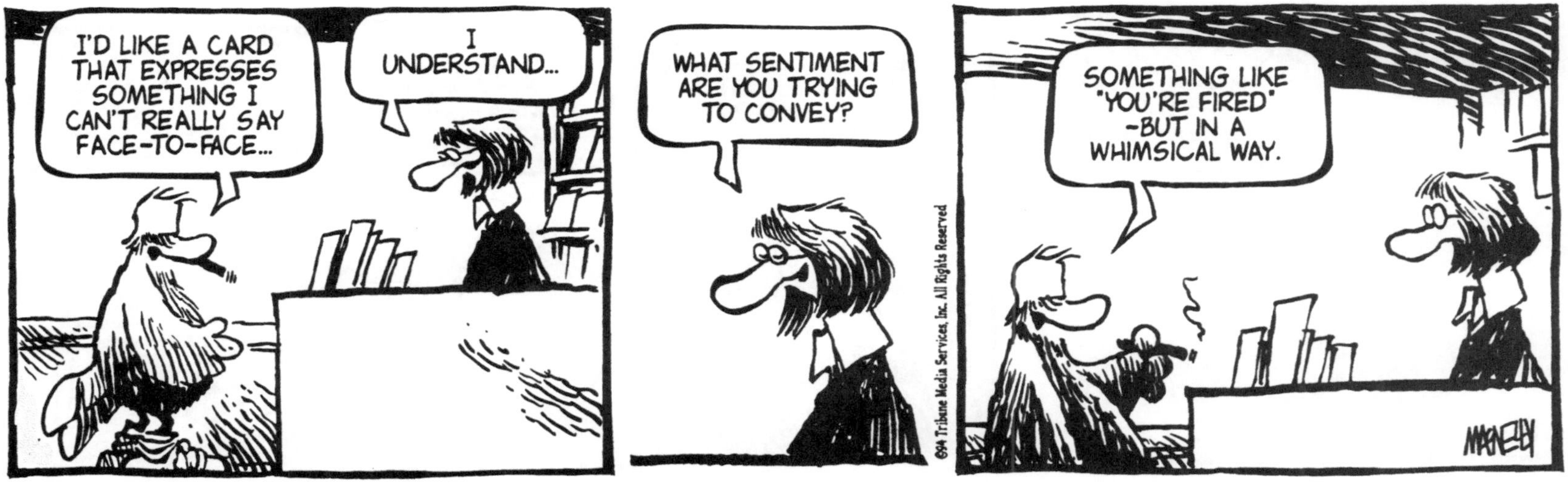
I'D LIKE A CARD THAT EXPRESSES SOMETHING I CAN'T REALLY SAY FACE-TO-FACE...
I UNDERSTAND...
WHAT SENTIMENT ARE YOU TRYING TO CONVEY?
SOMETHING LIKE "YOU'RE FIRED" -BUT IN A WHIMSICAL WAY.
©94 Tribune Media Services, Inc. All Rights Reserved
MACNELLY

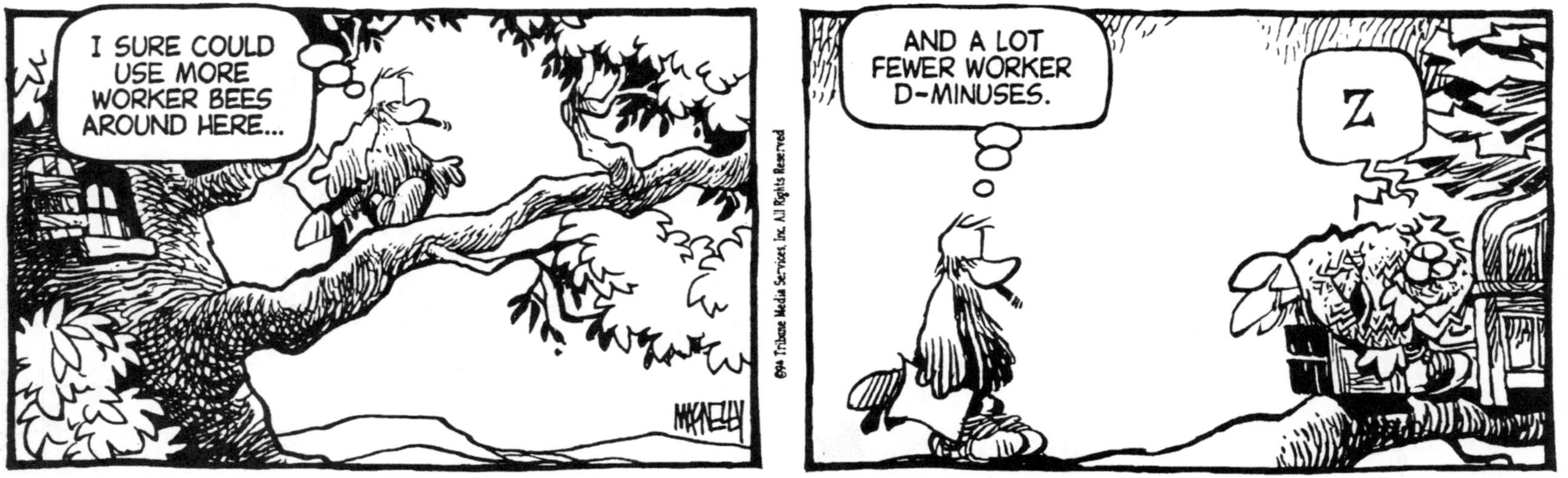
I SURE COULD USE MORE WORKER BEES AROUND HERE...
©94 Tribune Media Services, Inc. All Rights Reserved
AND A LOT FEWER WORKER D-MINUSES.
Z

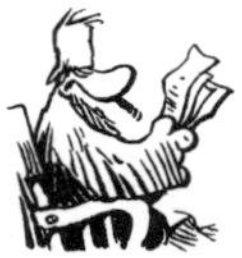

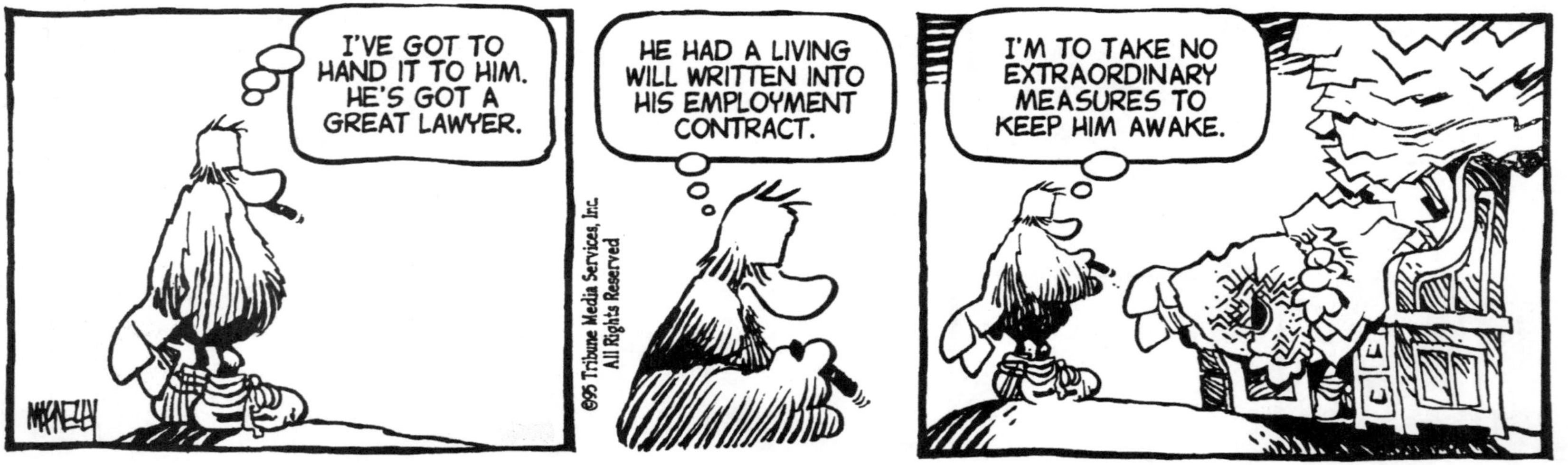
I'VE GOT TO HAND IT TO HIM. HE'S GOT A GREAT LAWYER.
©95 Tribune Media Services, Inc. All Rights Reserved
HE HAD A LIVING WILL WRITTEN INTO HIS EMPLOYMENT CONTRACT.
I'M TO TAKE NO EXTRAORDINARY MEASURES TO KEEP HIM AWAKE.

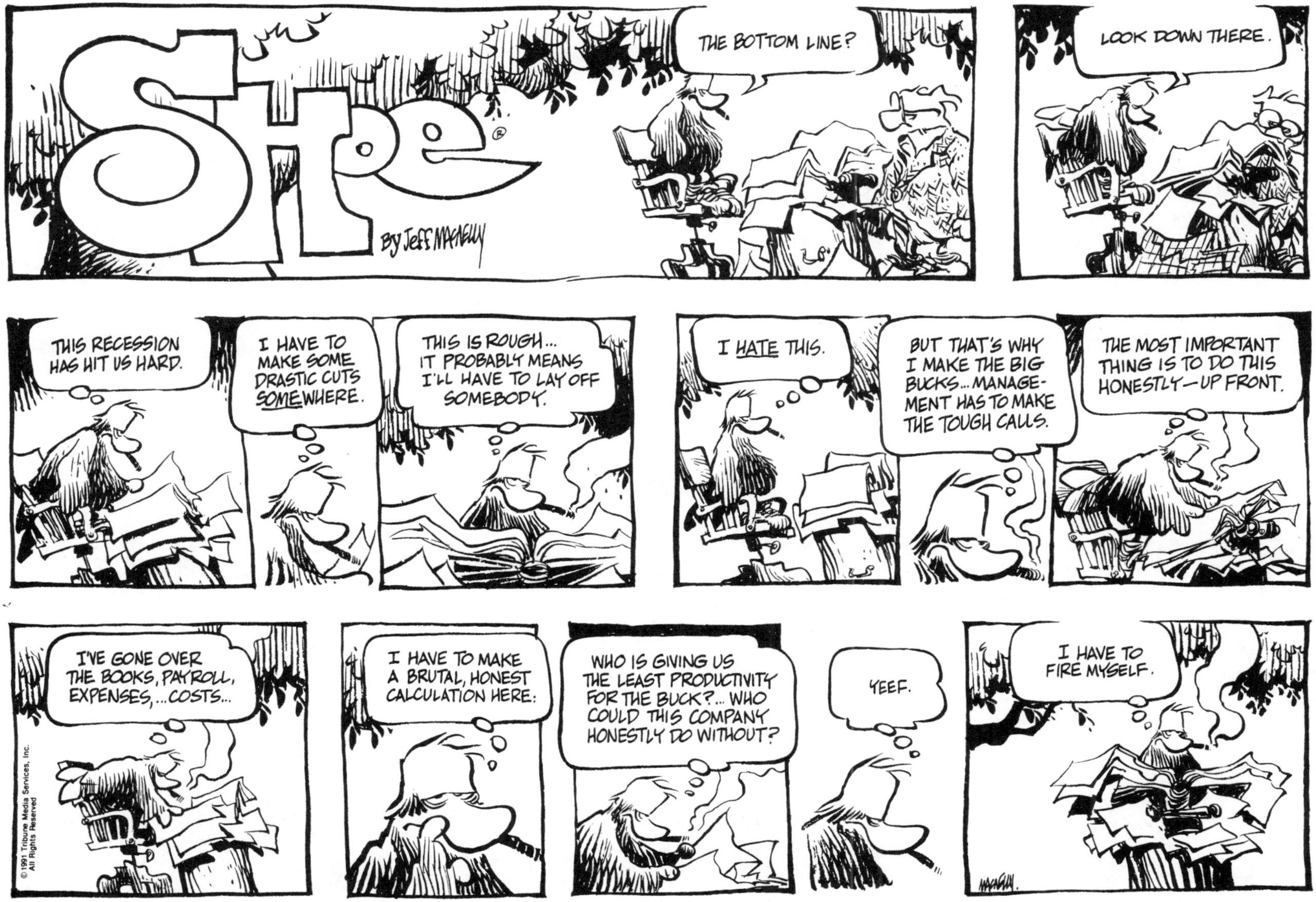
Shoe®
By Jeff MacNelly
THE BOTTOM LINE?
LOOK DOWN THERE.
THIS RECESSION HAS HIT US HARD.
I HAVE TO MAKE SOME DRASTIC CUTS SOMEWHERE.
THIS IS ROUGH... IT PROBABLY MEANS I'LL HAVE TO LAY OFF SOMEBODY.
I HATE THIS.
BUT THAT'S WHY I MAKE THE BIG BUCKS... MANAGEMENT HAS TO MAKE THE TOUGH CALLS.
THE MOST IMPORTANT THING IS TO DO THIS HONESTLY—UP FRONT.
I'VE GONE OVER THE BOOKS, PAYROLL, EXPENSES, ...COSTS...
© 1991 Tribune Media Services, Inc. All Rights Reserved
I HAVE TO MAKE A BRUTAL, HONEST CALCULATION HERE:
WHO IS GIVING US THE LEAST PRODUCTIVITY FOR THE BUCK?... WHO COULD THIS COMPANY HONESTLY DO WITHOUT?
YEEF.
I HAVE TO FIRE MYSELF.
MACNELLY

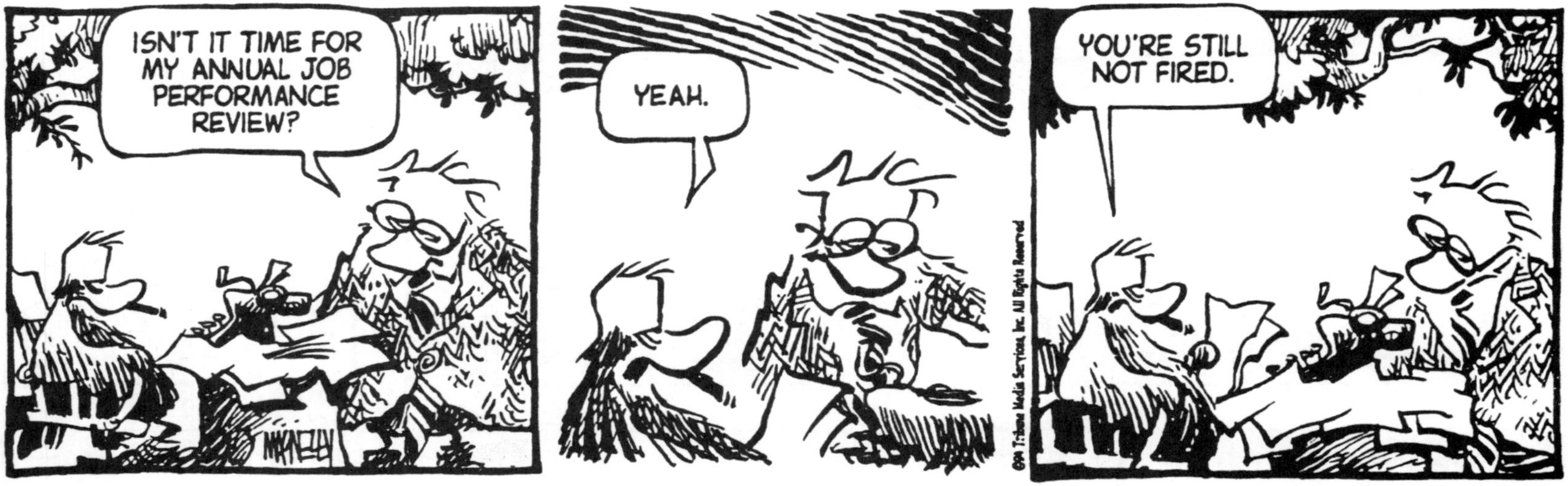
ISN'T IT TIME FOR MY ANNUAL JOB PERFORMANCE REVIEW?
YEAH.
YOU'RE STILL NOT FIRED.
MACNELLY

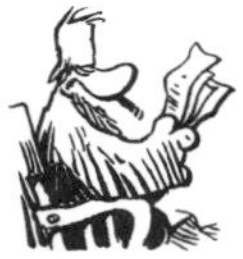

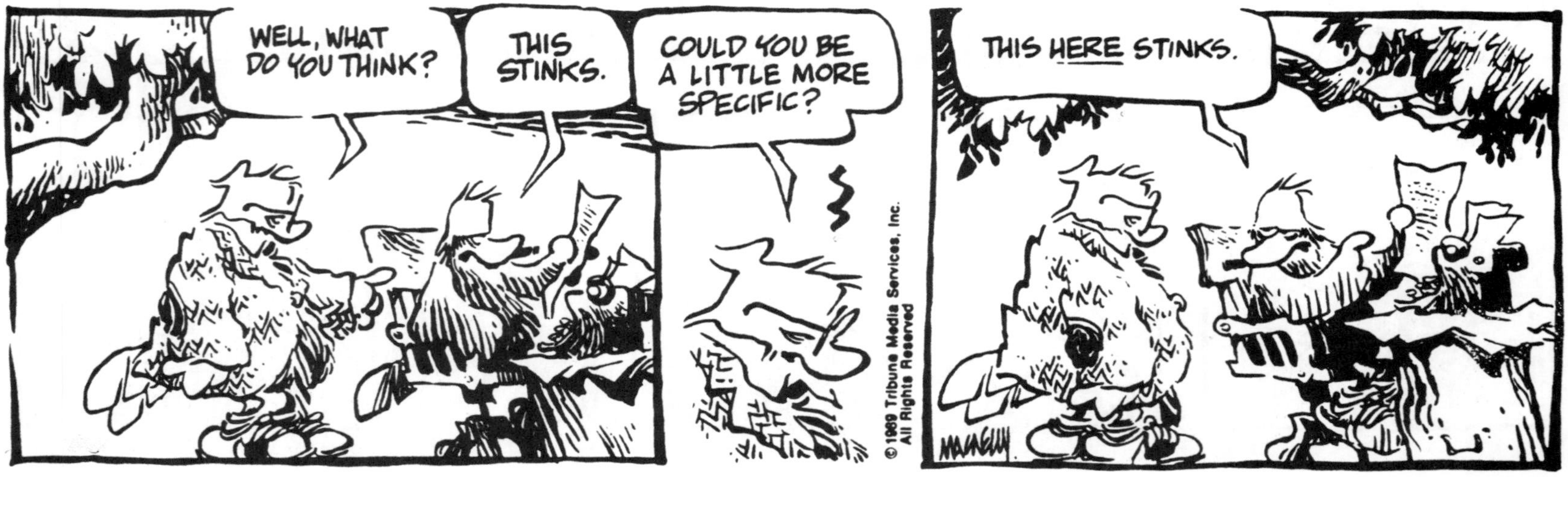
WELL, WHAT DO YOU THINK?
THIS STINKS.
COULD YOU BE A LITTLE MORE SPECIFIC?
THIS HERE STINKS.
MACNELLY

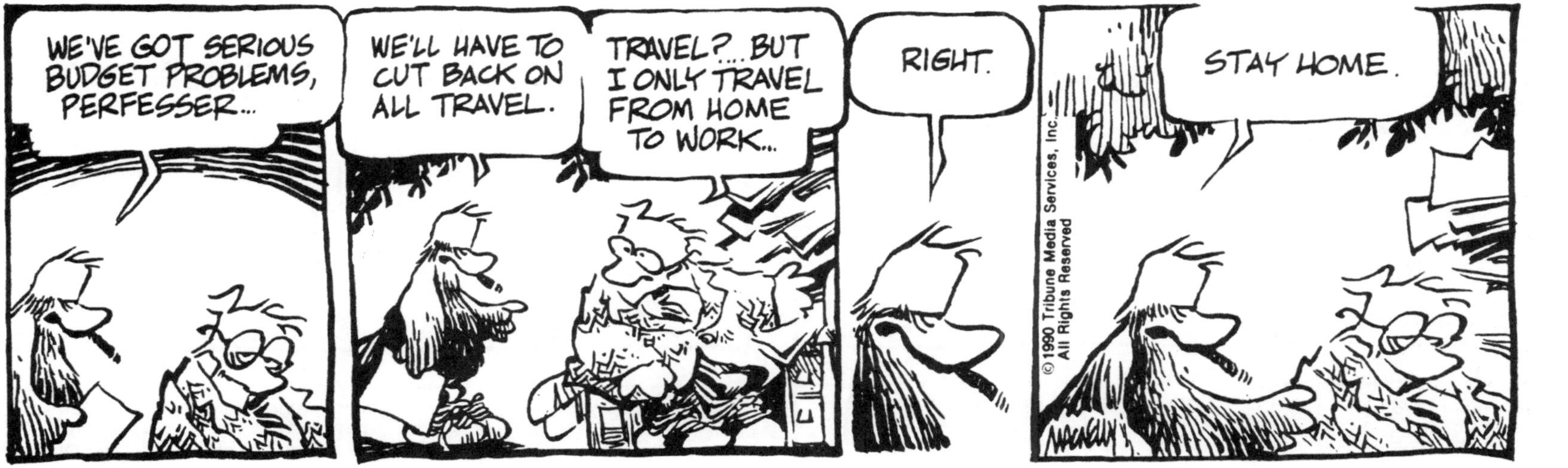
WE'VE GOT SERIOUS BUDGET PROBLEMS, PERFESSER...
WE'LL HAVE TO CUT BACK ON ALL TRAVEL.
TRAVEL?... BUT I ONLY TRAVEL FROM HOME TO WORK...
RIGHT.
STAY HOME.
© 1990 Tribune Media Services, Inc. All Rights Reserved

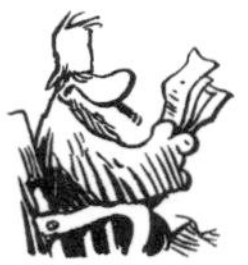

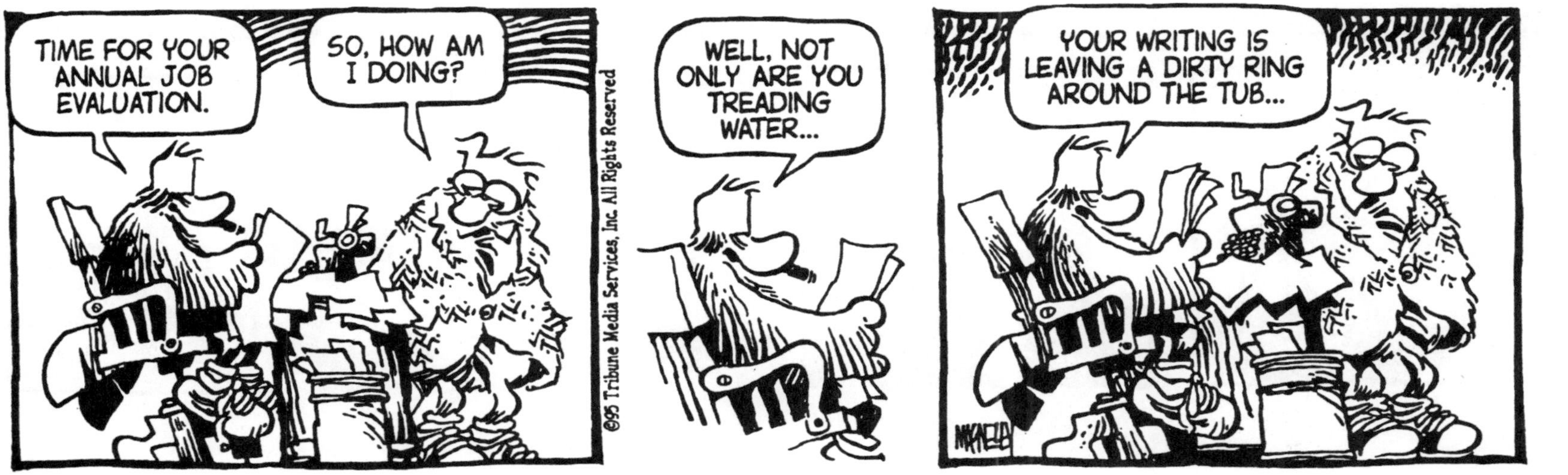
TIME FOR YOUR ANNUAL JOB EVALUATION.
SO, HOW AM I DOING?
WELL, NOT ONLY ARE YOU TREADING WATER...
YOUR WRITING IS LEAVING A DIRTY RING AROUND THE TUB...
©95 Tribune Media Services, Inc All Rights Reserved

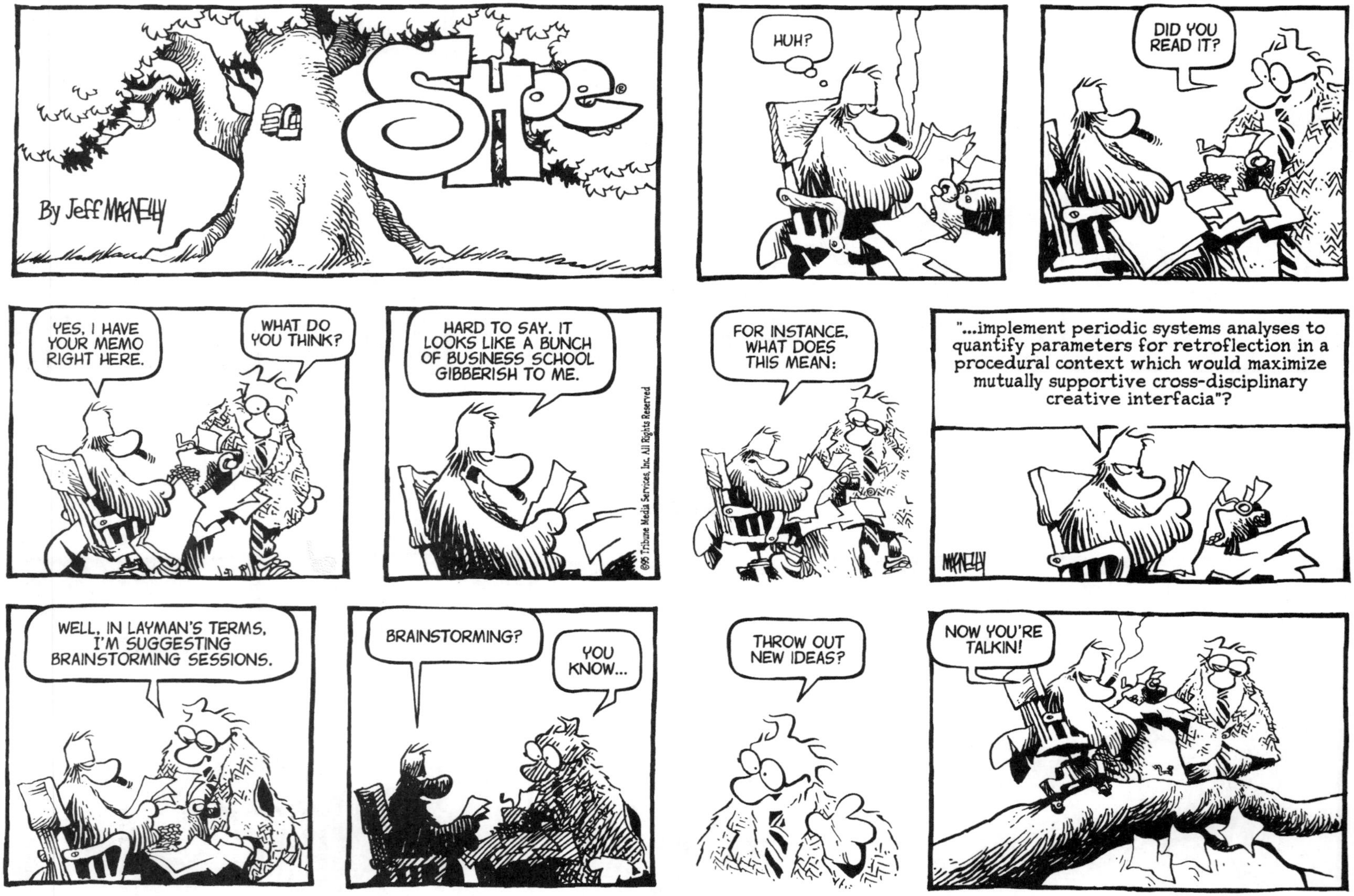

Shoe®
By Jeff MacNelly
HUH?
DID YOU READ IT?
YES, I HAVE YOUR MEMO RIGHT HERE.
WHAT DO YOU THINK?
HARD TO SAY. IT LOOKS LIKE A BUNCH OF BUSINESS SCHOOL GIBBERISH TO ME.
©95 Tribune Media Services, Inc. All Rights Reserved
FOR INSTANCE, WHAT DOES THIS MEAN:
"...implement periodic systems analyses to quantify parameters for retroflection in a procedural context which would maximize mutually supportive cross-disciplinary creative interfacia"?
MACNELLY
WELL, IN LAYMAN'S TERMS, I'M SUGGESTING BRAINSTORMING SESSIONS.
BRAINSTORMING?
YOU KNOW...
THROW OUT NEW IDEAS?
NOW YOU'RE TALKIN!

GO AHEAD! FIRE ME!! I GET GREAT UNEMPLOYMENT BENEFITS...

OH YEAH? LIKE WHAT?

WELL, I WON'T BE WORKING HERE — THAT'S ONE BIG UNEMPLOYMENT BENEFIT.

©1992 Tribune Media Services, Inc. All Rights Reserved

WELL, HOW DO YOU LIKE IT?

http://macnelly.com

THERE'S A LOT OF PAINFUL RECOGNITION FOR ME.

IT REMINDS ME I HIRED YOU.

©96 Tribune Media Services, Inc. All Rights Reserved

101

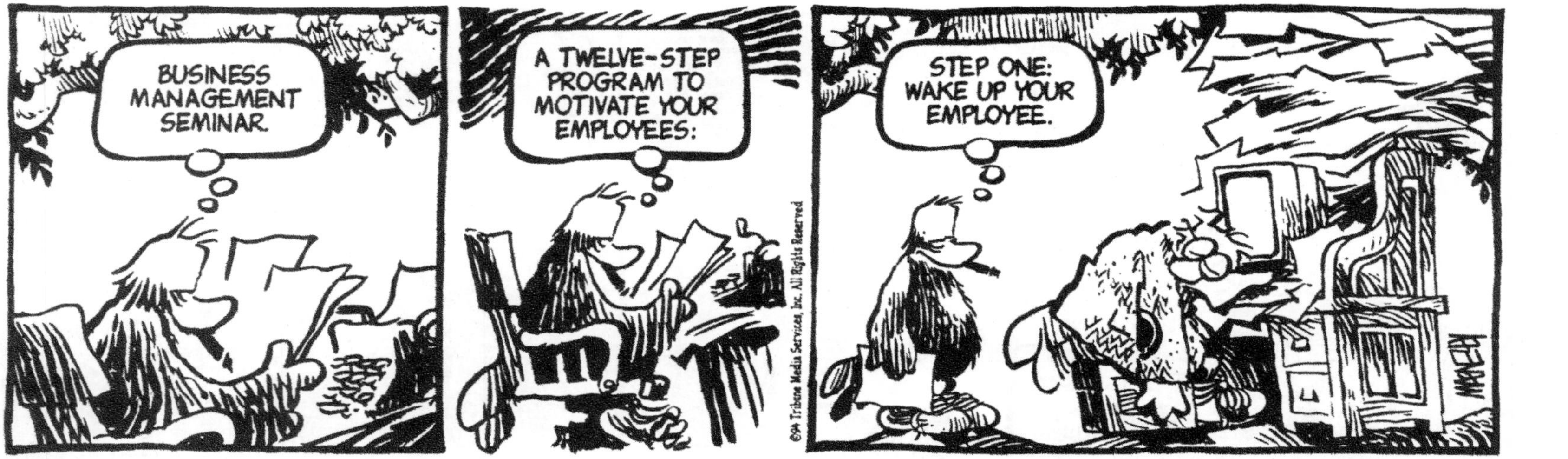
BUSINESS MANAGEMENT SEMINAR.
A TWELVE-STEP PROGRAM TO MOTIVATE YOUR EMPLOYEES:
STEP ONE: WAKE UP YOUR EMPLOYEE.
©94 Tribune Media Services, Inc. All Rights Reserved
MACNELLY

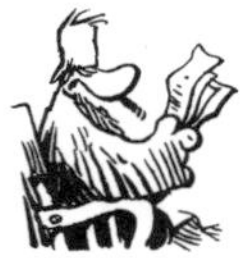

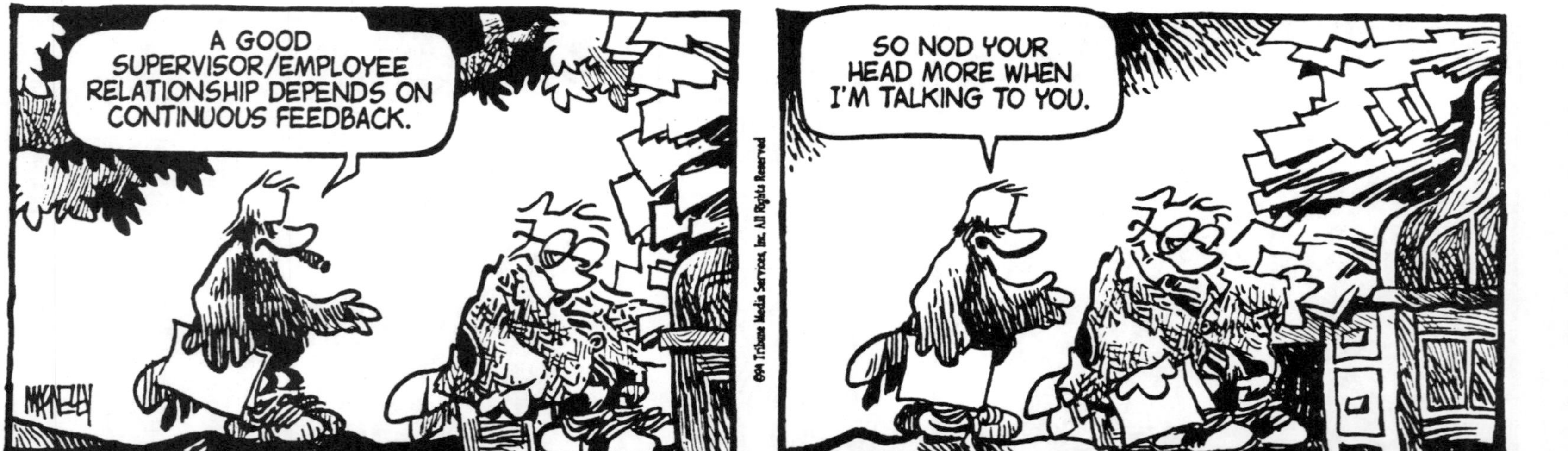
A GOOD SUPERVISOR/EMPLOYEE RELATIONSHIP DEPENDS ON CONTINUOUS FEEDBACK.
MACNELLY
©94 Tribune Media Services, Inc. All Rights Reserved
SO NOD YOUR HEAD MORE WHEN I'M TALKING TO YOU.

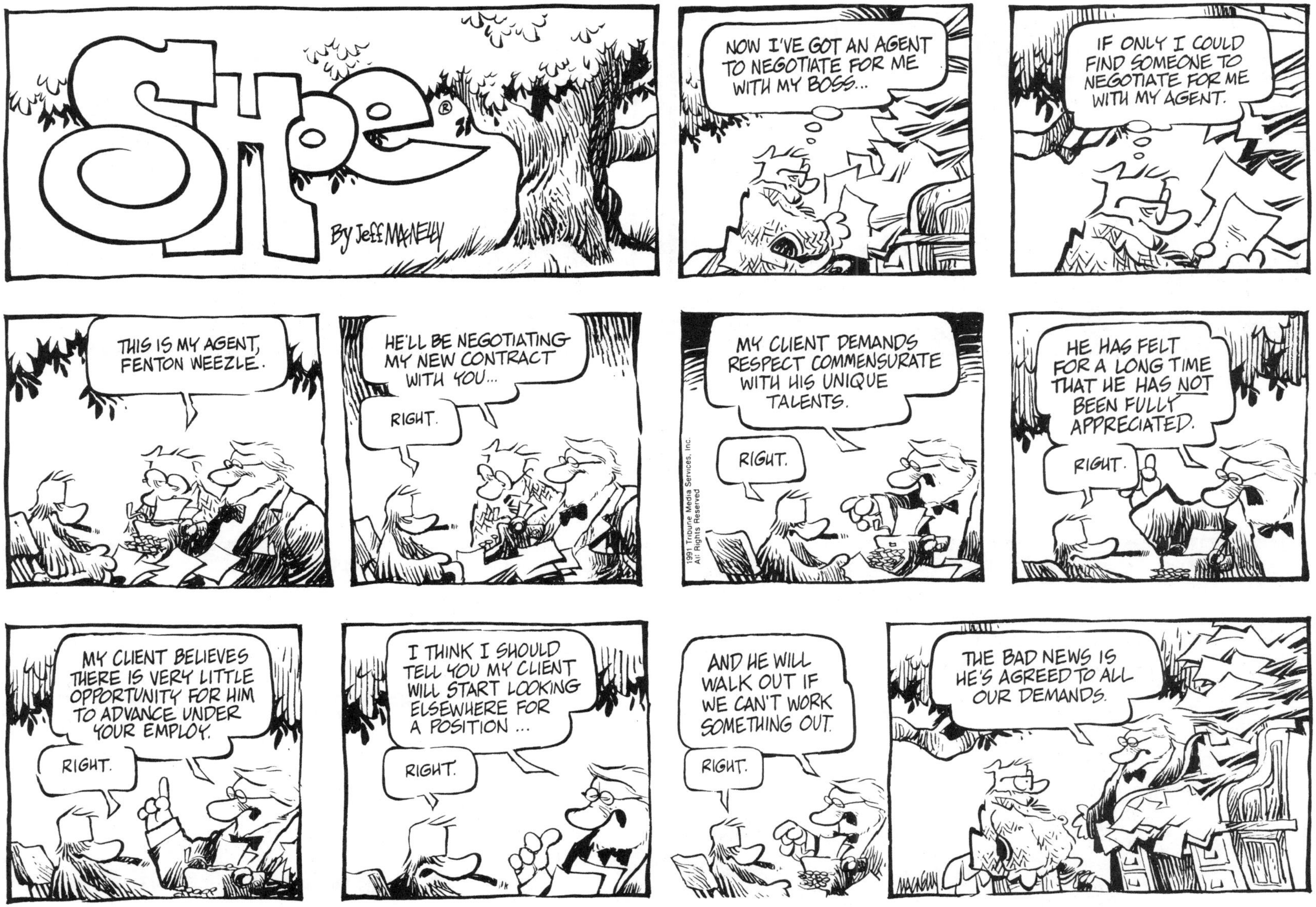
SHOE®
By Jeff MacNelly
NOW I'VE GOT AN AGENT TO NEGOTIATE FOR ME WITH MY BOSS...
IF ONLY I COULD FIND SOMEONE TO NEGOTIATE FOR ME WITH MY AGENT.
THIS IS MY AGENT, FENTON WEEZLE.
HE'LL BE NEGOTIATING MY NEW CONTRACT WITH YOU...
RIGHT.
MY CLIENT DEMANDS RESPECT COMMENSURATE WITH HIS UNIQUE TALENTS.
RIGHT.
HE HAS FELT FOR A LONG TIME THAT HE HAS NOT BEEN FULLY APPRECIATED.
RIGHT.
MY CLIENT BELIEVES THERE IS VERY LITTLE OPPORTUNITY FOR HIM TO ADVANCE UNDER YOUR EMPLOY.
RIGHT.
I THINK I SHOULD TELL YOU MY CLIENT WILL START LOOKING ELSEWHERE FOR A POSITION ...
RIGHT.
AND HE WILL WALK OUT IF WE CAN'T WORK SOMETHING OUT.
RIGHT.
THE BAD NEWS IS HE'S AGREED TO ALL OUR DEMANDS.
MACNELLY
1991 Tribune Media Services, Inc. All Rights Reserved

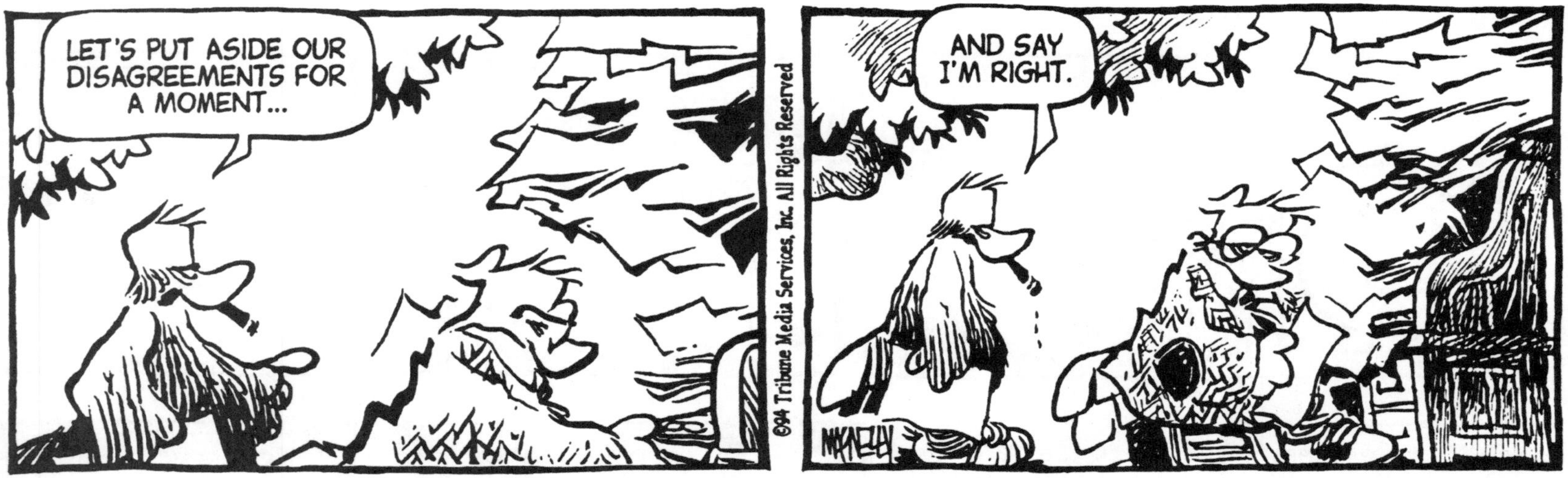
LET'S PUT ASIDE OUR DISAGREEMENTS FOR A MOMENT...
©94 Tribune Media Services, Inc. All Rights Reserved
AND SAY I'M RIGHT.
MACNELLY

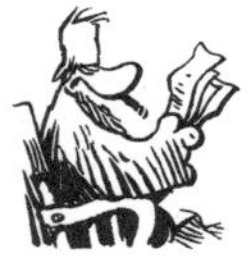

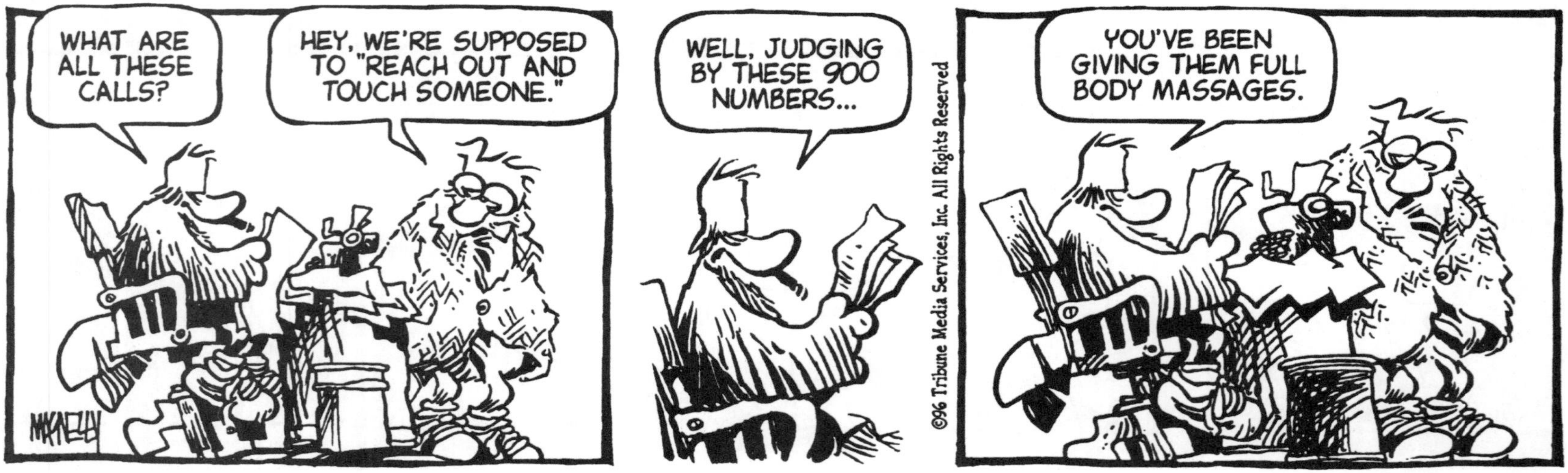
WHAT ARE ALL THESE CALLS?
HEY, WE'RE SUPPOSED TO "REACH OUT AND TOUCH SOMEONE."
MACNELLY
WELL, JUDGING BY THESE 900 NUMBERS...
©96 Tribune Media Services, Inc. All Rights Reserved
YOU'VE BEEN GIVING THEM FULL BODY MASSAGES.

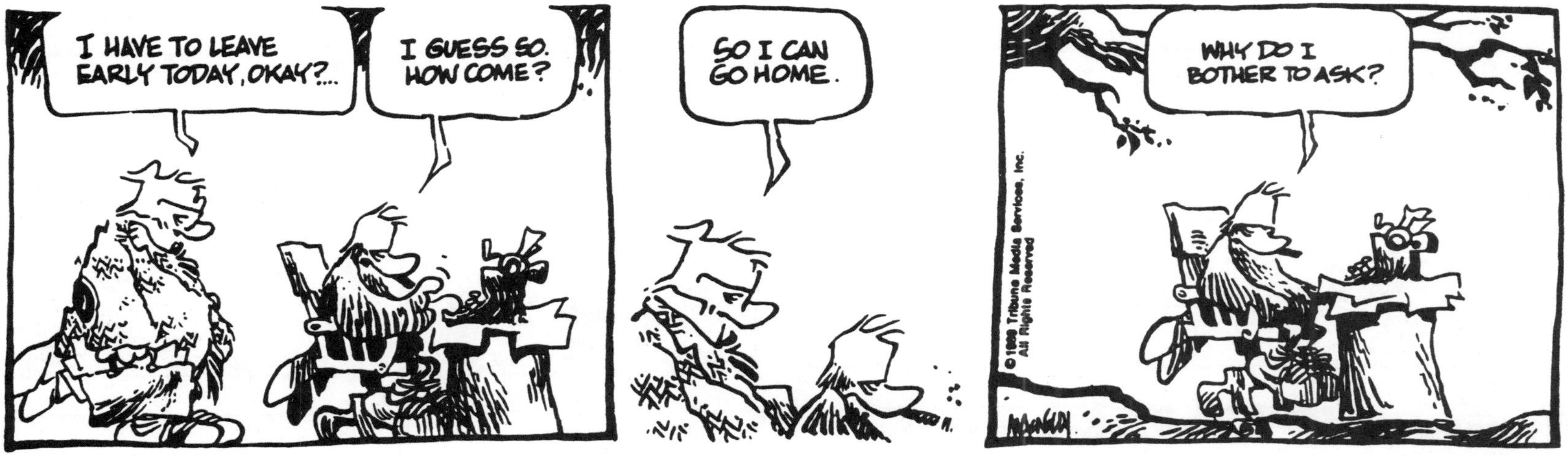
I HAVE TO LEAVE EARLY TODAY, OKAY?...
I GUESS SO. HOW COME?
SO I CAN GO HOME.
WHY DO I BOTHER TO ASK?

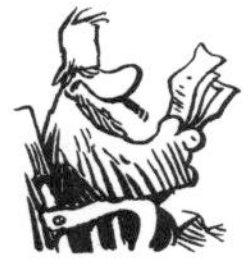

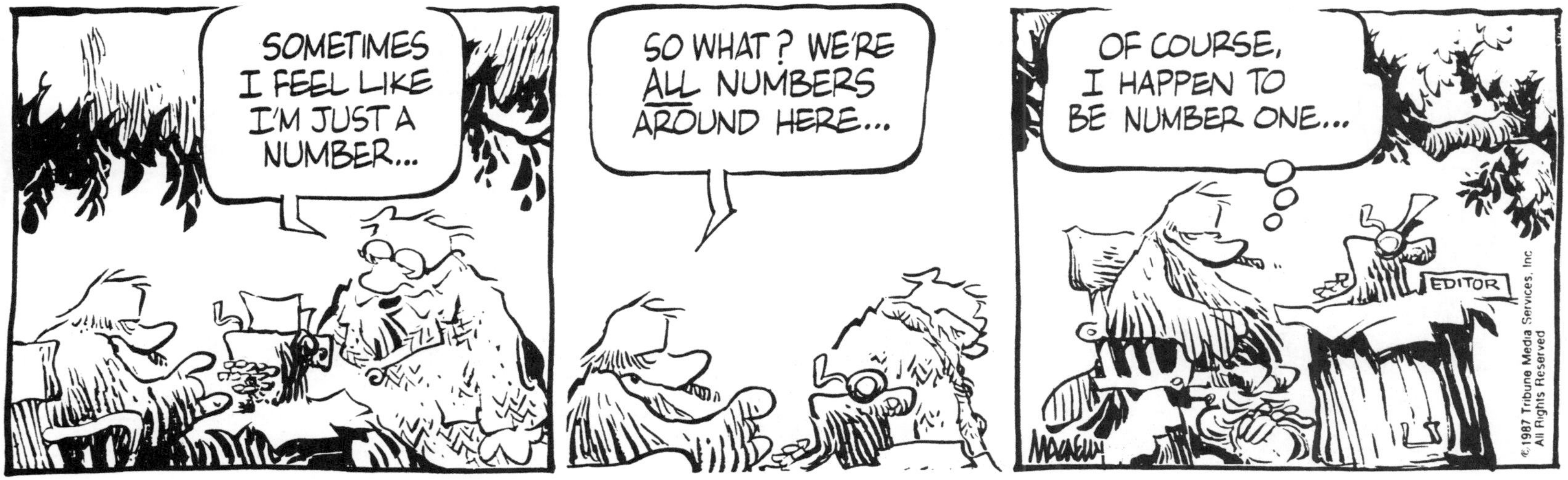
SOMETIMES I FEEL LIKE I'M JUST A NUMBER...
SO WHAT? WE'RE ALL NUMBERS AROUND HERE...
OF COURSE, I HAPPEN TO BE NUMBER ONE...
EDITOR
© 1987 Tribune Media Services, Inc.
All Rights Reserved

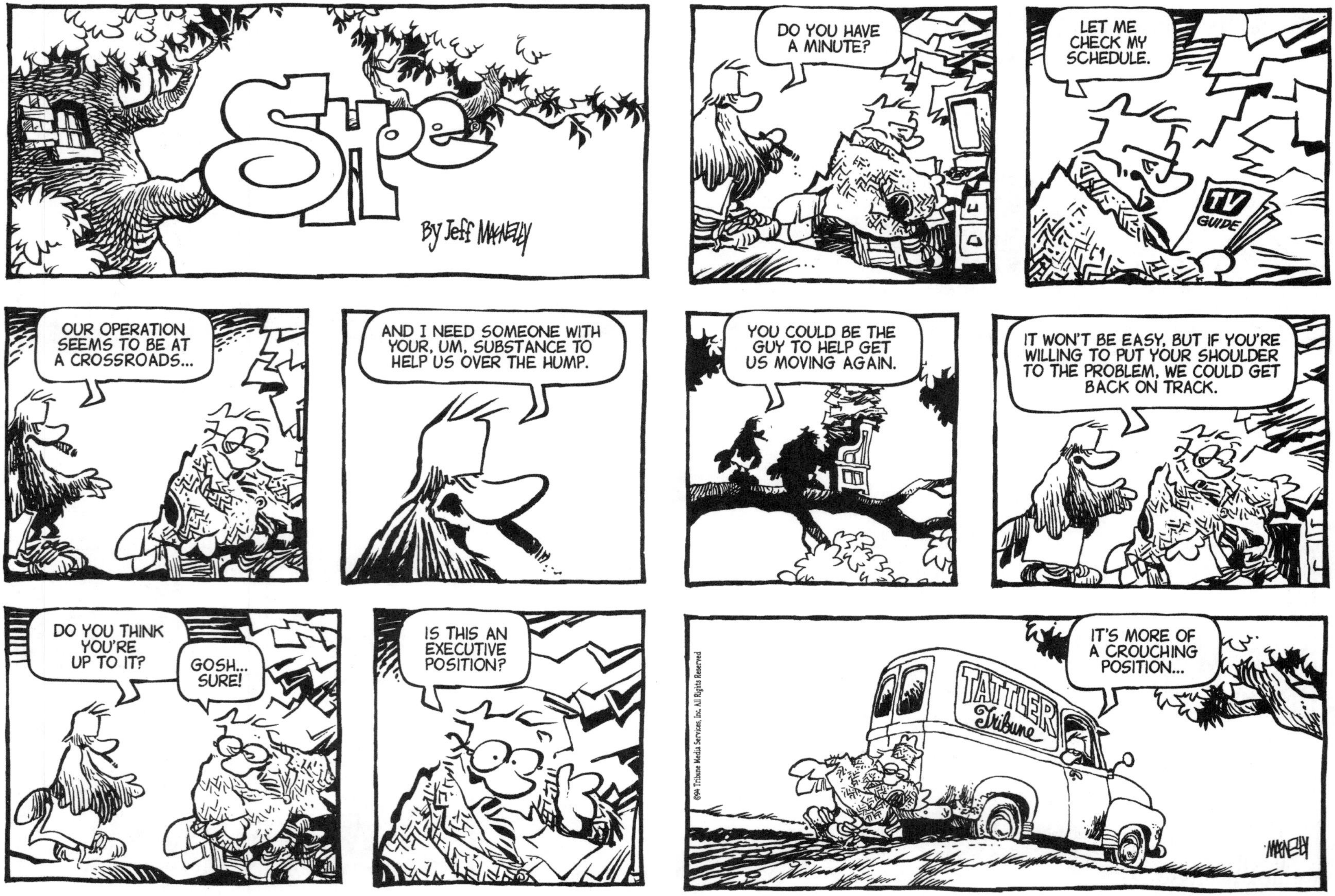
SHOE
By Jeff MacNelly
DO YOU HAVE A MINUTE?
LET ME CHECK MY SCHEDULE.
TV GUIDE
OUR OPERATION SEEMS TO BE AT A CROSSROADS...
AND I NEED SOMEONE WITH YOUR, UM, SUBSTANCE TO HELP US OVER THE HUMP.
YOU COULD BE THE GUY TO HELP GET US MOVING AGAIN.
IT WON'T BE EASY, BUT IF YOU'RE WILLING TO PUT YOUR SHOULDER TO THE PROBLEM, WE COULD GET BACK ON TRACK.
DO YOU THINK YOU'RE UP TO IT?
GOSH... SURE!
IS THIS AN EXECUTIVE POSITION?
©94 Tribune Media Services, Inc. All Rights Reserved
TATTLER Tribune
IT'S MORE OF A CROUCHING POSITION...
MACNELLY

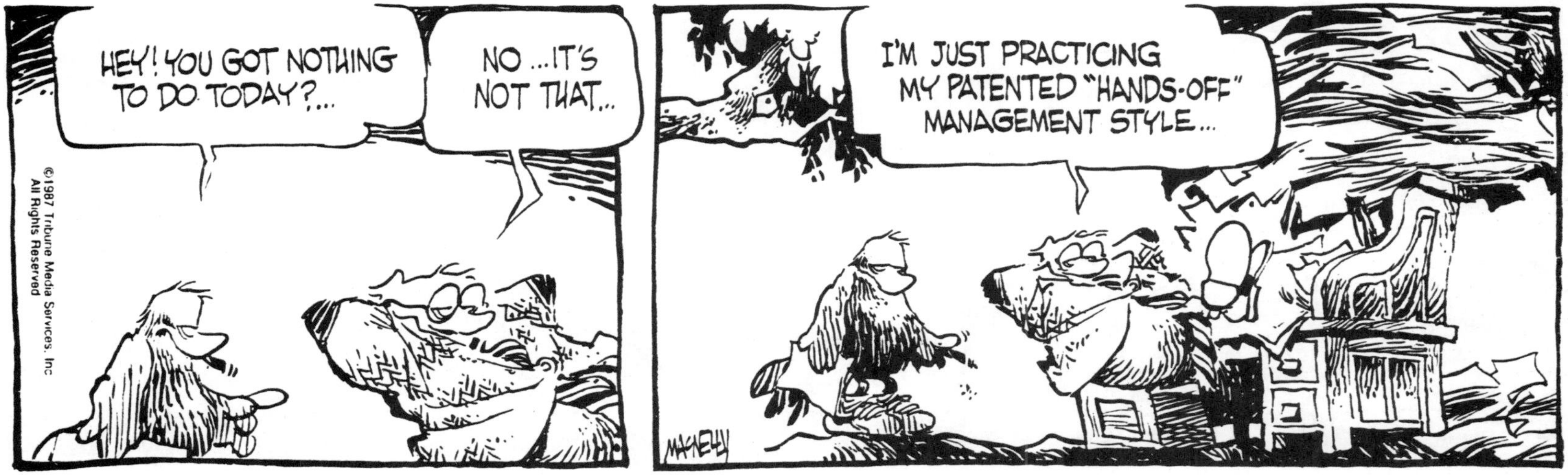
HEY! YOU GOT NOTHING TO DO TODAY?...
NO ...IT'S NOT THAT...
I'M JUST PRACTICING MY PATENTED "HANDS-OFF" MANAGEMENT STYLE...
©1987 Tribune Media Services, Inc
All Rights Reserved

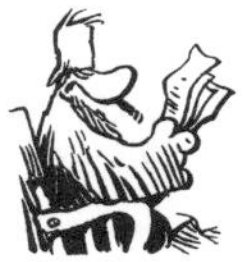

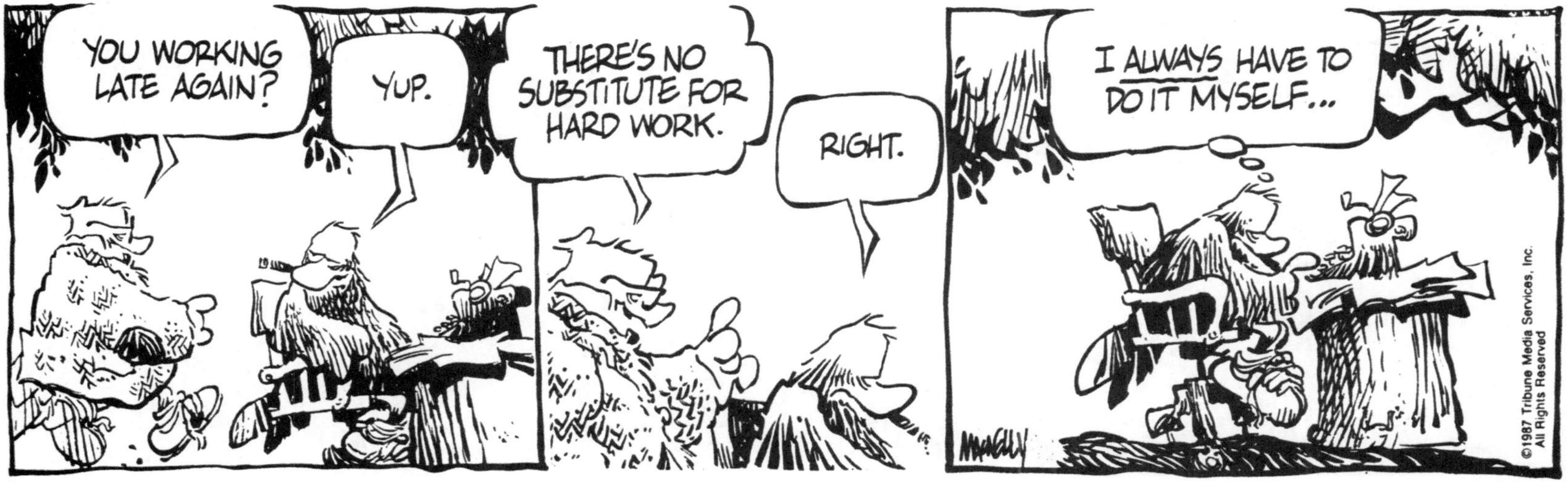
YOU WORKING LATE AGAIN?
YUP.
THERE'S NO SUBSTITUTE FOR HARD WORK.
RIGHT.
I ALWAYS HAVE TO DO IT MYSELF...
©1987 Tribune Media Services, Inc.
All Rights Reserved

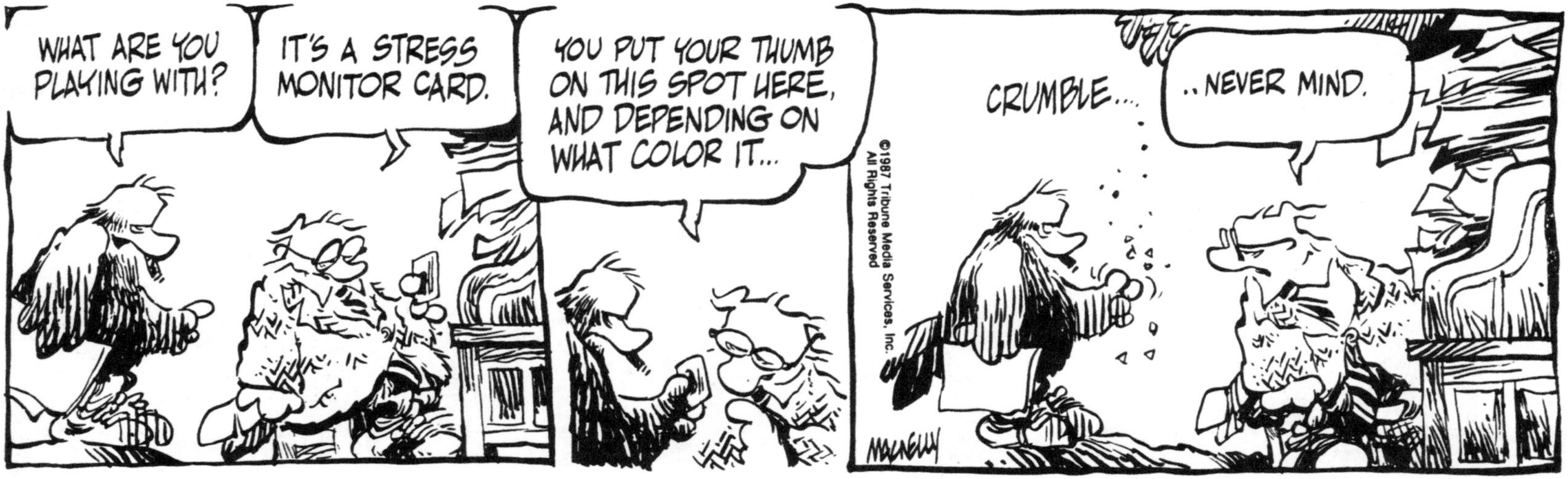
WHAT ARE YOU PLAYING WITH?
IT'S A STRESS MONITOR CARD.
YOU PUT YOUR THUMB ON THIS SPOT HERE, AND DEPENDING ON WHAT COLOR IT...
©1987 Tribune Media Services, Inc. All Rights Reserved
CRUMBLE....
..NEVER MIND.
MACNELLY

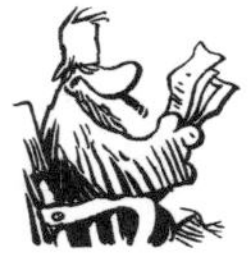

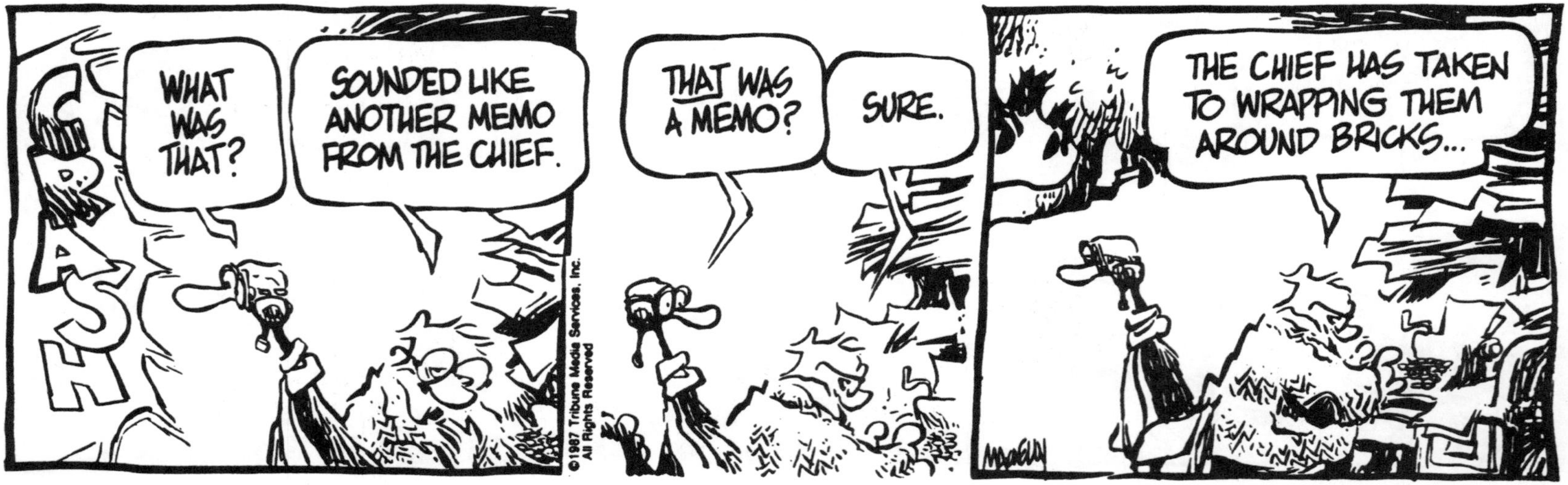
CRASH
WHAT WAS THAT?
SOUNDED LIKE ANOTHER MEMO FROM THE CHIEF.
©1987 Tribune Media Services, Inc. All Rights Reserved
THAT WAS A MEMO?
SURE.
THE CHIEF HAS TAKEN TO WRAPPING THEM AROUND BRICKS...
MACNELLY

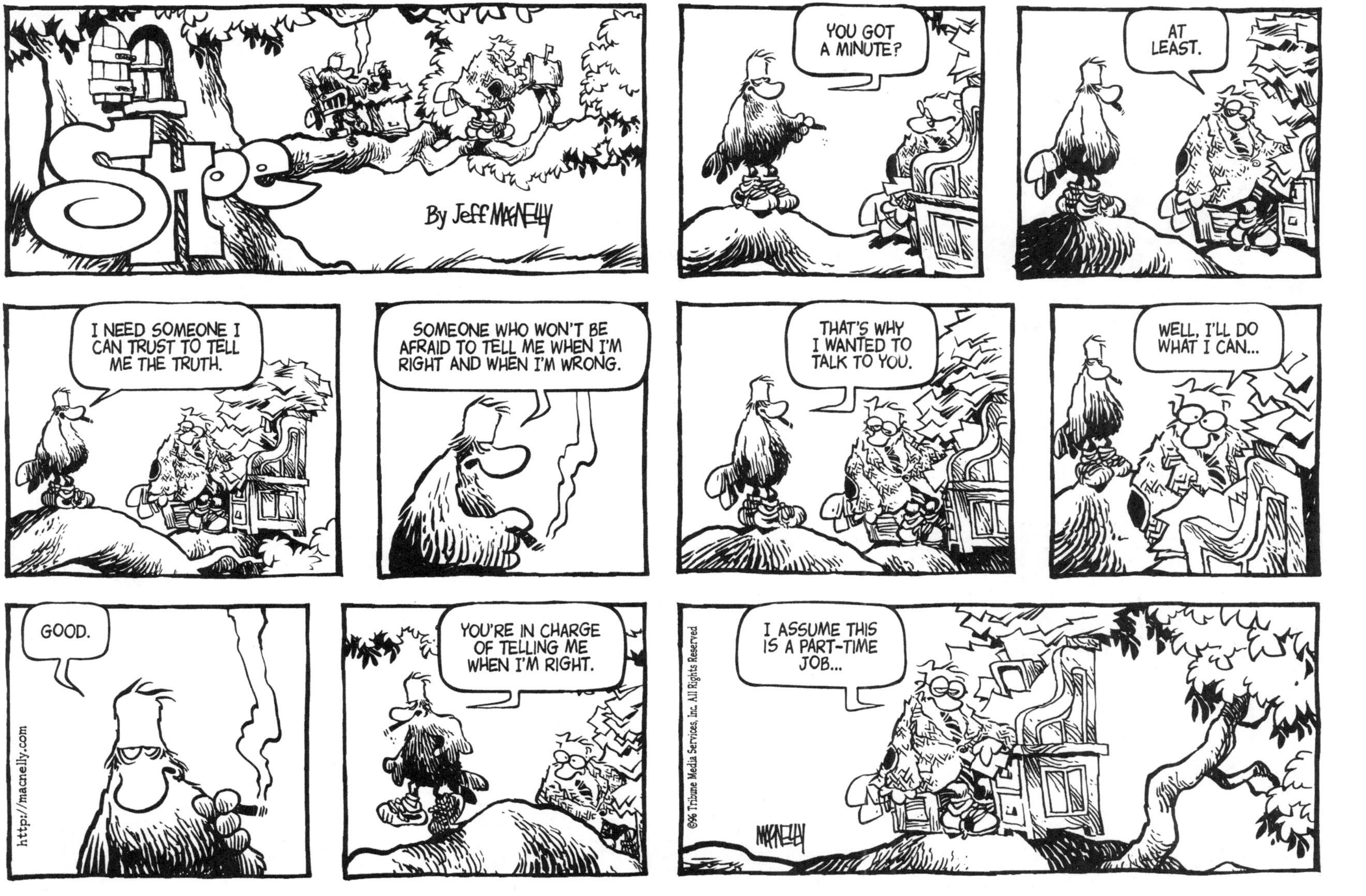
Shoe
By Jeff MacNelly
YOU GOT A MINUTE?
AT LEAST.
I NEED SOMEONE I CAN TRUST TO TELL ME THE TRUTH.
SOMEONE WHO WON'T BE AFRAID TO TELL ME WHEN I'M RIGHT AND WHEN I'M WRONG.
THAT'S WHY I WANTED TO TALK TO YOU.
WELL, I'LL DO WHAT I CAN...
GOOD.
http://macnelly.com
YOU'RE IN CHARGE OF TELLING ME WHEN I'M RIGHT.
I ASSUME THIS IS A PART-TIME JOB...
MACNELLY

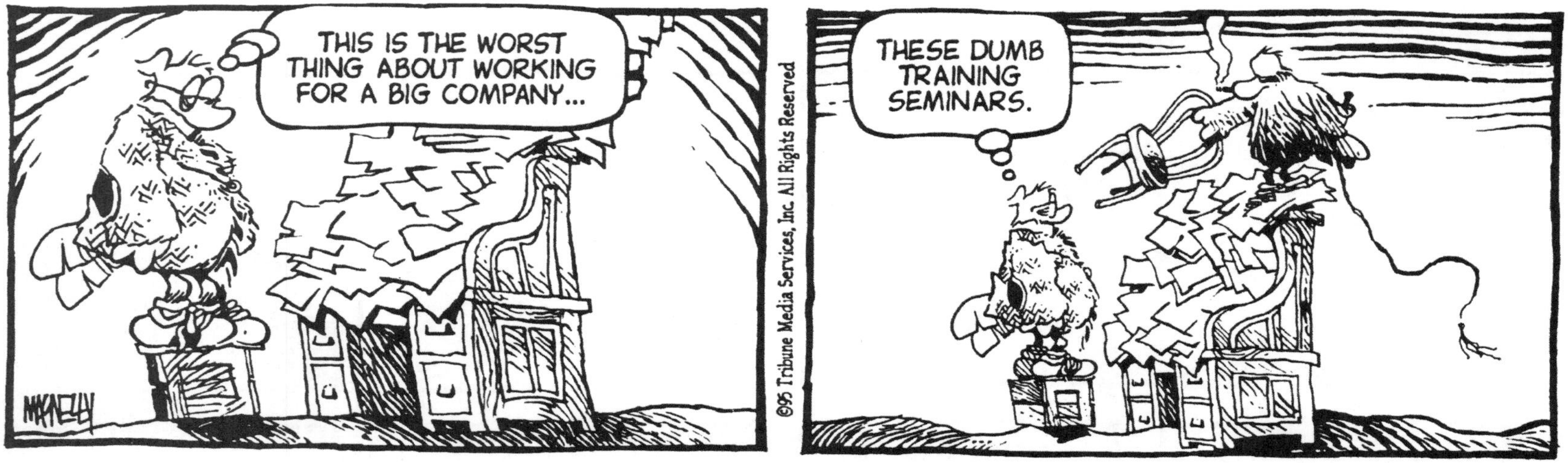
THIS IS THE WORST THING ABOUT WORKING FOR A BIG COMPANY...
THESE DUMB TRAINING SEMINARS.

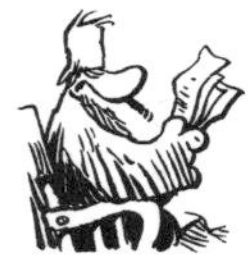

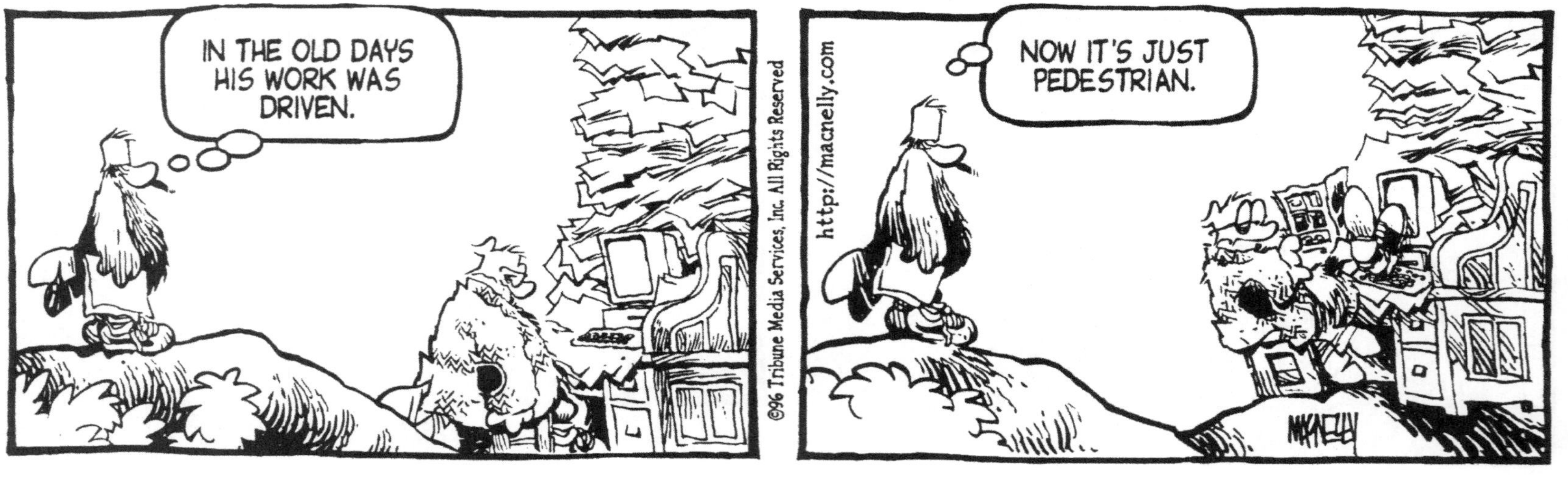
IN THE OLD DAYS HIS WORK WAS DRIVEN.
NOW IT'S JUST PEDESTRIAN.
http://macnelly.com

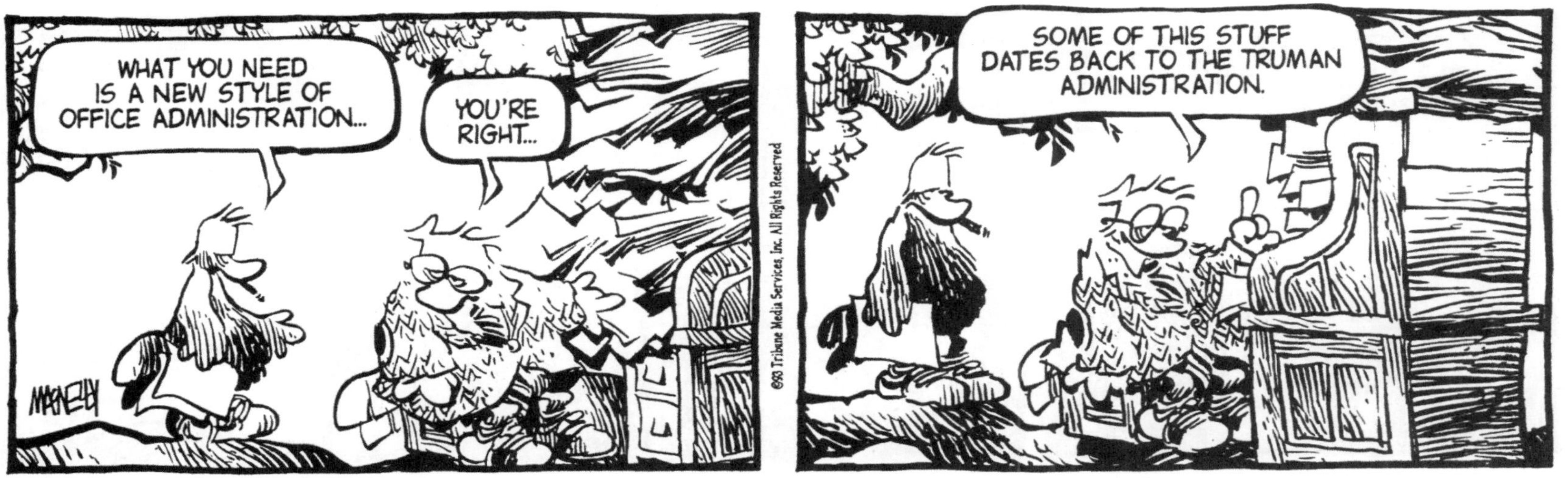
WHAT YOU NEED IS A NEW STYLE OF OFFICE ADMINISTRATION...
YOU'RE RIGHT...
SOME OF THIS STUFF DATES BACK TO THE TRUMAN ADMINISTRATION.
©93 Tribune Media Services, Inc. All Rights Reserved

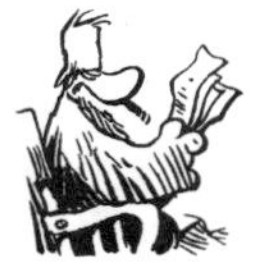

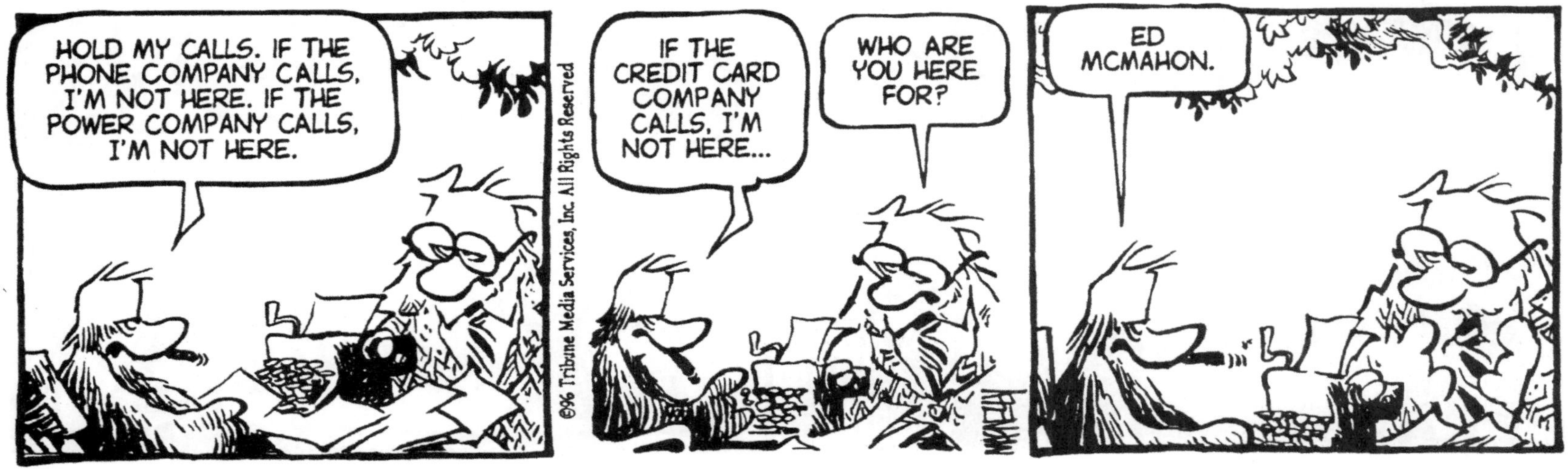
HOLD MY CALLS. IF THE PHONE COMPANY CALLS, I'M NOT HERE. IF THE POWER COMPANY CALLS, I'M NOT HERE.
IF THE CREDIT CARD COMPANY CALLS, I'M NOT HERE...
WHO ARE YOU HERE FOR?
ED MCMAHON.
©96 Tribune Media Services, Inc. All Rights Reserved

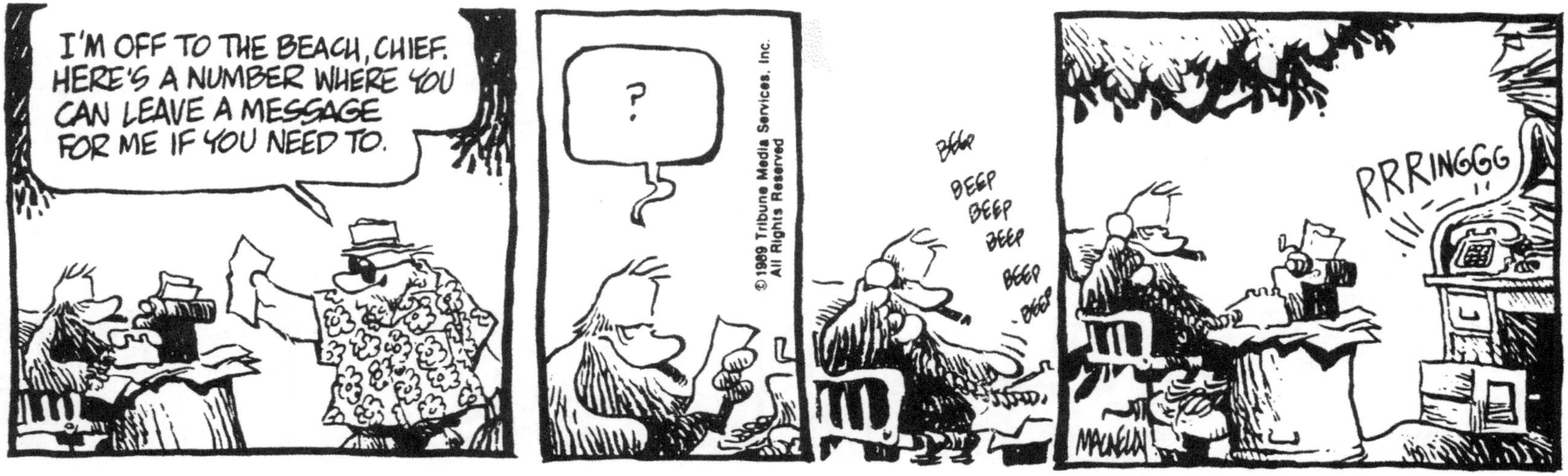
I'M OFF TO THE BEACH, CHIEF. HERE'S A NUMBER WHERE YOU CAN LEAVE A MESSAGE FOR ME IF YOU NEED TO.
?
© 1989 Tribune Media Services, Inc. All Rights Reserved
BEEP BEEP BEEP BEEP BEEP BEEP
RRRINGGG
MACNELLY

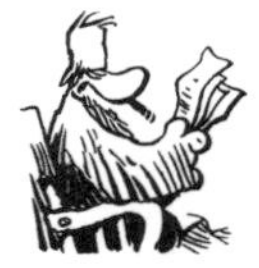

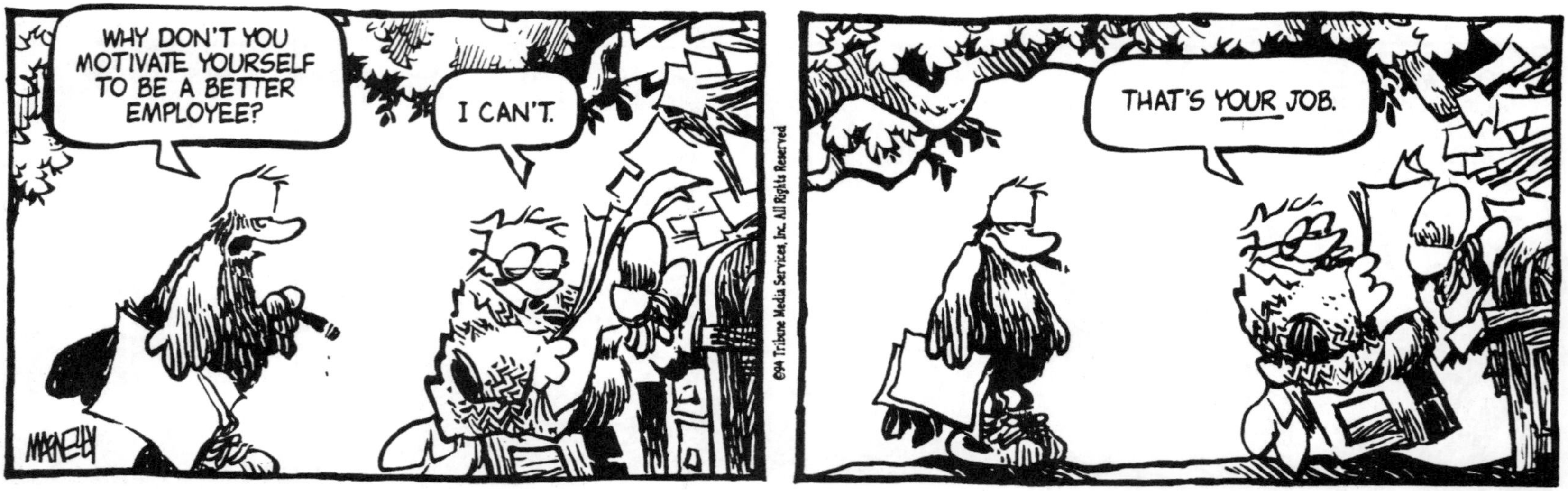
WHY DON'T YOU MOTIVATE YOURSELF TO BE A BETTER EMPLOYEE?
I CAN'T.
©94 Tribune Media Services, Inc. All Rights Reserved
MACNELLY
THAT'S YOUR JOB.

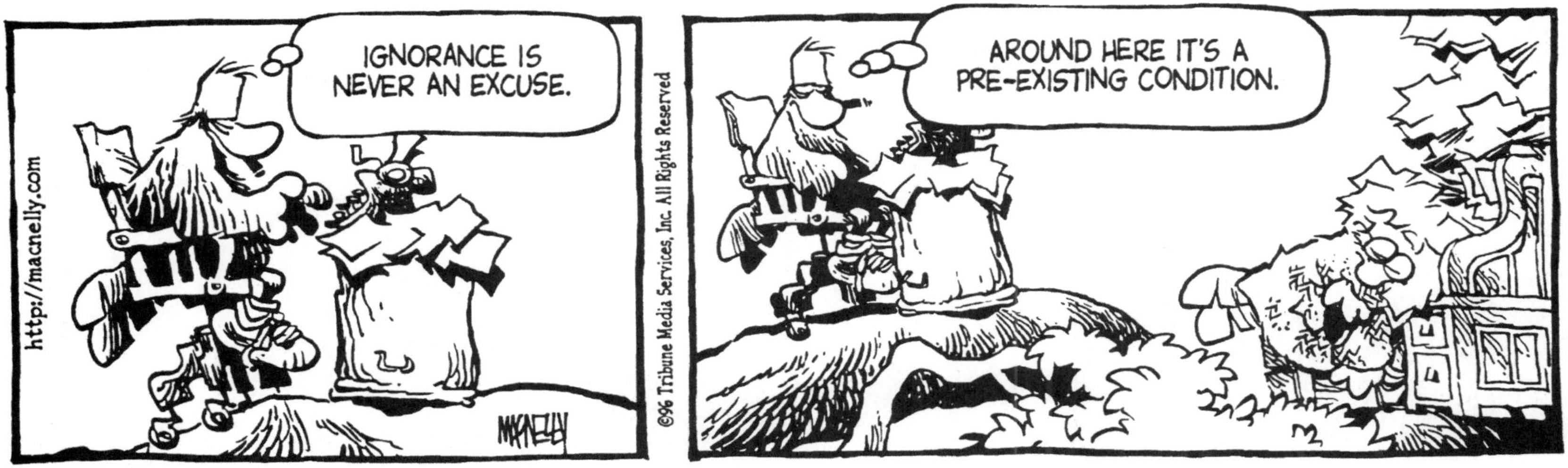
http://macnelly.com
IGNORANCE IS NEVER AN EXCUSE.
©96 Tribune Media Services, Inc. All Rights Reserved
AROUND HERE IT'S A PRE-EXISTING CONDITION.

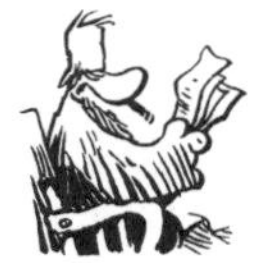

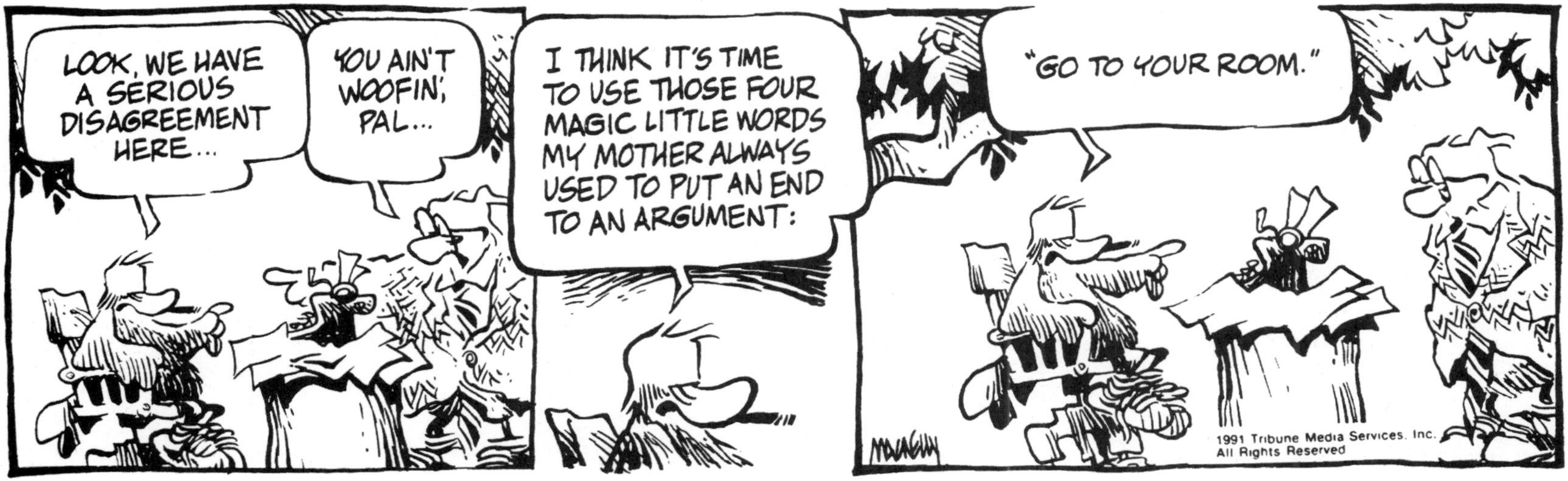
LOOK, WE HAVE A SERIOUS DISAGREEMENT HERE...
YOU AIN'T WOOFIN', PAL...
I THINK IT'S TIME TO USE THOSE FOUR MAGIC LITTLE WORDS MY MOTHER ALWAYS USED TO PUT AN END TO AN ARGUMENT:
"GO TO YOUR ROOM."
1991 Tribune Media Services, Inc.
All Rights Reserved